# IN OUR OWN WORDS:
## The Lives of Arizona Pioneer Women

# IN OUR OWN WORDS: The Lives of Arizona Pioneer Women

by

Barbara Marriott, Ph.D

Fireship Press
www.FireshipPress.com

ISBN-13: 978-1-934757-95-6
ISBN-10: 1-934757-95-0

BISAC Subject Headings:

| | |
|---|---|
| HIS036130 | HISTORY / United States / State & Local / Southwest (AZ, NM, OK, TX) |
| BIO022000 | BIOGRAPHY & AUTOBIOGRAPHY / Women |
| BIO002000 | BIOGRAPHY & AUTOBIOGRAPHY / Cultural Heritage |

*Address all correspondence to:*

Fireship Press, LLC
P.O. Box 68412
Tucson, AZ 85737

*Or visit our website at:*
www.FireshipPress.com

1.0

# Contents

For Minette who travels the hard trail of life, with the indomitable spirit of the pioneer women, while supplying love, kindness and computer advice to all.

Acknowledgements

Special thanks to my readers for their insightful comments: Betty Proffitt, Geri Redling, Kristi Riley, and Marge and Hal Rupard. Along the way in writing this book there were a number of guides including David Flake, Tim Udall, the Saint John's Historical Society, Brittany Chapman at The Church of Jesus Christ of Latter-Day Saints History Library, and Linda Richardson at the St. John's Stake LSD Family History Center; thanks for your information, tours, and pictures. Special thanks to Mike, my chauffeur, research assistance, and dinner partner, who kept me sane. The Arizona Federal Writers' Project interviews are achieved at the Arizona State Library, Archives and Public Record in Phoenix, Arizona.

# CHAPTER ONE
# From National Crisis to the Preservation of History

*All types and forms of folk storytelling and all minority groups-ethnic, regional, and occupational-are to be represented , in order to give a comprehensive picture of the composite America-how it lives and works and plays.*

*Benjamin A. Botkin,*
*Folklore Editor*
*Federal Writers Project*

## The Federal Writers Project

Rarely does a catastrophic situation produce a treasure. Yet in 1935 out of the economic chaos called The Great Depression a treasure was produced. The golden coins were the products of President Franklin D. Roosevelt's New Deal agencies and took form in a more modern infrastructure, a new blooming of the arts, and the capturing and preserving of our national history and our cultural ways.

The year was 1933 and Franklin Delano Roosevelt (FDR) just finished waging a political battle against Herbert Hoover for the Presidency; a battle he won with an overwhelming victory. FDR had only a few months to put together a cabinet that would help accomplish his biggest campaign promise. He would put unemployed Americans to work and end the depression. It was a promise of staggering proportion.

Unemployed men lining up for Free Coffee during the Depression. *(National Archives)*

In the beginning of Roosevelt's first year in office more than one third of the nation's laborers were out of work. While Roosevelt believed that financial welfare was an immediate aid he didn't want relief to become a habit for the country. He hoped to substitute work for relief. It was his philosophy that hiring men and women for meaningful work would accomplish not only the much needed update of America's infrastructure, but also give workers a precious commodity...their dignity.

He set about creating an alphabet soup of agencies funded by The Federal Emergency Relief Act. One of these agencies was the Works Progress Administration (WPA) which was established by executive order. Under the WPA the most controversial programs of Roosevelt's administration were developed. These programs, which offered employment to men and women of the Arts, were lumped under the title of Federal One and consisted of the Federal Arts Program (FAP), the Federal Music Program (FAM), the Federal Theater Program (FTP), The Federal Dance Program (FDP), the Historical Records Survey (HRS), and the Federal Writers Program (FWP).

Harry Hopkins the chief administrator of most of Roosevelt's New Deal programs was questioned about the wisdom of offering work to artists, writers and actors. His retort was succinct, "Hell, they've got to eat just like other people."

The Federal Writers Program, which was established on July 27, 1935, not only succeeded in giving jobs to those who were demographically or physically not suited for the requirements of other programs such as the Civil Conservation Corp, but also employed the most women of all the New Deal programs.

Its establishment was planned to employ experienced writers in key positions and hire those with less skill to fill the lower level jobs. Some of those who showed talent would be trained for writing and editing. According to the New Deal regulations most of the personnel had to be drawn from the relief rolls. This put a strain on the very core of the Federal One programs. Not all the necessary skills and talent needed could be found on the relief rolls.

A compromise of sorts was reached when non-relief workers were allowed to be hired in positions that required talent, specialized skill, and experience. It was this compromise that allowed such writers as Zora Neale Hurston, Studs Turkel, Max Bodenheim, and Saul Bellow to work in the Federal Writer's Program.

Keep moving
*(National Archives)*

A key element in all the New Deal projects was that the programs had to produce a very practical and useful product. Propaganda art that extolled the virtues of work, art that decorated public buildings, theater productions that entertained the workers along with dances and symphonies for them made the art, music, theater, and dance programs viable. For the Writers Program it was something special, something that turned out to be a golden treasure for America.

Washington hit upon a project when they realized that few Americans and foreigners really knew anything about the United States. For many years the world judged America by an archaic guide book called the *Baedeker's United States*. The book was first published in 1893, revised in 1909 and shockingly out of date by the thirties. Now here was a project worthy of the scope of the FWP...guide books of America, aptly named *The American Guide Series*.

The decision was based on sound reasoning. In the early thirties the automobile was just making a presence throughout the United States. But there was little available information on roads, scenic and historical sites, and country tours. Additionally there was emerging at this time an American character, although it was murky due to lack of clear definition and explanation. An understanding of who we were would spark national pride and provide a national identity. Regional guidebooks would encourage Americans to travel and view their national sites. And, probably most importantly, the guides would fit well with the improvements being done on our country's roads, parks and museums by other New Deal programs.

Guide books would encourage travel and reap an economic benefit for gas stations, hotels, restaurants, and other travel related industries. The guide books would also introduce fellow Americans and foreigners to the real America, extolling our beautiful land and its diversified people.

A standard format was established for the *American Guide Series*. The books were divided into history, art, industry and agriculture, geography, and city information. Suggested automobile tours complete with routes, history, sites and local color were at the end of the book. The photographs were usually supplied by another WPA organization, the Farm Security Administration. It was their original task to document farm workers and new settlements with photographs. However the photographers did not limit their talents to just these two subjects but succeeded in capturing America-the scenic and the people.

Henry Alsberg was selected as the director of The Federal Writers Project. In Roosevelt's New Deal Administration Alsberg held the position of assistant to Jacob Baker. Baker had the job of organizing all the new white-collar WPA programs and personnel.

Alsberg graduated Columbia law school at twenty but soon found law boring and turned to journalism, theater and travel. By the time he reached Washington and politics he had put time in as a newspaperman, an off-Broadway theater director and a playwright. However he was virtually unknown outside New York City.

The structure of the Federal Writers' Project was set up in layers with Washington the overall administrator. All copy was to come to Washington for final proofing and editing. Under Washington was the Regional Offices, and under them the State Directors that would make the writing assignments and manage the information collected.

It soon became apparent that regional guides would be too cumbersome and much too broad to appeal to the average user. Alsberg and his staff decided instead to produce a guide book for each of the 48 states, Puerto Rico, Alaska and several large cities.

The first book published in The American Guide Series was Idaho in 1937. *Arizona: A Guide to the Sunset State* was one of the last state guides to appear with its publication in April, 1940.

By its end the FWP far exceeded expectations. It not only produced a guide book for each state, but created over seven hundred titles by the time the program was closed out around 1943. The FWP not only produced the first authentic and comprehensive guides of our country but also launched the career of some of our finest writers including Nelson Algren, Saul Bellow, John Cheever, John Steinbeck, May Swenson, Frank Yerby, Margaret Walker and Richard Wright.

## The Arizona Staff

Once the program was conceived it didn't take long for Alsberg and his staff to lock horns with the Washington power-brokers who wanted to reward every native son and daughter and major campaign contributor with a plum job in the arts programs. The writer's project bore the brunt of this thinking. After all, it was visible talent that was needed in the other Federal One programs, but to the Washington mind anyone could write.

It was not only the top level of the writer's project that caused personnel problems. Since it was mandated that a majority of those hired had to come from the relief roles, a major vetting needed to be done to find workers that could research projects, gather and organize the data, and keep intelligent notes. State Directors were told to seek out lawyers, librarians, writers, journalist, archeologists, geographers, teachers, and college graduates on relief, or eligible for relief. As for the Arizona State Director, Alsberg was fortunate in finding the perfect candidate in Ross Santee.

Ross Santee was born August 16, 1888 in Thornburg, Iowa of Quaker parents. His father died when he was three years old and he spent his childhood first in Iowa and then in Illinois.

As a growing boy he enjoyed drawing, but his main art interest was the cartoons in the Chicago Record. He was a youth bent on the innocent pleasures of playing pool and creating mischief. In his youth he had no interest in writing. Santee believed his future lay in art.

Ross Santee
*(AHS #20763)*

Reading was another of his favorite pastimes and at the Moline public library he met the works of Mark Twain. He read everything by him he could get his hands on. The time spent with the works of this witty writer influenced Santee's future writing style. His western writings have a folksy, humorous flavor to them which was enormously appealing to a public starved for stories about America's west. While Santee wrote fiction hidden under that genre is a lot of biographical information.

After high school Santee enrolled in the Chicago Art Institute. Four years later he left for New York and sold his first piece of artwork to the editor of *Colliers*. He spent his time wandering the streets of New York sketching people and places, and it was these simple pieces that set his style and became his artistic trademark. Santee, like his art, believed in a straight forward, simple approach to life. This philosophy enabled him to become a true man of the west.

In 1915 Santee had enough of sophisticated cites. He wanted to get far away from New York. He decided a visit to his sister in Globe, Arizona would do it. Globe certainly was a far cry from New York. While New York was smooth, Globe was rough, while the city was packed with people, Globe was sparsely populated. New York had sky scrapers, Globe had mountains. New York had cosmopolitan dwellers, Arizona supplied Apache dwellers. Yet, it was here Santee realized his full potential as a writer and an artist making him one of the most important voices of the west.

Santee learned the ways of the west from the ground up, literally. Working for the Bar F Bar Ranch he admits he spent more time on his hands and knees than on a horse.

In 1920 Santee returned to the Chicago Art Institute to perfect his artistic style. He realized some success in 1922 when the National Gallery in New York City mounted an exhibition of his etchings. His art career was also enhanced when he sold some drawings to *Life* magazine and *Boy's Life*.

It was Mr. Crump, the editor of *Boy's Life*, who convinced Santee to write. In 1926 his book *Men and Horses* was published. This was followed by *Cowboy* in 1928, *The Pooch, 1931, Sleepy Black,* and *The Bar X Golf Course in 1933,* and *Spike: the Story of a Cowpuncher's Dog* in 1934. Santee published 14 books and several articles in his lifetime; however he never completely abandoned his art and embellished his stories with his simple but beautiful line drawings.

In 1935 when the Federal Writers Project was looking for a State Director for Arizona they were able to convince Santee to take the job. It was the perfect match. In Santee they had a recognized published author, an acclaimed artist, a resident of Arizona, and a true Arizona cowboy.

Santee set about finding field workers to collect the data. As the project got underway Washington realized that facts and figures such as miles and dates produced dull books. Alsberg's staff instructed their state directors to collect life histories which would translate into a truer and more meaningful depiction of America, its history and its citizens.

Santee chose Jose del Castillo for his Tucson field representative. Castillo was a lawyer and a graduate of the University of Arizona. He had connections to many communities in the Tucson area, among them the Mexican community, the legal community and, through Edith Stratton Kitt, Secretary of the Pioneers, a good connection to material on the history of Arizona. Not much is known about Castillo. All that remains of his work is a file in the Arizona Historical Society consisting of some interviews conducted with Mexican and Anglo informants and some correspondence.

Field workers were offered up to $22.77 a week and were not allowed to work over 24 hours a week. Apparently that was not enough for Castillo to live on and correspondence shows he sought other means of income. On September 26, 1938 Castillo wrote to Albright-Roewe Printing Company inquiring about self publishing some poems. In January, 1939 he applied for and was granted a Real Estate License and a few months later he received an inquiry from Columbia Music Publishers expressing an interest in seeing some of his poems and lyric writings.

Castillo filled out the required FWP forms with the precision of a lawyer. The first sheet of his interviews contained descriptive material of the informant. He was able to combine a degree of diplomacy with a large amount of honesty.

In one of his reports, after describing the home of Mrs. Carmen Lucero where the interview was held, he gave his impression of the informant, "Mrs. Lucero is a little woman, delicately wrinkled with age. She must have been a sweet small woman, properly raised. Her voice is delicate and gentle, and when it rings with animation her voice has a musical tinkle. She darns socks consistently and attends church twice a day."

Castillo's description of Mrs. Emilia Phy Smith was less than flattering. He describes her as "...a stout woman, always dressed in black. She has a strong nose and thick lips. She differs from her sisters who have more delicate features in facial shape. But her eyes are as candid as her frankness of speaking. Being so sensitive and sincere, she either hates a person or likes a person. She claims to be psychic."

In his description of Mrs. Belle Tully he was hardly diplomatic describing her as "...unwieldily (sic) fat. She is florid as an Irish could be. Her blue eyes look at you, calculating, considering. If you have heard any other opinion about her, this is the moment you have to throw it over-board and clean the slate of your mind—she might read it."

Some of Castillo's best work is in the gathering of folklore. From his notes it seems he was relentless in pursuing a story. For the folklore story on *The Jar* he spent almost a year trying to locate the original owner and solve the mystery of who buried the jar under a house and why there was a wax effigy, pierced with sharp pins, in the jar.

Castillo's most poignant pieces are interviews with men. In one piece a drifter's willingness to be interviewed depended on the fifty cents he would receive. The informant struggled to keep his pride, but it was evident he had little left.

All writings were published anonymously as was the art work. However the sketches in the *Arizona* guide book bear a strong resemblance to Santee's work. Although the writing was to be anonymous the reports in the collection of FWP papers in the Arizona State Archives show at least a dozen field representatives collected oral histories of Arizona women pioneers. Most of these reports bear the interviewer's name and in most cases the area where the interviewer worked.

The women pioneer interviewers and their areas, if identified, were: Jose del Castillo, Tucson; Kathlyn M. Lathrup, Duncan; Alfred Downing; Romella Gomez, Cochise County; Helen M. Smith, Cochise County; G.Reeve, Globe; John Vick, Cochise County; Agnes Huran, Phoenix; Grey and Ensign, Yavapai County; Edward J. Kelley; Pearl Udall Nelson; and Roberta Flake Clayton, Phoenix, Snowflake and Navajo County. There probably were other information compilers but these are the only names that appear on the Women Pioneer interview papers.

Of all the field representatives Roberta Flake Clayton was the most prolific. From 1936 until 1941 she was responsible for 81 of the 122 interviews, a whopping 66%.

Clayton herself was a worthy subject for an interview. Born in Beaver, Utah on August 19, 1877 she was only weeks old when her parents set out to settle the Little Colorado River area. Her father, William Flake settled his pioneer group near the Little Colorado River, but after several months of fighting floods that broke through several dams he looked for a new settlement site. He found just the place in the Stinson's Ranch located in a lush valley. Flake made arrangements to buy the ranch from James Stinson for 500 head of good Utah cattle.

On his way to Utah to make arrangements for the cattle he met Erastas Snow and his group. The Snow group was abandoning Taylor, a small settlement they had founded. It proved to be unsuccessful due to constant flooding and harsh weather.

Snow proposed he and Flake join forces and pioneers in the new town, which would be named by combining their names. And so, Snowflake, Arizona was born.

Roberta grew up in Snowflake and was married at the age of 19 to Joseph Ramsey the son of Ralph Ramsey a renowned wood carver. Roberta had been warned by her family that Joseph was not the best choice for a husband and she soon found that to be true. Eventually she divorced the scoundrel but not before they had a son, Milton Flake Ramsey, who was killed in World War I.

Eventually Roberta married again, this time to James William Clayton. There are five children listed in this family but some may be adopted as their dates of birth indicate she was between forty and sixty years old. Her husband died in 1935 leaving her with a houseful of children and no money. It is rumored that he invested heavily in Mexico and lost everything leaving Roberta destitute.

Nineteen thirty five was the middle of the Great Depression years. Roberta needed an income, and being an intelligent, well education woman she found employment with the FWP. Her keen interest in history combined with a personal knowledge and acquaintance of Arizona's original Mormon pioneers made her an ideal interviewer.

Because of her Church of Jesus Christ of Latter–day Saints (LDS) affiliation she had an entry into the early Mormon families. She was further helped by that culture's respect for, and value of, family history. But, perhaps the most overriding reason for the prolific amount of Mormon Pioneer interviews was money. Roberta needed funds to support her family.

Roberta was a valued addition to Santee's staff not only for the above reasons but also because she was a writer. She had turned her Mother Lucy's diary into a book, authored plays, pageants and wrote poetry.

Roberta continued writing after her employment with the FWP ended producing five books including *Pioneer Women of Arizona* (1965?), *Pioneer Men of Arizona* (1974); *To the Last Frontier* 1976; *Rhymes, Rhythms and Rhapsodies;* and *Diaries for My Children.* An active member of the Church of Jesus Christ of Latter-day Saints she served as a counselor, President of the Relief Society and a member of the Pioneers of Navajo and Apache Counties.

She lived a full life, was highly respected in her community and is described as outspoken, opinionated women, a bright, active woman who lived to be 103 and who left a legacy in Arizona's pioneer women's oral histories.

## Destination Arizona

The Arizona's Pioneer Women interviewed by the Federal Writers' Project migration into Arizona between 1870 and 1890. During this time Arizona's population jumped from 9,658 in 1870 to 88,243 in 1890.

Arizona with its 113,998 square miles is bisected by the Gila River and its tributaries which nip the southern portion of the capital city of Phoenix. The northern section is noted for its pines, grass lands and rugged topography which include the San Francisco Mountains and the Grand Canyon. Several small rivers and streams water this land inviting agriculture and ranching. It was into this part of the state that the majority of Mormon settled.

South of the Gila River is desert land through which, on occasion, run the San Cruz and the San Pedro Rivers. This is the land first explored by the Spanish Conquistadors, and later settled by the people from old Mexico.

With the Gadsden Purchase in 1853 potential migrants saw their chances for land under the America flag increase. Additionally, the northern part of the state had been investigated by the Mormon Battalion that marched through Arizona in 1856 on their way to California. They brought back tales of a lush land waiting for development and promising much for the farmer and rancher.

These reports encouraged Brigham Young to call Latter-day Saints to settle the land following the philosophy that to govern is to populate.

During the territorial days of the eighteen hundreds the northern section was Indian land, and as such was vulnerable to Indian raids and attacks, primarily from the Apaches. Here and there were a few forts (or camps) set up by select Mormons sent in advance for the purpose of support of the migrants. Jacob Hamblett was part of this advance guard. During the Indian Wars and after the Civil War the Army established camps and forts like Fort Apache and Camp Grant. But mostly the land was a rough, untamed wilderness where one made his or her own life, or died trying if not from hostile Indians, then from hunger or disease.

The Mormon migration was primarily focused in the untamed north along the Little Colorado. Starting as early as 1850 Mormon's staked claims to sections of this Indian land, sometimes heading as far south as the Mesa/Phoenix area. Here they surveyed the land creating villages and towns out of nothing but the desolate land. They dammed the rivers and streams, made their land arable and farmed.

Most Hispanic women pioneers settled in cities and towns with a Hispanic history such as Bisbee, Tucson and Tombstone. The men were miners, freighters, or purveyors of wood and water. They continued their lives much as they had lived them in Mexico. Their houses were the one story adobes of their native land, their language that of Mexico, the streets were dirt. They lived their life as they had in their native land; the only change was the venue.

The non-Mormon women who came settled in or near Phoenix, Tucson, Tombstone, Prescott or other small towns. For them the change was the culture and way of life. Ranching was new to them as were the dusty trails for roads, the outlaws, the lack of water, and the isolation of the villages and ranches.

## Different Cultures, One Land

These interviews represent more than a window on Arizona frontier life in the late nineteenth and early twentieth century. They offer insights into two distinct cultures of the time. One is of the Mormon Church composed mostly of Anglo Saxons; the other is the Mexican culture which was already deeply rooted in parts of Arizona. There was also a group of non-Mormons of various other religions, or no religious affiliation, who came out west for a variety of reasons. They did not come out as a group, as the Mormon's did, to colonize the land, nor did they come out to join their families on what had been their traditional land, as the Mexicans. Most of them came into the Arizona Territory in small family groups and tended toward the towns where work was to be found. While these women did not belong to either of the two major pioneer cultures they still experienced and suffered many of the same hardships and deprivations.

The Mormons headed out to unsettled land, built towns and put in place their own governing political, social and economic structures. The Mexican Americans mostly settled in established frontier towns like Bisbee, Tucson and Tombstone. Those who were not Mormons or Mexicans settled in scantily populated areas, in unpopulated areas with good grazing land where they established ranches, or in frontier towns where they owned or worked in businesses.

The economic base of the Mormon towns was agrarian and ranching. Commercial businesses were established as needed based on the demands of the town population.

The Mexican America pioneers worked at commercial endeavors which supplied services and goods such as freighting, wood, domestic and general labor. A few wealthy Mexican American townspeople owned businesses; some had established sheep or cattle ranches and they employed members of the lower Mexican economic class to work for them.

The Mexican Americans were an independent lot; the early Mormon settlers depended on each other. This dependence had a name, The United Way, a communal way of living. Upon arriving at their wilderness destination the Mormons proceeded immediately to do two things. One, survey the land and plot out the town, and two, establish the United Way of sharing the work.

When the newly arrived Mexican American immigrant arrived at his or her destination during this period of time the first efforts were put to finding work and finding a place to live. Earlier Mexican arrivals had founded the towns, which went back as far as 1700. By this time those towns were well established.

Religion played a big part in the behaviors and values of Arizona's early settlers. The Mormons practiced polygamy and many households consisted of more than one wife, each with her children, and a common Father. Their households were extremely large; fifteen people in a house were not uncommon.

The Mexican Americans were staunch Catholics and their marriages consisted of one man and one woman. The Catholic women were brought up under strict rules where dances were frowned upon and courting was supervised and approved of by the parents. The Mormon women grew up attending dances and song fests, singing, dancing, and musical talent played a big part in their frontier lives and in their courting rituals.

In the Mexican Catholic community it was not uncommon for the husband to be chosen by the parents and couples were monogamous. Mormon women had some say in choice of husband, and had the right to approve or disapprove of their husband taking another wife.

Exactly how strict these cultural behaviors were followed is difficult to say, but it seems that for the most part they were adhered to by the majority of the two societies.

When on the frontier the two cultures initially met with friction and mistrust. The fights and killings that occurred in St. John's, Arizona between the Mexicans and the Mormons were an example of the rubbing together of two different sets of cultural values.

Sometimes the cultural wars were prompted by economic reasons. Many early Mexican settlers on the frontier were sheep herders. The Mormons preferred cattle ranching. The wars were over land, grass, and other resources.

This mix of very different cultures was superimposed onto the existing indigenous native, the American Indian. They saw their land being taken over as ranches, farms and towns were established. When the Native Americans saw their resources, such as water and wood being used in ways they did not approve or understand; ways that left them with less, their reaction was either to make friends with the intruders, or kill them.

The reactions, beliefs, and eye witness accounts of the meeting of these cultures can be read in the life interviews. As these women talked about their lives, and the lives of their neighbors, they were reporting on the meeting and finally the blending of these cultures.

Thus, these interviews are more than the life of a person or a family; they are a personal view of the making of America and the blending of many cultures into the American Culture.

And, that is specifically what the directors of the Federal Writer's Project wanted. When the decision was made to do the state guidebooks they wanted more than facts and figures. They wanted examples and an explanation of the "American Way", Americans in all their differences and in their sameness.

Washington ordered their interviewers to talk to members of various socio-economic groups and members of various cultures. While other states interviewed ex-slaves and their families, or Welsh coal miners, Arizona's biggest pioneer culture groups were the Mexican Americans and the Mormons. Both represented, in their own way, religions that controlled demographics. The manifestation of these controls was represented in their every day behaviors reported by the women in that culture and make interesting reading for their contrasts. It is unfortunate that Native Americans were not interviewed. Arizona did publish some studies on several Indian tribes under the FWP. These are explicit explanations of the cultures, but are not oral histories.

## The Format

The FWP planned two series of cultural studies. One was to focus on folklore and the other was a social-ethnic study. The latter information was organized around ethnic and religious groups, regions and communities with an emphasis on ways of living and cultural diversity.

The interview instructions were simple. All material was to be taken from oral sources *exactly as heard.* It was this mandate that produced the rich oral histories of the FWP now found in our archives including the former slave narratives in the south and the stories of Arizona's pioneer women.

There were over 700 stories of Arizona men and women collected by the FWP field representatives. Some of them are merely short biographies and some run to pages of interview material. Included in the later are 122 interviews with Arizona Pioneer women.

Each interviewer had his or her own style. This produced copy in a variety of formats and style. Some, such as Roberta Flake Clayton, wrote in the third person. Helen Smith and Jose del Castillo wrote up their interviews in the first person. Consequently some of the grammar is poor, after all many of the pioneers had little education; also not many of the interviewers were professional authors.

Additionally the language can be stilted, or flowery, even difficult to follow, but remember this was in the mid thirties, and much popular literature of the times followed this style. However the stories are rich with unique words and expressions of the times.

The Federal Writer's Project probably contributed to a style change in American literature from the more formal, flowery, or stilted language to a simpler more emotional style as avant-garde young authors were given a chance to write and publish.

The Arizona Pioneer Women's interviews took place from 1935 to 1941. Most of the interviews were with the actual pioneer women; some were life stories related by their family descendants, as told to them. It is evident that there was not a mandated format or questionnaire for these interviews. Although Jose del Castillo's interviews are preceded by a description of the interviewee and the physical surroundings of the location of the interview, the rest are not. While most of the interviews contain some demographic information such as date of birth, parent, marriage, children and education, others are stories of a particular time or incident. However what makes them such a treasure is that they do represent the reality of the times, or what was perceived by the interviewee to be the reality.

Some of the interviews read like stories out of a novel, and because of that others seem almost mundane. But all of the stories are laced with hardship, self-doubts, and sacrifices. Hard work runs though each one, not as a theme, but as an integrated part of life.

These interviews, as told to the Federal Writers' Project workers, are snapshots in words that freeze in time snippets of the frontier life of Arizona's pioneer women. Some are horrifying, some are tender, and some are even funny. They serve as a measure of the capabilities of women under the most arduous conditions and are reproduced here in their original forms to preserve the language and feelings of the women interviewed and of the times.

Taken all together these oral history interviews go a long way in explaining the so called American Persona as it was and as it has become.

## The Pioneer Women

In some cases a whole family of females is represented. But, not every interview addressed the same topics. Therefore, there is demographic information on some, but not on all. Some interviews relate the westward trek. Others mention their childhood, and the Mexican women in particular tell their folklore beliefs. Yet, even though there are differences in the type of collected information, all of it produces an overview that depicts the various lifestyles and cultures that were a reality on Arizona's frontier in 1800 and early 1900.

The family names of many of the women in this book can still be found in Arizona in places of historical significance or in descendants who are playing important roles in the state. I have included a Name Index at the end to facilitate locating the stories of specific people. I have also included a Place Index to facilitate gathering information about specific locales, whenever they were given. See also the map just before the Place Index.

# CHAPTER TWO
# Backgrounds

*The pioneer women who came west were not superwomen with extraordinary talents and a thirst for adventure; but were women whose goals were simple: getting through each day, achieving contentment, and finding a place in life.*

Other than these simple desires were there any other traits they shared? Was there a demographic, or an experience that they had in common in their earlier lives; a similar social standing, the same educational background? Besides the strong Mormon ties of many, they are a remarkably diverse group.

While courage was an asset for Arizona's pioneer women, the biggest virtue was their innocence of not knowing what they were to face in the journey and their new frontier life. But, sometimes in life courage is not enough. A good deal of innocence can achieve unbelievable goals. This lack of knowledge caused them to answer their problems with innovativeness, and hard work. Few complained, as least not much and not for long. They accepted what they faced as the norm. After all you really don't know what you don't know.

Economically there were a few from wealthy families and some from abject poverty. They represented several religions, and no religion. They were born in Europe, in the eastern and southern parts of the United States, in America's west. They first saw life in mansions, log cabins, and covered wagons.

Some were teenage brides; a few were in their twenties or older when they took their vows. Although education was a prized commodity among the pioneer women there were those who were illiterate, and those who taught school. The families of some were close and loving; others lived a neglected or abusive family life when they were young.

Was there a significant event that happened to these women in their childhood or early lives? An event so powerful it shaped them into strong, determined women, the stuff pioneers are made from?

If any did experience an event, it did not manifest itself in the same form for all the women. A look at their early family life bears little similarity between the women. What marked their early years: their father's occupation, place of birth, loss of loved ones, their parents' economic situation, marriage—none were predictors of the role these women would play in settling the west.

Yet, these experiences and their childhood environments had to have an impact on making them the type of women they became. For such a diversified group to funnel into the frontier, and for so many of them to meet and conquer the hardship is a phenomenal achievement.

They covered the spectrum in demographics, and this is what makes them so interesting. There was no one dominating characteristic that defined the pioneer women except their gender. Girl and woman they came to Arizona Territory, met the challenges, and succeeded.

While the original pioneers are gone, their names still mark Arizona in places, (for example Snowflake, Arizona and Kartchner Caverns); and their decedents can still be found in many of the towns and cities in Arizona including business signs, and on the rolls of Arizona's public servants (such as Mo Udall and Jeff Flake, U.S. Congressmen.)

Since there was no required format for the interviewers to follow, demographic information, when reported, was written in different styles. Some of the demographic information is reported in a very dramatic manner, some is factual, and here also is the bare-bones type of reporting or none at all.

Roberta Flake Clayton gathered demographic information on almost all of her subjects. There are several common threads among the Mormon women. However, the interviews by other reporters that covered non-Mormon women, while scant, do provide contrasts which give us a balanced picture of the early lives of pioneer women.

What there is in demographic information gives us some insight into who these original pioneer women were and how they saw their childhood. It is doubtful that any of them had thoughts of creating a legacy and a model for future generations. Yet the characteristics that define western women were shaped by them.

## Elizabeth Adelide Hoopes Allen

Interviewer: Roberta Flake Clayton
Phoenix

She was the daughter of Warner and Priscilla Gifford Hoopes. It was always their belief that this little daughter was the first child born in a humble covered wagon, of the hundreds of Mormon Pioneers who were driven from their homes in Missouri. The incident occurred in Pottawattamie County, Iowa on September 8, 1847. Her early life was spent in the moving and wanderings of this much maligned people.

Mr. Hoopes was a shoemaker by trade; and a good one at that. Every old boot, shoe or bit of leather obtainable was made up for his own and his neighbors families. His services were always in great demand, as he accepted leather for his work. Thus he kept his own well shod.

Mr. Hoopes took his family into Buchanan County, near St. Joseph, Mississippi in 1855. His wife was in very poor health, and it was hoped that she might improve. Most of those early pioneers could turn their hands to many kinds of work. Here Warner became a charcoal burner, and as there was great demand for charcoal from the blacksmith shops and furnaces, he became quite prosperous.

"Even in this part of the world we found a strong sentiment against the Saints and their religion. One night we entertained an Elder McGaw who had stopped at our place on his return trip from a mission to England. He told my father that he felt impressed that he, my father, should remove his family immediately to Florence, Nebraska and there prepare to immigrate to Utah. He repeated the advice that night and again the next morning.

After he started away, he returned and advised him to go right away and leave his family to dispose of the property and follow later. My father was loath to leave his prosperous situation and heeded not the council.

About a week later a non-Mormon family was burned in their house and the Mormons were accused of committing the deed. Four of the brethren were arrested, but were proven innocent and released. However, that decision of the court did not satisfy the hellish mob, which then made plans to kill them.

They were warned by a friend, but my father didn't believe any harm would befall him. The sheriff of Buchanan County called for my father and offered him protection, and yet he refused to accept, for he "knew of no enemies," he said. But after a few days when he had reconsidered, he began to feel a little uneasy. One night he felt that he had better not be found at home. Consequently he left for the woods in the back of the house, with the understanding that should friends come my mother was to call him; if enemies should come she was to blow the dinner horn, signifying that he should hasten farther into the denseness.

Some time during the night my mother was awakened by some voices outside. She listened and recognized the voices of the mob making plans to take my father away. After they had stationed their guards at the doors and windows with the intention of shooting him down, should he attempt to escape, she arose, and taking the dinner horn blew three loud blasts.

The leader of the mob, thinking it a signal for him to return, wrestled the horn from her and blew it repeatedly. Finally my mother told him that the longer and louder he blew the horn, the farther and faster my Father was going in the opposite direction.

The mob grew more angry, but she told them that if they had come like gentlemen she would have called him and he would have returned. Furiously they took to the woods where they hunted all night for Father and Mr. Lincoln, but all without avail.

The next day they returned and tried to persuade my mother to give up that "terrible religion", saying that if she would do so, herself and children would be well cared for.

The following night my father and Mr. Lincoln returned and were taken to prison by the Sheriff for protection from the mob. They remained there for ten months, and were then proven innocent and released. Thus the money my father had accumulated was spent for lawyer fees and we were reduced to a state of poverty. However Mother was energetic and made willow baskets for us children to sell to help sustain our lives. Our last cow was sold to pay our steamboat fare to Florence, Nebraska where we waited some time for my father to join us."

### Clara Styron Armstrong

Interviewer: G. W. Reeve
Globe

Clara Styron was born in Seguin, Texas in 1864. Her father, William Wallace Styron, was Sheriff of that county at the time of Clara's advent into this world, which office he held for eight years.

When Clara was two years old, her father moved with his family to the plains, at a place later known as Cleburne, Texas, and builds his house there. This was known as the first house in Cleburne. He engaged in the cattle business, buying and selling beef cattle, and started a meat business. Starting with a little butcher shop, killing and butchering his own beef, he built up a butchering business that gave employment to from sixty to seventy men. He would buy "feeders" (thin range stock) and fatten them and butcher and see them as beef.

In 1882 Mr. Styron moved his family to George's Creek, where he ran a large farm and ranch. It was here that Clara graduated into a full-fledged cowgirl, riding the range and assisting with the management of the ranch.

### Pauline Mymie Barall Aremijo

Interviewer: Kathlyn M. Lathrop
Duncan

I was born Pauline Mymie Barall, in 1848, in that little strip of country called France-Italy, which was ceded by Italy to France years before I was born. Most of the people there were half-breed French Italians. My mother was pure Italian, and my father a French soldier.

In our native land it is a custom of the people to manage all the details of their children's marriage, at any age they think suitable. The parents of the prospective groom, makes a marriage deal with the parents of the prospective bride. The feelings of neither of the young people are considered. The match is made by the parents and the wedding announced, and there is no law to prevent it. I was fourteen years of age when my adored father told me I must marry Tony.

Tony was going to America and he must take a native bride along, there was no use to resist, tears got me nowhere. I knew I must obey my father's command. I hated Tony, but felt sorry for him I knew he did not want me.

When according to the marriage contract he called to pay me court, and as soon as we were left alone in the parlor, Tony said to me, "Mymie, I know this is most unjust to you as well as to myself, but we both know the law and command of our respected fathers—there is no way out, we must obey! But, even in America, the law of our Church still dominates us, we can never be divorced."

But when we sailed for America, I felt a vast relief somehow. I would be dominated by Tony alone. My people and his people would not be ordering me around. And if Tony, like most men I know, got fresh and started to mistreat me, I could defend myself, even if I had to shoot him.

**Edna Price Armbrust**
Interviewer: Alfred E. Downing
Flagstaff

Arizona's climate has lured many within her boarders. The pioneer parents of Edna Price were among the first to settle here in search of good health. When she was a year and half old, they had gone from Ohio to Los Angeles in the interests of Mrs. Price's health. But the moist climate there was unsuitable for the Mother, and three years later, in 1890 they retraced their steps to Flagstaff, Arizona. Their homestead was located in the little valley which is now covered by Lake Mary, an artificial lake created in about 1906.

Edna Price was married at the age of 19 to Eric Crouse in 1908. The marriage was unhappy. Her marriage to Charles B. Rudd was a union with a representative of one of the outstanding Arizona pioneer families. He came out West in a wagon train led by his father, who educated himself after four children were born to him. He died in 1929 at the age of 65. Her marriage to Mr. Armbrust came in 1934.

**May Arthur Bates**
Interviewer: Helen M. Smith
Cochise County

My mother's people lived in California, and I was born there in 1878. My father, Bob Arthur, brought us to Tombstone when I was very young, too young to remember anything that happened there. We remained in Tombstone about two years then returned to California.

Very soon my father was sent for by the Old Dominion Mining Company of Globe. He was a machinist and blacksmith, and he was to oversee the installation of the machinery at the O.D. Mine.

The company built us a little house of logs. It was perhaps two miles from the mine on a hillside as all buildings in Globe were. I remember there was a wash in front, and that Father built a rude bridge across the wash, since the only road which approached the house came from the other side of this wash. Immediately behind us was a hill, and there we had a dugout where we stored supplies, etc.

## Fried Zeigler Bourn

Interviewer: Roberta Flake Clayton
Navajo County

In the year 1831 after a slow tortuous trip of several weeks because of delays owing to floods and lack of transportation facilities, Mrs. Bourn came to Denver from New York.

Nothing ever escaped her notice, and her inquiring mind went back to the cause of floods and their control, instead of complaining at conditions as most of her fellow travelers were.

Her interest in flood control led to their prevention through reforestation. Because of her work along these lines, and her efforts to have forestry taught in the schools of the state, she became acquainted with and a good friend of Guifford Pinchot, appointed by President Teddy Roosevelt to look after lands under public domain.

Fitted by nature as a teacher and being able to speak three foreign languages: German, French, and Swedish, her services were much sought after in settlement work. She was instrumental in organizing and conducting free kindergartens in localities where the people were too poor to afford to pay. Her knowledge of German helped her to assist many a German Jew in Denver to adjust themselves to new surroundings, and to each other.

Mrs. Bourn's husband was an invalid for many years before his death, which placed upon her the necessity of providing for herself and her one child, made permanently deaf by illness.

They acquired a ranch in Colorado and went into the cattle business. Mrs. Bourn had to drive several miles to the Post Office in the winter time through banks of snow. She saw again the necessity for planting trees when she would pas half a dozen, or more, carcasses of cattle which had died through lack of shelter and protection that trees might have offered.

During a trip to Washington en route to Philadelphia, to put her son in school there, she appeared before the Committee on Land Affairs to obtain title to her land and while there was instrumental in helping to pass laws beneficial to the stock men of Colorado.

Her interest and intelligent research in forestry, soil erosion and conservation and the articles written by her, brought much favorable comment. And may we say, in a way, was responsible for those subjects being taught in the schools in Colorado, and in some of the states resulted in large burned out areas being replanted from seed imported into this country from Europe, principally the Norway Pine.

Through her indefatigable efforts along all these and many other lines, Mrs. Bourn's health failed. She sought the salubrious climate of Arizona, where she found not only health but a vast field of pioneering along the lines in which she had been so successful in her former home.

Having an "underprivileged" child of her own, and knowing the handicap placed upon those unfortunate, Mrs. Bourn immediately set about finding a remedy and her home in Gilbert was turned into a training school for this group. Soon she outgrew the small town of Gilbert and she taught in a vocational school held in the basement of the Monroe school.

Not only did she teach sewing, cooking, are of children and health subjects to the hundreds of women and girls who came to her school, but she interspersed citizenship, and kindred subjects to the men who gathered in t the noon hour and after school closed at night. She taught them how to sign checks, conduct their business, to speak and write English, and show loyalty to their adopted country. Instead of 9 'till 4 o'clock school hers extended to 9 sat night.

She was never too tired to give ear to their troubles and unlike many who merely sympathized; Mrs. Bourn went to work doing something about it. She had enough influence among those who had power to establish centers where her work could be carried on. For years she kept one or more afflicted children in her home.

## Ella Emily Burk Merrill Brown

Interviewer: Roberta Flake Clayton
Navajo County

Ella Brown was born in the little town of Farmington, Davis County, Utah, on August 9th, 1855, just 7 years after her pioneer parents reached there. She was the sixth in a family of ten children.

Her father was Allen Burk and her mother, Emily Jane Smith, a sister of Let Smith, a man noted in early Utah and Arizona history as being afraid of neither man nor the devil and who finally, while protecting his property, met his death t the hands of a Navajo Indian.

Ella's home was 18 miles from Salt Lake City, and frequently went there with her parents. Because of its location near headquarters, Farmington had exceptionally good schools and to these Ella and other members attended.

Benjamin Brown
*(St. Johns LDS Family History Files)*

The Burk family management devolved almost entirely on the Mother who partook some of her noted brother Lot's executive ability. Allen Burk was never bothered, never in a hurry and took things as they came without complaint. They were moderately comfortable for the early days until one year of sickness, the serious illness of the hard working Mother, and the death of a sister, reduced them to near want.

Tom Merrill was not exactly the parent's choice, it was decidedly Ella's, who loved to hear him sing, play the guitar or mandolin and watch him step dance which he could do better than anyone in these parts, was the life of every party, so they were married when she was 17.

Because they moved around so much they were in very straightened circumstances when she became a widow. After all were married but the baby she accepted the hand of a neighbor, Benjamin Brown.

Ella was the mother of 10 children, 4 of whom died in infancy. She raised three girls and three boys to maturity.

**Miriam O. Bugbee**
Interviewer: Roberta Flake Clayton
Phoenix

On December 2, 1881 on what is known as the Greenhaw Addition, little Miriam was born. Ever the pioneer, Mr. Greenhaw moved out about 13 miles west on the desert and took up a ranch. He had a section and a half of land and specialized in raising fine horses. Miriam was only five years old at that time, but on this ranch her childhood and early girlhood was spent. Here she attended her first school.

After graduating from the little country school, Miria came into Phoenix and attended the Larson School. As there were very inadequate facilities for higher education in Arizona at that time, and as the mother knew the value of education, the Greenhaws allowed their oldest son and daughter to go to Pasadena, California where they graduated from the Thropt Polytechnic, now the Cal Tech College.

Mr. Greenhaw was a gifted pianist and violinist. Her mother was one of education and refinement and was a gracious hostess. There were eight children, five of whom grew to maturity.

Aside from these home entertainments in which the children of the family took their part, Paul playing the violin by his father's accompaniment while the others gave readings and told stories. There were occasional dances and always horseback riding and the proverbial horse and buggy.

When Miriam graduated from college she expected to become a teacher and it was no little disappointment to her mother that she met and married Clinton H. Bugbee.

## Catherine Barlow Burton

Interviewer: Roberta Flake Clayton
Phoenix

Catherine, or Kate as she was always called, was the daughter of James Madison and Bleets de la Motte Barlow. Her parents came west from Kentucky, walking across the plains from the Missouri River to the Great Salt Lake. When their shoes wore out these faithful pioneers wrapped their wounded bleeding feet in "gunny sacks."

Kate was born May 9, 1861 in her father's big home near the famous Beehive House in Salt Lake City, Utah.

James M. Barlow was one of the first jewelers in Salt Lake City, and his work was one of the highest order. He made the most intricate designs in long earrings, so popular in those early days, bracelets, rings, broaches, etc.

Kate was the fourth child in her mother's family of six children. Her schooling did not begin until she was seven years old as she had to go more than a mile to school.

Her marriage ceremony was performed by Joseph F. Smith, afterward President of the L.D.S. Church. The wedding presents were many and very expensive as both families were well to do.

Kate is the mother of twelve children. Only once has death come to her immediate family and that was when a Doctor administered the wrong medicine to her baby and killed him.

## Achsah May Hatch Decker

Interviewer: Roberta Flake Clayton
Contributed by her daughter Helen E. Decker
Navajo County

Achsah May Hatch was born August 29, 1875 at Franklin, Idaho, the daughter of Lorenzo Hill and Catherine Karren Hatch. She came of a long line of Vermont Hatches and at least one English Ratcliff who jumped out of a two story building in order to marry the man she loved.

Her parents were among the first Arizona pioneers. In fact, at the early age of three months Achsah May found herself a completely initiated and active pioneer.

Strange to say 'twas written in the stars that Louis Addison Decker and Achsah May would someday meet and wed. Both of them had been saved from drowning when young children. When Achsah May first met Louis, he was singing at an annual M.I. A. convention entertainment. She thought Louis was slightly off key and laughed at him, but a few months later when he sang, "I love you truly", she thought he was definitely in tune.

On October 1, 1897 they were married in the Temple in Salt Lake City, Utah. They settled in a snug and neat log cabin in Taylor, Arizona. There the stork stopped by at intervals until he had left them ten children.

**Juanita Gonzales Fellows**
Interviewer: Roberta Flake Clayton
Phoenix

Three weeks is rather an early age to begin pioneering but that is as old as little Juanita was when her parents Jacob and Eulalie Gonzales moved from San Miguel to Guymas, Sonora, Mexico. The tiny daughter and only child of this couple was born October 18, 1865. Her father was part owner of a ranch and large herd of cattle. He bade his young wife goodbye one morning to go and look after his cattle interests. The next day word was brought to her that he had been murdered by renegade Apaches.

Juanita's grandfather went and brought home the lifeless body and buried it. The young wife was inconsolable, and for a year lingered between life and death. Little Juanita was given all the love of her poor mother's heart, as she so resembled her father.

Conditions in Mexico at that time were in such a turmoil that life and property were unsafe. Young Jacob's partners robbed the widow of all that the Apaches left. The Government was unstable. Law and order unknown. After being robbed many times and being unable to obtain redress and having four of his sons conscripted into the army, Grandfather Gonzales disposed of his large land holdings in Sonora and came to Arizona. He brought his family including his widowed daughter. Juanita was nine years old at that time. They located in Tempe.

Eulalie Gonzales was beautiful, with her olive skin, large dark eyes and luxurious black hair. Many suitors came to woo her in her new home. Finally she married William Osborne. As a stepfather, William Osborne was all that could be desired, always kind and generous to Juanita. Juanita went to the American schools but she also had a Spanish instructor to teach her the language and legends of her people.

When she was seventeen she married William Wallace Fellows. Mr. Fellows was an engineer at the Vulture Mine. The eldest child; a daughter, was born at the mine, and then they moved to Tempe where the other nine were born; five girls and five boys. Two of each died when they were small.

## Prudence Jane Kartchner Flake

Interviewer: Roberta Clayton
Snowflake

In Utah, just south of Salt Lake lies a little vale that in the early settlement of that land was called "Little Cottonwood." Here was born to William D. Kartchner and Margaret Jane Casteel Kartchner on March 15, 1850, a little baby girl, she was the second daughter and third child to bless their home. Her father was of sturdy Pennsylvania Dutch stock, and her mother's descent is from the Royal families of Flanders, with known ancestors back to 1410.

When but a few weeks old, owning to unfavorable living conditions, baby Prudence took a severe cold which settled in her lungs weakening them so that all her life when she took cold she had difficulty in breathing.

Prudence's school days were spent in various places. Often she would only get three months schooling during the winter's term. She always made the best of her opportunities.

When she decided at the age of eighteen to marry she accepted the offer of William J. Flake. He asked her to become his wife, and to accompany him on the trip he was taking. They were married ten years before Prudence had any children of her own. During this time she continued as a member of the church choir, and to gratify her desire for higher growth and development, attended school.

To satisfy her longing for children she adopted a little girl, but finally gave her up. Prudence's health had begun to fail, her old lung trouble developed into asthma, so her husband took her to the Temple to be blessed for her health and there she was promised a son. This promise was later fulfilled for she became the mother of seven children, two of them were sons. Three of her children died in infancy, the eldest of the sons lived to be two years old before he passed away.

**Carmen Flynn**
Interviewer: Romelia Gomez
Cochise County

Mrs. Flynn did not come to Bisbee until after her marriage to Mr. Bernardino Flynn, around 1890. Here Mr. Flynn secured work in the smelter as foreman of the plant where the "adobitos" of the ore were made. He had working under him many Mexicans, and according to Mrs. Flynn, he was well liked by them.

The Flynns lived in a large building on Naco Road, somewhere around the place where the fire station now stands. They bought water from "aguadores" who brought it to them in water bags. Sometimes Mrs. Flynn would have to go up to the office on Main Street to pretest that she hadn't had any water delivered to her for two or three days, saying that her barrel was getting empty. The man in charge there would then tell her, jokingly, to pray a lot so that it would rain and there would then be plenty of water for everyone. Their firewood was also brought from "leneros" with their burros'. Mr. Flynn always bought it by the cord.

In Mexico Mr. Flynn attended very few dances because she didn't like them. In Bisbee she didn't attend any at all, going out very seldom to fiestas or community affairs. She has never gone to a movie and the only place she remembers going to was the Opera House, where she saw two or three plays given by actors from Mexico.

She has always been very reluctant to witness any scenes or occurrences like fire, accidents, etc., even to the point of not coming out of her house to see an accident which occurred in front of her house. She just doesn't like to see such things and isn't a bit interested in them.

**Mary Louisa Whitmore Garner**
Interviewer: Roberta Clayton
Navajo County

Soon after her arrival she was married to Samuel Price and by him had four children, three boys and a baby girl that died at the age of three months

With marriage life began in earnest for Mary. Raised as she was in comparative luxury, it was pretty hard to be deprived of the actual necessities of life and share in the poverty of the early pioneers. Often times she longed for her home and its comforts. She never allowed a disloyal thought to her church enter her head, nor a murmuring word to escape her lips. With her sweet voice resounding she would drive away the "blues" while she bathed and put the children to bed long enough to wash, dry, iron and mend their clothes so they could put them on again. The three little boys had lots of enforced rest periods.

Two great sorrows came to Mary in her early married life, one the loss of her husband, and the other, her brother, James M, who with a companion was murdered by Indians when they were out rounding up cattle. Their bodies were buried under the snow, were recovered and taken to their homes in Salt Lake for burial.

Although left a widow with three small sons, almost destitute of the necessities, she possessed a spirit of cheerfulness and love, always trying to make others happy regardless of her lot.

Mary again married, this time to David Garner, who had been a member of the Mormon Battalion, and a pioneer of 1847, by whom she had one child, a daughter. Many a time she took her baby girl on one arm and a basket to eggs on the other and walked four miles to the store and back to get some necessary article.

Again she was deprived of her husband and companion.

Later she moved to Springville, Utah. One of her boys, who had remained in Ogden, was stricken very seriously ill and sent for his mother to come to his bedside.

She went by rail and arriving in Salt Lake City she had to change trains. While trying to find out when she could leave a switch engine backed up, struck her, and threw her across the track catching her feet and crushing them. She was also cut severely over the right eye from which she nearly bled to death before she was taken to a hospital.

She was so terribly injured that the Doctor told her afterward that if it had been on a battlefield she wouldn't even have been picked up, as death seemed so evident.

So serious was the accident, and so little hope was held out for her recovery, that the doctors waited for an hour after the amputation of her one leg, six inches below the knee, before they took off the other. She took very little chloroform and was conscious and realized all her pain and suffering, which was so intense that she slept none at all until the third night, when in a fitful nap she was given assurance in a dream that she would live. Maimed and crippled though she was, she was glad that she could live for the children's sake.

This dream was a great consolation to her during the three months that she was allowed to lie flat on her back in the hospital without once even being turned on her side. The Doctor who attended her at first either thought it a useless task, or was drunk at the time, as the flesh was never drawn over the ends of the bones and for a long time these s ere as tender as one's eye.

The doctor's said they were sure she would die, but she lived for 40 years thereafter. She brought suit for damages against the railroad company, but the only witness she had, that she could count on, was mysteriously drowned in the Weaver River leaving a wife and two little children. All Mary ever got for her two priceless feet was a thousand dollars, just about enough to pay her hospital bill.

When at last she was brought home to her baby girl, then seven years old, she forced a smile of cheerfulness and as she took her little daughter in her arms, assured her they would get along somehow as they had one pair of good feet between them, and little Elizabeth was always willing to loan hers for her mother's comfort. Such is the background in the life of this pioneer woman who with two artificial feet, and two crutches came to Arizona in 1884. Not a dependent by any means, but as a useful, beloved, independent citizen.

## Mary Elizabeth Greenwalt

Interviewer: Kathlyn M. Lathrop
Duncan

Perhaps my story will shed some light on the subject of "Child Marriage" which the world today seems to be making such a fuss about. In that part of the Ozarks where I was born, April 6, 1873, child marriage was not so unusual as they are in other parts of the world today.

I became a bride at the age of twelve, and my husband was fifteen, there wasn't any fuss or to do about it either. True, we were a little young to take up the duties of marriage, I can see that now, but nobody thought anything about it then. Even so, I can also see that a lot worse things could have happened to me without marriage at that age.

I was born two days after my father was shot and killed in a moonshiner's feud. It was the Sharp-McCullock feud. Pa was Jack

Sharp, the last of the male Sharps of that generation except my two small brothers, John and Ike, who were mere babies at the time.

The man who killed Pa was Jasper McCullock, he and his small son, three years old-were all the McCullock men left from that feud. After old Jasper killed Pa of course he took Pa's still, but he promised to look after Ma and her brood of eight youngsters, which he did.

Ma died when I was born, and the children were left to the mercy of old Jasper. Sister Jane, who was the oldest, was only eleven, she was promptly married off to old John Shaw, he was fifty, or sixty, I reckon. The other six children were sent to live with Jane. Jasper's wife, Mary, insisted on keeping me and raising me herself—old Jasper done the raising with his bull whip.

Old Jasper didn't come home from the still only about once a month or so, but when he did he came in roaring like a shaggy, old redheaded lion and swinging that bull whip; he slept with that whip hanging on the head of his bed, his rifle within reach and a jug of moonshine handy.

Ed McCullock and me were the youngest in the family, and after Aunt Mary died and old Jasper got killed in an explosion at the still, Granny McCullock said that she thought it best for Ed and me to get married. We did and Granny lived with us.

A few months after Ed and me were married, Granny decided she had had too much trouble there in the Ozarks and she wanted to go over into Kansas where she had some relatives on her side of the house; she had married old Ed McCullock, old Jasper's father, when she was only fourteen, and hadn't seen any of her people since.

We settled on a one horse affair farm about twenty three miles from where the town of Leon, Kansas is now. Ed and John located what they thought might be a silver mine, it was lead however, not far from our house, and after they had the crops all laid by that summer they decided to do some mining.

They had a tunnel about sixty feet back in the hill and were using powder to blast out the ore. Granny and me were standing in the front door or our cabin watching the blasting. Suddenly there was a louder boom than before and we seen the bodies of both men sail into the air with the dirt and rocks. I still done' know just what all did happen then. The next thing I knew it was almost a week later. What had been found of the bodies of Ed and John were buried and I had become the mother of a pair of twins.

At Granny's suggestion we sold off everything but a milk cow, a buggy horse, the chickens, and a pig, bought a house in the village and moved in where I could get a little work around for people to help out. At eighteen I met and married Clarence Greenwalt.

Not that I wanted to get rid of my twins, but just to pacify Granny I let her keep them and that settled her objections to my marriage to some extent. That was in 1890, and Clarence and me moved off to the coal mines in Oklahoma. Clarence and me had six children.

Then one morning I walked with Clarence out to the gate when he started off to his work. He kissed me goodbye and went off signing "When you and I were Young Maggie." I stood there watching him out of sight; I could hear his voice long after I couldn't see him.

About noon that day word came that there had been a cave-in in the mine, fourteen men were trapped; nine of those men were killed, six were found within a few hours, but Clarence and two more were not found for three days, three thousand years to me. I have made my home with my brother Ike Sharp at Bisbee, Arizona since 1919.

## Manuel Armenta Gonzales

Interviewer: Jose del Castillo
Tucson

I was born Manuela Armenta on January 14, 1864, in Tubutana, District of Altar, Sonora, Mexico. I married Senor Nazario Tapia Gonzales. I have one brother Oreol Gastelum Armenta.

I came to Tucson when I was eight years old, traveling on a horse cart with my mother. We went back to Mexico, and seven years later, I returned, an orphan, with my aunt Refugio Gastelum, and her husband, Ramon Gonzales, and made our home in the United States. We lived in the San Pedro Valley.

In Mexico, my father obtained most of the money by making soap and selling it. At that time we were living, as the Holy Scripture has it, "like the children of the Limbo." We knew not how or from where we received our food, all we knew was that we had it, and we made the most of it. My father had a fruit grove that grew quince, apples, apricots, and other such fruits.

At Tanque Verde, my husband worked for Mrs. Inez de Oury. We then moved to Alcala Ranch near Tanque Verde. The owner of this ranch was Guadalupe Alcala and his wife who was my husband's sister, Delores de Alcala. We lived at the Alcala Ranch until my last child was born, then we moved to the El Oso Ranch on the old road to Nogales. After leaving El Oso we moved to Rincon.

My children were: Nazario, Maria, Jose, and Manuel. Five of my children are dead: Juana, Guadalupe, Carlos, Cleotilue, and Cruz.

We lost some land that was once Baboquivari Grant, at that time a Mexican possession, and we also lost some land in Tubac.

## Victoria Fredona Gooch

Interviewer: Kathlyn M. Lathro
Duncan

I was born in Fall County, Texas, January 22, 1871. I am the 6th of a family of nine children. I came to make my home in Duncan, Arizona, June 23, 1911. So, I have missed the thrilling frontier life of the territorial days in Arizona but I have not missed all of the frontier days in Texas, and pioneer life "in-the-raw" in the territorial days in the Oklahoma Strip.

My mother, Angline Malalie Blevins, was born September 26, 1855, in eastern Missouri. She is the daughter of half-breed Cherokee woman named Jane Blevins, and a German trader named Andrew Blevins. There were three of the children, one girl and two boys.

## Sarah A. Packer Higgins

Interviewer: Helen M. Smith
Cochise County

I was born in Greenriver, Utah; July 29, 1867 I lived the more or less uneventful life of the Mormon child until I was nine years old when I was crippled with rheumatism. We wore hand knit heavy stockings and heavy shoes to school. Someone had been irrigating and the road was under water. I sat all day in school with my shoes and stockings soaked, and have walked on crutches all the rest of my life in consequences.

Sixty one years is a long time to go on crutches, but in spite of my affliction I seem to have accomplished as much and enjoyed as much as the ordinary women. I had ten children and raised nine of them, and it seems as I look back that I managed to care for them as well as other mothers of my acquaintance.

I was married in Utah in 1886, and shortly after we started for Arizona in company with other of our relatives.

## Miriam Dalton Hancock

Interviewer: Roberta Flake Clayton
Navajo County

Born of pioneer parents, Miriam Dalton herself became a pioneer. She was born February 1st, 1864, at Virgin City, Kane County, Utah, the daughter of John and Ann Casewell Williams Dalton.

When only a child of eight years Miriam says she had to go out to work and earn her living, working for a neighbor with whom she stayed for 2 years.

When she was 10 her mother had a paralytic stroke and the whole care of her devolved on Miriam and her sister Jemima, who afterwards became Mrs. Simon Murphy. They carried their tiny little mother, who at her best never weighed more than eighty pounds, around in their arms like she was a baby.

As soon as her help could be dispensed with at home, Miriam again sought employment that by the little she could earn besides her own board and keep might be used to assist the family. "When I was 15 years old I came home one day and found Mother with no shoes to wear. I took the only ones I had off my feet and put them on hers, and I, myself, went barefooted, though I was almost a grown young lady. Under other conditions this exposure would have been rather humiliating, but for my dear little Mother, no sacrifice was too great for me to make."

For almost a year she kept company with Lyman Hancock. They were married in the autumn of 1880. Their bridal trip was made in a covered wagon to St. George, Utah. There they remained during the winter and until May of the next year. Upon their return, Miriam and her husband went to live at Snowflake Camp, as Pinedale was then called, taking up a homestead. They were among the first permanent settlers. Mrs. Hancock is the mother of 13 children, 9 of whom grew to maturity.

## Emma Swanson Hansen

Interviewer: Roberta Clayton
Navajo County

Emma Swanson Hansen is truly representative of those who early fought the elements to make the desert a fit and habitable place for white man to enjoy and be glad and proud to call home. She was the second child born to Swedish immigrant parents in Spanish Fork, Utah, March 3, 1863.

In was in this place that golden haired Emma received her education for which her father paid in produce from his farm. Not all the children of her day were thus favored for many families were not able to part with any of their produce to pay even for a meager education.

Not all the education she possessed was learned in the log school house where slab boards were made into crude seats and where writing was done on slates. Emma was a sturdy Swedish girl and her parents taught her how to make the soil bring forth its bounties. In her childhood she worked long hours hoeing weeds, digging potatoes, milking cows and doing other tasks bout the farm.

It was shortly after her eighteenth birthday March 2nd, 1881 that this girl with a youthful round face, honest blue eyes and golden wavy hair became the wife of Joseph C. Hansen.

Joseph had also spent his life in Spanish Fork until he was chosen to help make a settlement on the Little Colorado River in Arizona. He lived there for three years and had come back to Spanish Fork for a winter's visit during 1880-1881. In the spring of 1881 he turned his face again southward taking with him his wife Emma.

**Loretta Ellsworth Hansen**
Interviewer: Roberta Flake Clayton
Navajo County

Rettie, the daughter of Edaund and Mary Ann Bates Ellsworth was born April 12, 1868 at West Weber, Utah. The home at that time consisted of two rooms and there were twelve in the family. The boys slept in the barn.

At the early age of nine, Rettie began the duties of Motherhood, assisted by two of her sisters. Twin girls were born in the home and she took over the care of one of them, while Nellie and Julia took the other. The hardest part of this child raising was when the babies had to be fed at night and the little mothers would have to get up and heat the milk over a coal oil lamp. Their labors of love were rewarded, and Effie and Ellie grew up to be beautiful women.

When Rettie was eleven years old there was a terrible outbreak of diphtheria in the little town which took the lives of many of the children, among them a very dear little friend of Rettie's. She and five other members of the Ellsworth children were stricken at the same time, and when Rettie heard of her little pal's death wanted to go too. She would put her feet out from under the bed covers so she could catch cold, and when medicine was left by her bed she would empty it out. But Fate decreed it otherwise; for instead of Rettie going, two brothers and a sister were taken all three within four weeks.

When she was seventeen Rettie promised to became the wife of Hans Hanson, Jr., a fine young man she had known since coming to Arizona.

## Mary Adsersen Hansen

Interviewer: Roberta Flake Clayton
Navajo County

Far away in Tange, Jylland, Denmark, on September 28, 1849 to Peter Adsersen and his wife, Annie Catherine Lauriteen was born a baby girl, destined to play an important role in the pioneer life of Arizona, as was also her only sister, Kristen. Peter was a tailor by trade, and his wife a milliner and the daughters assisted their parents, thus learning both useful arts.

Mary and her mother emigrated to America about 1860, and settle in the town of Washington in Utah. Kristen had come with some friends four years previously and shortly after her arrival had become the wife of Hans Hansen, one of her own countrymen. When her third child was born she and the infant son both died, and her mother and sister took the two remaining children.

On May 15, 1865 Mary married her sister's husband and became the mother of 11 children, six sons and five daughters. After their marriage they took Hans Junior, the daughter Annie remained with her grandmother.

## Louesa Park Harper

Interviewer: Roberta Flake Clayton
Contributed by her daughter Louesa Rogers

My mother, Louesa Park Harper, was born December 13, 1845, at Winter Quarters Nebraska. She emigrated with her parents, John and Louisa Smith Park to Utah in 1847.

Her parents were both emigrants from the old world. Her mother born June 24, 1818, at Faranhorn, Kent County, England, came with her parents in 1820, and settled in Canada. John Park coming from Scotland as a young man met and married Louisa early in 1840.

They left Canada in 1845 with two wagons and four yoke of cattle. They passed through Nauvoo, Ill., and joined the company at Winter Quarters, where their fourth child was born and where they remained during the winter of 1846-47, in the spring going on with John Taylor's Company.

Upon their arrival in Salt Lake City, they build a log cabin on the old Fort Square, now known as Pioneer Square. It was a great relief to have even a log house to live in as they had lived in their wagon boxes what time they had spent since leaving Canada.

There was great excitement when Johnson's army entered the valley. This family along with others determined to defend their homes and their belongings. The Army, while appearing to be a menace was a blessing in disguise. The settlers found a ready market for all their surplus produce, and were able to trade for all kinds of provisions, clothing and work animals.

When Louesa was nineteen her older sister, Mary Ann, married and went to Murray, Salt Lake County to live. Louesa went with them. Here she met Harvey John Harper, son of Charles and Lavina Dilworth Harper, who lived in Big Cottonwood. Louesa Park and Harvey John Harper were married December 29, 1866, Salt Lake City, Utah and made their home at Big Cottonwood.

## Happylona Sanford Hunt

Interviewer: Roberta Flake Clayton
Snowflake

Born in a home of plenty, Happy or Hap, and Later Aunt Hap as she was called, never knew what it was to go hungry as so many pioneers did. When she was born, February 18, 1855, her parents, Cyrus and Sylvia Clark Sanford, were in very favorable circumstances. They were among the first emigrants to Utah, but by thrift, frugality and good management they had plenty for their ten children, the first and last of whom came in pairs.

The eldest twins were Almira and Alvira, and the last two were Happylona and Saphronia. There was only one brother, but he early learned to take his part against all of these girls, and was a match for all of them.

Whether it was her natural sweetness and fun loving disposition or because she was the child of the parents' mature years, Hap was always the favorite of her father, who petted and spoiled her dreadfully, at least so said her older sisters. An occurrence caused them all to humor her, when she had typhoid fever.

Long months she suffered from this dread disease, but won out and was getting nearly well, when one day a crowd of her young friends came with a sleigh and four prancing horses and pressured her mother to let her go riding with them. Very reluctantly the mother consented. With all their care Hap took cold and had a relapse and was much worse than at first. For many long months she lay between life and death. She was not able to leave the house for almost a year.

Along with her many friends were many young men admirers, yet she saved her great store of love for a man much older than herself, and who had buried one wife by whom he had had a large family, some of the children older than Hap. There was great excitement in the home of John Hunt when the children waited for him to bring from Springville, Utah, his new wife. Though they were married March 19, 1887, she did not come to her husband's home in Snowflake, Arizona until the following October. Never blessed with children of her own, she mothered every one belonging to her husband, from the eldest to the youngest.

## Virlinda Jennings

Interviewer: Kathlyn M. Lathrop
Duncan

I was born in Smith County, Republic of Texas, December 26, 1845, just four days before the little republic became the possession of the United States of America. I reckon you'd call me a "Squalling Christmas Present" that has lasted 94 years, come December 25, 1939.

My memory is quite clear on the most important things that have happened in my own life, but I have had no schooling—that is book learning—and I don't recall, clearly, all the exact dates of things that happened to my people when those first bloody pages of Texas history were in the making.

I reckon we best start with some of the things I was taught to "never forget" in childhood: My grandfather, William Hamilton Smith, and his bride of a few months, her name was Sarah Tyler, came to Texas from Tennessee with a colony of about 300 families back in 1821. I do not remember just which colony.

They settled in a community on the Colorado River, which later became the city of Columbus. Then when Grandfather's land grant was given him, he moved to Nacogdoches County. Smith County was organized from Nacogdoches County, when I was about one year old, and was named for General James Smith, who was an uncle of Grandfather. The town of Tyler was named for my grandmother's father, and built on his land grant.

Grandfather Smith died at the Alamo, and of course, his only son—my father—fell heir to the plantation where he was born, and where I was born, which was in Smith County by that time. Father was away fighting in the war when I was born.

When he came home from the war on New Year's Day, 1846, he was somewhat surprised to find he had a daughter and not a son to follow in his footsteps. And, Mother said she was surprised to learn that Texas was no longer a republic of its own, but now belonged to the United States of America.

My childhood was no different to other girls who were born in that age and brought up on the Texas frontiers. We learned to cook, wash, iron, piece quilts, spin and weave cloth, and make all our own clothes, and knit our hosiery from yarns that we made ourselves. Of course we had Negros to do most of the work, but that did not mean that we girls were to be brought up in idleness. No siree!

I was only about 16 years old when the Civil War broke out, and had been married three years. I had a son almost two years old. Girls married young those days you know. We were considered grow-up, or marriageable age as soon as we developed into womanhood.

I married Buck Jennings two months after I met him. He had come to Texas from Missouri, less than a year before that. He was just a young adventurer, whom nobody seemed to know much about, seeking to make a fortune all his very own in the wild and woolly west.

## Olive Jewell

Interviewer: Helen M. Smith
Cochise County

I was born in Mississippi in 1865 and came to Arizona with my mother and a sister in 1884. My mother was a widow, and except for a married brother in Mississippi, we were all the family. We went to Snowflake, a small Mormon settlement. My sister and I worked out as hired girls, farm hands, and any other work we could get. We were allowed all the wheat we could glean for our own use; altogether we managed to make a good living.

Typhoid broke out in the camp, of a virulent type, and almost all in camp took it. My sister died, and for awhile my mother's life was despaired of, but I was not even sick. I was quite worn out, though, from nursing so many sick. There were a great many deaths, sometimes three or four from one family. It was a terrible experience.

Soon after that we went to Utah, where I was married in the Temple to Leonard Jewell. Returning to Arizona, we went to Safford, where my husband farmed and raised castle. While living there three children were born to us, and one died of measles.

**Ellen Jane Parks Johnstun**
Interviewer: Roberta Flake Clayton
Phoenix

I was born July 12, 1844 at Sheffield, Yorkshire, England. My parents were Samuel and Ellen Wright Parks. My early life was spent in Sheffield. Father was born in Dublin, Ireland but is of English blood. Grandfather was a chain maker and was sent for to Ireland to carry on his trade. At one time he was making an enormous chain. When asked why he was making such a big one he answered, "To tie up the Pope and Priest and Devil together."

My mother had five children, I being the oldest of them, three girls and two boys. When I was about five years old we had small pox and one of my sisters died. My parents were very devout Christians and often carried me twelve miles to church when I was a baby.

I remember how I loved to hear the band and when it paraded I would follow all over Sheffield. These were officers and bands getting recruits for the Crimean War. My father went to America to avoid this draft.

About September 1854, my Father sailed for America. Our home had been guarded for three weeks to get him in the Army. He was not financially able to bring Mother and us so he went and settled at Alton, Illinois. He was a mechanic and made iron machinery. Just as soon as he got settled he borrowed money from a wealthy farmer to send for us. We sailed April 26, 1855.

I was married in January, on the 26, 1863 to William James Johnstun. He was twenty years older than I and had been married before. He was a hostler at the stage line in Salt Lake so that was our first home. Later he went to work for Jenson Stoddard. Mr. Stoddard was pretty well fixed. He was called to go and help colonize Arizona but did not want to go, so William volunteered to go in his place.

## Annella Hunt Kartchner

Interviewer: Roberta Flake Clayton
Navajo County

Annella Hunt was born February 15, 1862 at Colton, California, near San Bernardino. Her parents were John Hunt, son of Captain Jefferson Hunt of the Mormon Battalion, and Lois Pratt Hunt, a lady of high culture and beauty.

Their home at the time of Annella's birth was located near the Santa Ana River, and on the morning of February 15, as the family were seated t the breakfast table, their house was surrounded by floodwaters, overflowing the low banks of the river.

John Hunt hurriedly hitched up his team and they drove to his sister Harriet Mayfield's home which was on higher ground farther from the river. Here at midnight of that day Annella Hunt was born.

When Annella was a year old, the family made the journey by team across the great American desert and settled in Beaver City, Utah. Their three small daughters had whooping cough during that journey. Just before leaving California John Hunt had all his family vaccinated, even Baby Annella just past a year old. This precaution proved to be a very great blessing to them all fifteen years later.

They lived in Beaver for eleven years and the family went to good schools. Besides the three older daughters, two brothers and three other sisters were born here. John Hunt was sheriff of Beaver County during the entire time and his family had many anxious times when he was after men who had committed serious crimes, or had escaped from jail.

He finally decided to move away from Beaver and took his family to a small settlement on the Sevier River, where they remained for two years. They next joined a group of pioneers who were going into Arizona, or New Mexico, where new settlements were being made.

In the fall of 1878, John Hunt was called to be the Bishop of the new Snowflake settlement, on Silver Creek. Now, began Annella Hunt's long active life in Snowflake where she served in every sort of capacity. She was the teacher of the first little school in Snowflake in the spring of 1879. The following winter she also taught the first school in the town of Taylor, three miles south of Snowflake. In the fall of 1881 Annella and her oldest sister, Ida, taught the Snowflake school and in the spring of 1882 they taught the school in Taylor. Three or four months were as long as the county funds permitted the school to continue.

The three oldest Hunt sisters, Ida, May and Annella, had passed a Teacher's Examination under Mr. James Stinson, who was County Judge and they had certificates which entitled them to teach in Arizona schools.

In September 1883, Annella Hunt left her home to become the bride of Orin Kartchner. They made the long journey by team to be married in the Temple at St. George, Utah, traveling in company with a brother of the bridegroom. They were married October 11, 1883. They remained in Utah nearly two months.

## Margaret Jane Casteel Kartchner

Interviewer: Roberta Flake Clayton
Navajo County

Margaret Jane Casteel was born September 1, 1825 in Cooper County, Missouri. Her parents were Jacob Israel Casteel and Sarah Nowlin Casteel. There may have been more than the six children whose names are known but there were six brothers and sisters at least. Their names were Mary (St. Mary), Emmeline (Savage), Margaret (Kartchner), James, Joshua, and Francis Steven, called "Frank", who made a journey down the Missouri River, supposedly to Texas and never returned. His fate was never known and this was a great source for mourning by his mother and brother and sisters.

The Casteel blood was of French extraction with mixtures of English, Scotch and Irish. They were evidently of devout Christian faith, for Margaret's father's family consisted of eight brothers and one sister were given bible names throughout. They were: Abraham, Isaac, Jacob, Israel, Shadrack, Meshach, Abednego, Daniel, Benjamin, and Mary.

Very little is known of Margaret's life until she was eighteen years of age, when she married William Decatur Kartchner, on March 17, 1844 in the city of Nauvoo, Illinois.

## Rebecca Steward Kartchner

Interviewer: Roberta Flake Clayton
Phoenix

It has been many long years since I was a baby in my mother's arms. I will never forget what she told me many times that she never wanted me. That she was ashamed to take me any place, but

I am still here in this old dreary world, and have gone through all that a girl needs to go through.

I can remember since I was six years old, I was a big, fat, girl , as big around as I was tall, with large blue eyes and black hair. I would fall down standing still I was so clumsy. No one seemed to care for me but my brother George. He was a blue eyed boy with brown curly hair. He was two years older than I. Everybody loved him, but he was my old standby. My name was Rebecca and George knew when he called on Becky he always got what he wanted done.

We lived in the back woods of Alabama. Ours was a two-room log house. It was a mile from the road by a big mountain with a little stream of clear water running close by. George and I spent many happy hours wading in the water. We were always barefoot, my parents being too poor to buy shoes.

My father drank all the time. He made his own whiskey. I was afraid of him because he would come home drunk every night, abuse Mother and beat us poor little hungry children. He said I wasn't his child and would knock me over in the corner where Mother had a pile of cotton to have the seeds picked out.

Mother would card and spin and make clothes for us children to wear. After father would get just so drunk he would go to sleep, then Mother would have all us children sit around the fireplace and pick cotton seed. She would throw on a piece of fat pine so we could see, we had no lamps. I was so afraid father would wake that I would get close to Mother. All of us would sit in silence, look back in the dark corner once in awhile to see that he stills slept, then we would bend over the cotton we were picking until our brains were nearly cooked. After awhile we would go to bed, George, my baby sister Evaline and I would sleep in a pile or cotton with an old quilt over us and I would cry myself to sleep. If I heard a little noise I would think father was coming and would lay close to George. When morning came we would get up and eat our breakfast, which was only a piece of corn bread, then we would go out to play.

One day Mother went to the field to plow as Father made her do all the farm work. While us children were alone we did some queer things. This day George said, "Come here Becky, lets plow with our old cat." So we put a rope around her neck but she would only lay down. We whipped her but still she wouldn't go. I carried her to a big rock, put her head on it and George hit her head with another big rock. That was the last of her.

While this was going on and we were watching the cat Father stepped up. His eyes were red and he couldn't stand still. He took out his knife. When it was opened it was exactly twelve inches long. He staggered back and cut a peach tree limb, caught me by the arm, put my head between his knees, pulled up my dress and whipped me until I stood in a puddle of blood.

When he raised up he fell face downward on the ground and laid there for awhile. George ran to the house. I got in a big bunch of bushes, put my hand over my mouth and cried until I could cry no longer. After awhile my big sister came and took me to the house and put me to bed.

All the clothes I had to wear was a belt waisted dress that touched the ground, long sleeves and high neck. I had no underwear or anything else. When my dress got so dirty it didn't smell very good, then Mother would put me to bed and wash it. All the boys wore were long shirts and no pants.

There were thirteen of us children to make cloths for and Mother had her heart and hands full as she had most all the farm work to do besides caring for as many children and making our clothes. All Father thought of was whiskey and bad women. He drank so much he was nearly blind and when he was sober he professed to be a hard-shelled Baptist preacher.

In the year of eighteen hundred and seventy six, two men came through where we lived and stayed a week with my people. They talked to them about the west. They said it was the only place to live, there were lots of pretty women there and lots of money. Many of the men believed what they told and were anxious to go. These two men said people ate flour bread out west all the year around, worked two horses at a time, men wore underwear and had blue shirts to work in, women had rub-boards to clean their clothes and stoves to cook on and bought coffee that was parched. They said there were even no bed bugs to wake you at night. I would sit still and listen and although I was little I understood many things the older people talked about.

While these men were to our place Father stayed sober, we children didn't have to work, he bought some bacon to eat, Mother made biscuits for breakfast and we could have one piece, with a little grease on it. Soon all the people began making plans to go west.

Father and twenty-five more families went on to Arizona. They traveled another month and stopped on the Little Colorado River.

We were all so naked that Mother took the tent and made us girls some dresses and the boys' shirts and pants.

**Cora Lee Mefford Keegan**
Interviewer: Kathlyn M. Lathrop
Prescott

Cora Lee Mefford was born in Shelbyville, Missouri, May 31st, 1867. She came to Prescott, Arizona with her parents in 1878. She married James Keegen, 1884 and became the mother of eight children. Cora was one of the "Bells of Society" in the early days of Prescott. Her father was one of the important business men of this section.

"Blacksmith Jim" was born in Scotland, 1857. He came to America when a lad of three years. He settled in Prescott, Arizona at the age of twenty one, and went into the blacksmith business. Blacksmith Jim, prior to his appearance in Prescott, rode the Old Chisholm Trail following the great herds from the Texas plains to Kansas City. But, like a lot of the men that laid the foundation for sane civilization in this wild and wooly west, Blacksmith Jim left his family "broke." Cora Keegen, typical of the courage of all western women, went into the Hand Laundry Business.

**Caroline Marion Williams Kimball**
Interviewer: Roberta Flake Clayton
Contributed by her daughter Effie Kimball Merrill
Phoenix

Mother was the daughter of Thomas S. and Alvina W. Williams, she was born April 24th, 1843, Nauvoo Illinois. With her parents she joined the famous Mormon battalion which arrived in Salt Lake City July 29, 1847.

Mother grew up to be a beautiful girl, and was educated in the Salt Lake Schools. Her father was one of the largest freighters in Salt Lake in the early days. He ran sixteen mule teams from Salt Lake to California, hauling dry goods and groceries. When Mother was thirteen, her father gave her a beautiful locket and chain made out of gold from California. He also gave her pretty silk to make some dresses.

When she was only sixteen years old she met Father, David P. Kimball. They were married on the 13th of April, 1857 when Mother was only seventeen years old.

## May Hunt Larson

Interviewer: Roberta Flake Clayton
Snowflake

Coming from a line of school teachers on her mother's side it is no wonder May Hunt Larson was blessed with an exceptionally brilliant mind. This combined with the determination of Grandmother Hunt to master difficulties who at the age of 71 years learned to write. The courage of her Grandfather, Captain Jefferson Hunt, of Mormon Battalion fame, and the leadership of her father, John Hunt, who for over 30 years directed the affairs of the town of Snowflake, makes of her an invaluable asset to any community.

She is the daughter of John Hunt and Lois Pratt. She was born May 5, 1869, in San Bernadine, California, the second of eight children, six girls and two boys.

When she was nine months old, she was very ill with influenza, which deprived her of the sight of one eye; but somehow she had managed to see as much, and read and study more, than most people with two eyes.

When she was three years old, her parents moved from California to Beaver, Utah. Here she went to her first school as soon as she could talk well, her mother's sister, Louisa Pratt, being the teacher. Later she attended school taught by her grandmother, Louisa B. Pratt, and to another of her mother's sisters, Ellen Pratt McGary.

From 13 to 16 years old she was a member of a select private school taught by Richard S. Horne, or Teacher Horne as his pupils called him. That was the last school she ever attended.

She was married to Alof Larson, October 26, 1881, and for 55 years they have lived together. Thirteen children were born to them, six of whom died, four in infancy and two in young manhood.

## Gertrude Bryan Leeper

Interviewer: Special Staff of Writers
Phoenix

She was born in Gainesville, Cook County, Texas, and is a daughter of Porter Reese and Louise Catherine (Hammer) North, the Father of whom was a school teacher by profession and a rancher by vocation. Her maternal grandfather, Samuel Hammer, was a pioneer settler in Tennessee.

She attended the public schools of Tennessee, and completed her education in Carson-Newman College, at Jefferson City, Tennessee.

She was married on June 14, 1907, to Wylie Milton Leeper, an attorney of Sandridge, Tennessee, and in 1918 they established their permanent home in Phoenix, Arizona.

## Carmen Lucero

Interviewer: Jose del Castillo
Tucson

I was born the thirteenth of January, 1860 in Tucson. It was outside the Presidio. The Mexicans were going away, the soldiers evacuating the fort, heading for Sonora when the American troops came in.

My grandfather, Juan Gonzales, was an officer of the Mexican troops in Tucson. He took care of the prisoners. Many Mexicans, who wanted to stay, if they choose, remained. Grandfather had married Ramona Ruelas, who were native here. The family had everything; cattle, lands—all that tract southwest of Congress Street cut by the railroad tracks of which the Southern Pacific sanatorium now used to be the station. Grandpa while courting grandmother serenaded her. They had a daughter, my mother.

My father was coming from Sonora at the time the Mexicans left Tucson. He met them coming out and spoke to them. They discouraged him and wanted him to join them and go back to Mexico; Father's name is Lorenzo Renteria. He was carrying his violin with him, slung across his shoulders.

He was an aficionado and played well the violin by ear. He was the first violinist in Tucson. He played for the Americans who liked to hear him play the Mexican airs. It was new to them. He played for their dances, and during fiestas. He was invited to many places and was popular. He fell in love with the daughter of Don Juan Gonzales and married her.

I was about three years old I think when they built the San Agustin Church. We went to church when there was a priest and that was at the church of San Cosmo del Tucson, at the foot of the Sentinel Peak.

## Sophia De La Mare McLaws

Interviewer: Rae Rose Kirkham
Joseph City

"Before I was married," she began as her eyes twinkled kindly, "I was Sophia De La Mere. My father's name was Philip De La Mare, a Frenchman. President John Taylor, of the Mormon Church, while on a mission in France, met my Father on the Island of Jersey. President Taylor had been instructed to bring something of value to Utah from abroad, so he and Phillip De La Mare went to France where President Taylor purchased my father's sugar mill. Together they brought it from Paris, France, the pioneer sugar beet factory, to America.

I was born in Tooele, Utah. In 1875, I was married to John McLaws, we were among those called from various counties of Utah by Brigham Young to colonize the Little Colorado River in Arizona. I have had thirteen children born in this settlement. Mine was the first male child to arrive in Joseph City, August 3, 1876. I was eighteen years old then.

I remember the rebels coming into Utah even. Also, the old stage coaches that passed thru Tooele with pictures of Jefferson Davis painted vividly on the side. Right under his picture was printed the words, "Will hang Jeff Davis on the sour apple tree as we go marching on."

How well I remember the tragedy of President Lincoln's assassination. The word came by slow mail teams to Salt Lake City. I was only eight years old but how plain my childhood is to me!

## Mary Ann Smith McNeil

Interviewer: Roberta Flake Clayton
Navajo County

Born July 2, 1853, the daughter of William and Mary Hibbert Smith emigrated to America in 1856 on the ship *Speedwell*. The family made its way to Missouri where they remained for awhile outfitting for the West.

They obtained a team of oxen and a wagon and made their way to Salt Lake City with a group of other pioneers landing there when Mary Ann was ten years old.

Because of only one wagon and it containing all the family possessions, Mary Ann had to walk most of the way. Sometimes when she was too tired she would ride on the long reach pole that stuck four feet behind the wagon. This was far from comfortable, however, and not very safe.

When they settled down it was in Bountiful, Davis County, Utah, where at the age of fifteen Mary Ann was married to John C. McNeil. Their first home was a one room dugout and here their first child, Sarah Alice was born.

## Dona Apolonia Mendoza

Interviewer: Romelia Gomez
Cochise County

Dona Apolonia doesn't know in what year her family came to Bisbee, but insists that they were one of the first families in Zacatecas Canyon, for their rude "jacalito" was one of the three then comprising Zacatecas, most of which was covered with trees and bushes.

Apolonia and an older sister attended school at Central for a short while, during which time she says they learned nothing at all, so their mother took them out of school so that they could help her in earning the family's living, which she did by taking in washing from families living on Chihuahua Hill. Apolonia's duty was to go back and forth bringing and returning the laundry. Often during these occasions she was offered a dime by Mexican families so that she would take lunches to their men folk from Chihuahua Hill to the smelter, which was then in Bisbee.

Another one of her tasks was to draw the water used for washing the clothes from a little well near their home in Zacatecas. This she did by taking it up in a pail, for the well was very small and quite shallow.

Once, while engaged in this task, some of her playmates mischievously pushed her head first into the well. This in itself was nothing dangerous, for ordinarily she could have gotten out quite easily. In falling she accidentally loosened rock, which fell and struck her on the forehead making a bad cut.

Her mother not approving of dances, the girls were never taken to any, nor were they allowed to go to shows or fiestas of any kind. They never attended church services either, but this was because they didn't care to or didn't have time.

When Apolonia married, at the age of 12, she and her husband moved further down on Brewery Gulch. When he went off and deserted her, leaving her with two small daughters, she was left with no alternative but to go out to work. She has been working ever since.

### Effie Isabell Kimball Merrill

Interviewer: Unknown
Hackberry

She is Effie Isabell Kimball Merrill, daughter of David P. and Caroline Williams Kimball, born in Salt Lake City, Utah, May 4, 1849. Until she was four years of age the Kimbells lived there. The first move was to Bear Lake, Idaho, where they remained three years, moving back to Salt Lake City. They built them a good home and were very happy when her father was selected by Brigham Young to help colonize Arizona. Consequently in 1877 they began this journey.

When they reached Hayden's Mill sat what is now Tempe, he directed them to a place they named Lehi. Here they began building homes and getting out water for irrigation and there began Effie's first real schooling, though her mother had begun teaching her children their letters and multiplication table and other rudiments of education. Pioneer Mothers found this a very effective means of preventing quarreling that might result from too much being thrown together as were the children on those long journeys. This first school was taught by Zulu Pomeroy whom Effie learned to love sincerely.

After about 3 years at Lehi, her father again moved; this time to Cochise County to a little settlement called St. David in his honor. Soon about sixty families settled there and a pretty little town was the result. First a large fort was built of white stone. Here the newcomers lived until they had homes of their own to move into.

The Merrill Family were among the first white people to settle here and it was here Effie met a dashing young man whom everyone liked, who was destined to became her future husband. It did not take them long to decide they were meant for each other, for at 14 years of age she became the bride of Orrin Merrill.

Effie is the mother of 13 children, five girls and eight boys. She had lost two grown sons, two grown daughters and one babe.

## Sarah Emma Kartchner Miller

Interviewer: Roberta Flake Clayton
Navajo County

Being the first white child of American parentage born in the state of Colorado, and accompanying her parents who reached Salt Lake Valley, July 29, 1847, then to California, July 1, 1851, to Beaver City, Utah in 1857, in May 1866 they moved to the "Muddy" which is now Overton, Nevada, back to Utah in 1871 where they settled in Panguich. Finally to Arizona in 1877, living first at a camp on the Little Colorado River known as Taylor, and then to Snowflake in August 1878.

She was born in Pueblo, Colorado, August 17, 1846 where her parents, William Decatur and Margaret Jane Casteel Kartchner, with a group of other emigrants from Mississippi, where awaiting the arrival of the Mormon Pioneers who were preparing to leave Illinois for the great Salt Lake Valley.

Because of the sickness of her mother and the care of a large family, Sarah was early pressed into service. At the age of seven she learned to cook, preparing the meals for the others. In spite of her household tasks, Sarah learned to spin and weave taking the raw wool, carding and spinning it into yarn, then weaving it into cloth and making all kinds of clothing.

On June 1, 1877, Sarah became the wife of Ninian Miller, and their delayed honeymoon trip began in November of that year when they started with their father's family and other families for the Indian infested land of Arizona. This trip lasted almost three months, but the honeymoon continued until the death of her husband, December 14, 1912.

## Sarah McNeil Mills

Interviewer: Roberta Flake Clayton
Navajo County

Sarah was born May 7, 1870 in Bountiful, Davis County, Utah and came to Arizona in 1879 with her parents John C. and Maryanne Smith McNeil.

In the spring of 1880 Mr. McNeil moved his family to the Indian Reservation settling at a small place called Forest Dale where there was perhaps a half a dozen other families, engaged in farming. Of these early days Sarah says, "My brothers, sisters and myself have played with the Indian children, worked with them and eaten with them. We have eaten everything they did except rats.

We drew the line there." In the fall when the pinion nuts were ripe and the rats had them stored away in their big community 'nutteries' for the winter, the Indians would rob the nests and then out of the kindness of their hearts, I suppose so that the rats wouldn't starve during the cold winter, would eat them too; but no rats for the little McNeils, although many times they knew the pangs of hunger in those pioneer days.

There were very few schools in these little settlements in those days. Sarah's first teacher was a blind woman called Aunt Abbie Thayne. It is said that her sense of hearing was so keen that she could distinguish the slightest sound and of touch so delicate that she pieced a quilt of small calico pieces and in the whole quilt there was only one piece that was wrong side out and she said she knew when she made the mistake but was too tired to rectify it.

The few weeks Sarah went to this school completed her scholastic training, but no one would know it from her ability to read and write. She is the mother of 10 children, eight of whom are living.

**Charlotte Ann Tanner Nelson**
Interviewer: Roberta Flake Clayton
Navajo County

She was born in Ogden, Utah on May 5, 1870. Her parents were Seth Benjamin and Charlotte Ann Levi Tanner. When she was only two and a half years of age her mother died, leaving seven small children, the eldest, John being fifteen at the time. Because of her tender years, the other children were very kind to her, particularly John, who by his love and care of her won her undying affection.

At a very early age Ann began making herself useful in the world, first, by carrying water and doing other small tasks for an invalid, and then at the age of four, becoming the eyes of her Grandmother Levi who had lost her sight. During two years she was always near to lead her grandmother wherever she went. She had learned to do many things, among them to knit her own stockings.

It wasn't from choice that Ann became a pioneer of Arizona. She had been living with her grandmother when her father came for her in December 1876. She says, "I had such a horror of Arizona, the land of Indians and wild animals, that when Father came I hid under the bed and cried myself to sleep. The next morning when they were ready to start, my Uncle Sidney had to take me to town and literally dump me into the wagon with my father and brothers and my new step-mother. The latter was a Danish woman and had no experience with children nor American ways and could scarcely speak a word of English. She had been a dressmaker and was a very fine seamstress but the trouble was, in those days we had very little to sew."

The Tanners arrived at Moenkopi, Arizona on January 2, 1877. Ann used to spend her Sundays roaming over the hills hunting rubies or down at the river fishing. One day the girls got tired trying to fish with a bent hook and having no seine they improvised some by taking off their long sleeved petticoats, tying the neck and wrists then dragging them through the water. They caught plenty of fish, more than they could carry. But, they caught something else when they got home with their lace trimmed petticoats completely ruined by the red mud of the Little Colorado.

Her father was instructed to go to the place on this river where emigrants first contacted it and there to build a granary where travelers from Arizona bound for Utah could store their grain and other feed for their horses on the return trip.

While there he built a two-room log house for his family to live in. It had a mud roof. A steady rain of long duration caused the roof to leak. Her father was not there, so Ann and her sister climbed up, and were going to put a heavy wagon cover over it to keep the rain from ruining everything within.

Ann got too near to the edge and slipped and fell to the ground hitting the back of her head on a large rock. She lay unconscious for fifty hours and from this fall developed weak eyes and ears and a sickness that lasted a year.

At this time the country was filled with desperadoes and cattle thieves. Ann and her sister were now to be detectives reporting to the sheriff the color of the eyes and hair of every man that passed.

While the family was living on the Little Colorado a long continued rain brought the river up filling their house with red muddy water to the depth of two feet. The women and children had to be taken to the hills on a hastily improvised raft. They then moved to Moab.

One time the two girls went for the milk cows. They had to cross a dry arroyo on their way. A heavy rain fell and when they returned they found the arroyo a raging torrent. The girls were wet and cold and must get home but how to cross this swollen stream they knew not. They each took hold of a cow's tail with both hands and drove the cows into the treacherous stream. The girls held on for dear life and the cows swam across taking the girls with them.

On January 13, 1886 Ann was married to Price William Nelson.

## Ann Jane Peel Noble

Interviewer: Roberta Flake Clayton
Snowflake

Her father, Benjamin Peel, was a nephew of Sir Robert Peel, famed Premier of England. Benjamin and his brave wife, Nancy Turnbull had been disinherited and driven from home for having dared to join the Mormons. How and when they reached America is unrecorded. Their two children, Ann Jane and Robert were born and grew to school age in St. Louis. Ann Jane Noble was born February 15, 1852 at St. Louis, Missouri.

Nancy Turnbull
*(St. Johns LDS Family History Files)*

The father, a calico printer in Manchester, turned to whitewashing, plastering, and painting in the New World. Let this little touch of workmanship indicate the grain of the Peel tribe: Summoned one day to whitewash a fine home, he found all the floors bare, and the furniture covered. He insisted on restoring the rooms as they were before beginning the job. "I put my whitewash only on the walls," he said proudly.

Benjamin Peel, an Englishman, was threatened with draft into the southern army, a cause he detested. This fact brought to a head the long cherished, long delayed journey to Utah.

Jane's parents settled in Bountiful, Utah, where she lived until her marriage, January 31, 1870. She was married to Edward A. Noble soon after his return from a four year mission to England.

## Ethelinda Murray Osborne

Interviewer: Roberta Flake Clayton
Phoenix

Her parents, William P. and Margaret White Murray were living in Burleson County, Texas, when on April 5th, 1857 Ethelinda was born. She was one of seven children. They were no longer privileged to enjoy the love and devotion of their mother, as she passed away when the children were small.

In the month of May 1870, her father brought his family west en route to California. They were driving oxen, and had a large herd of loose cattle. The trip was hard on the stock because of scarcity of grass and water. Whenever both of these necessities were found in the same local, many days, or even weeks, were spent there until the supply was exhausted. Hence, it was December before the company reached Maricopa. Mr. Murray heard of the possibilities of the valley of the Salt River, so leaving his outfit there, he came on. He was so delighted with what he found that he let the company go on to California without him.

Ethelinda's father did not live along to enjoy his new home. The following May he passed away leaving his smaller children in the care of a married daughter and older members of the family.

Whether it was because she had no home or Mother, because she was so attractive, or because she and young William Osborne were so much in love, Ethelinda and he were married before she was seventeen.

The trials of early days taught her to bear stoically whatever comes. Because there were no doctors for miles around in those early days she did not look upon childbirth as a condition to be dreaded. When sickness came to her children she mixed common sense with herbs, roots and simple remedies for their care and was successful in raising a family of strong healthy boys and girls.

Everything that could not be produced here had to be freighted in from California. Screens for the windows and doors were unknown. The flies were terrible, as were the centipedes, scorpions, and tarantulas.

## Alzada Sophia Kartchner Palmer

Interviewer: Roberta Flake Clayton
Navajo County

Alzada Sophia Kartchner Palmer was born January 3, 1858, at Lower Waters, Mohave Crossing, California near what is now San Bernardino. She was the daughter of William Decatur Kartchner and Margaret Jane Casteel. They were pioneers in California at this time, and were just preparing to leave for Beaver, Utah to pioneer the desert lands when their daughter Alzada was born.

The night after she was born, her brother James, who was two years of age, died. The journey then was delayed three or four days to let the mother rest. The father prepared the little boy for burial in an old fashioned metal churn, sealing it tightly. They took him to Parowan, Utah to bury him.

The Kartchner family moved into Beaver, where they made their home for eight years. Their home was humble but a heaven on earth. They were all musicians, some played violins, Alzada played the accordion, and they all danced and sang. Three or four spinning wheels were put in one room where all could work together and enjoy real companionship and a wealth of family love. Alzada wove cloth when she was so small she could hardly reach to put the band on the wheel. They spun their own thread as well as wove the cloth. One year her sister Sarah wove four hundred yards of cloth. It was here in Beaver that Alzada first went to school.

In her diary she mentions the caroling on Christmas morning, how she looked forward to the wonderful Christmas songs and spirit.

In 1871 they went to Panguich where they built a log house of two rooms also a blacksmith shop as her father was a blacksmith. In this home as always they made work a pleasure and were taught by example as well as precept to be good sports and make life pleasant in the face of difficulties. In her own words she says, "I was proud of my parents. They were honest and true."

It was in Panguich that she met Alma Z. Palmer whom she married on May 11, 1874.

## Lucy Bedford Phillips

Interviewer: Kathlyn M. Lathrop
Duncan

I was born Lucy Laurenda Bedford, November 11, 1861, at Llanotown, Texas. My parents came to Texas with their parents when they were very small children, along about 1830, with a colony from Mississippi.

My parents were old timers in Texas by the time I came along. They had learned the pitfalls and dangers of this wild country. They could endure the hardships, and live and let live, and they could teach us children how to live and enjoy life in spite of the dangers, horrors, and hardships.

I don't remember anything about the Civil War, of course, as I was just a baby when it broke out, but I do know that every able bodied man amongst my relatives went to the war, and left their wives and children to fight Indians and live if they could.

The men folk in my family were all mighty fighters, and the women were no cowards by a long shot! My grandfather, father, uncles, and cousins were all Confederates. My brothers were all too young to go to the Civil War.

I remember when Father came home from the war, that is, I have a hazy recollection of it. Maybe, because I have heard them talk about it so much. How happy everybody was to have the men folk home to help fight Indians.

## Mary Langdon Pitt

Interviewer: Kathlyn M. Lathrop
Duncan

I was born September 17, 1867, in Buffalo, New York. My parents were each an only child, and of English-American aristocracy. My mother died at my birth and I was left o be brought up by my grandmother, who was the only relative I had left in the world except my father.

Shortly after Mother's death, my father, John Barry Langdon, left New York State to find solace in travel and adventure in the west. He was not, so grandmother taught me, seeking a fortune, for that he already had through inheritance.

There were letters from time to time, but not regularly, a mail service in those days depended upon whether or not the pony express rider happened to get through alive.

Grandmother brought me up properly, according to her own ideas. I had an old Irish biddy nurse through my baby days, a French governess through childhood, and English tutors by the score. But, I seen so very little of Grandmother. She was always so very busy with her social obligations that she had little time to bother with me.

She never talked to me about my parents, or much of anything else, as to that matter, unless it happened to be some ultimatum she had to deliver. She took long trips, but where she went or what she did; I was not allowed to know. At times I have wondered if she might have visited Father. I was not permitted to read any of Father's letters. I was told as much, or as little, as she cared to tell me and the letters were locked in her desk.

At the age of sixteen I was sent to a girl's finishing school up in the State of Maine, and I knew nothing about that sixth letter from Father until I returned home, three years later. I came home to Grandmother's funeral. I discovered I was not the rich heiress I was supposed to be. Grandmother's fortune had completely vanished and mine had vanished with it. It sees incredible that Grandmother could have squandered all the wealth of those two aristocratic families, Langdon and Rowden, but it was certainly all gone, and I was left practically penniless. Grandmother committed suicide.

Grandmother died on Christmas Day, 1886, and of course, that ended my school days. With the sale of furniture, clothing, bits of heirlooms, and jewelry which by some miracle of fate Grandmother's creditors failed to take I had just five thousand dollars in the bank; a conservative amount for three months expenses according to the money I had been used to spending.

In January 1887, I went to New York City to try to earn a living teaching painting. I had no trouble getting a class and managed to live very well, not in luxury, of course, but well enough until 1893, when I took a notion to come to Arizona. I decided to come to Clifton, June 5, 1893. I taught painting and music up to 1898 when I married George Pitt.

**Nina Malinda Leavitt Porter**
Interviewer: Roberta Flake Clayton
Navajo County

Nina Leavitt, daughter of George and Sarah Angeline Porter Leavitt, was born in Richville, Morgan County, Utah, November 23, 1861.

The Leavitt family, like many of the Pioneer families, spent their earlier years in humble circumstances with few of the comforts of life. Nina spent a great deal of her early life working for families for low wages assisting with the means thus obtained in keeping her mother and the family.

Schools were few and rudimentary, and the school room in which Nina attended may well be described as poorly furnished. Around the walls were shelves on wooden pegs and rude supports, in front of which were split log benches without backs, which served for the period of study as well as recitation. Only the three Rs and spelling were taught. Teachers were poorly paid and poorly prepared for their work. Nina's mother, with an education far surpassed today by our eighth grade students, was one of the teachers of that day.

Nina was married September 4, 1879, to Sanford Marius Porter, son of Sanford Porter, Jr. and Emma Ensign.

## Mary Ann Cheshire Ramsay

Interviewer: Roberta Flake Clayton
Navajo County

Mary Ann was born in Kensworth, England, August 28, 1841, the oldest child of George and Elizabeth Keys Chesire. For generations her family had resided in that vicinity and by honest toil and strictest economy had eked out a living. Eight children were born to this worthy couple, and as each child became old enough, he or she had to share in responsibilities.

As Mary Ann was a delicate child and could not receive the necessary attention because of the arrival of the other children, she was taken into the home of an uncle and aunt who had no children and who loved and cared for her as their own.

Being of a very independent disposition, Mary Ann could not remain idle and accepted their kindness, so at the age fourteen she began learning the millinery trade. At 18 she went to Luten, a larger town about six miles from her home, where there was a greater demand for the work she had now become quite proficient in. Here she rented a room and as she went to the shop in the morning she would take her food to the bakery to be cooked for her, getting it on her return from work.

On June 4, 1863 all of her family but the eldest son, who was in the army, set sail from their beloved England for the New World.

An ox team and covered wagon were obtained in Missouri and with them the family journeyed westward. But on wagon for nine people and their belongings doesn't provide much comfort so Mary Ann rode part of the way on a thrashing machine that was being brought to Salt Lake, and part of the time she walked.

At the age of 28, Mary Ann Cheshire was united in marriage to Ralph Ramsay, but she kept up the millinery business and established a store on Main Street. This venture was also successful but after their two oldest children were born her husband became restless and moved to several places, even down into Mexico before they finally settled in Snowflake, Arizona in 1891.

**Ruth Campkin Randall**
Interviewer: Roberta Flake Clayton
Navajo County

Beginning her pioneering at the age of five was the experience of Ruth Campkin Randall. She was born in St Louis Missouri, January 2, 1845. Her early childhood was spent there. In the year 1850 her parents, George and Elizabeth Campkin left their home in Missouri to come west with the Mormons.

Leaving early in the year 1850 they continued their journey across the Plains arriving in Utah that fall. Here they established quarters in the old Fort, where they resided the first winter during which time her father built them a home and they moved into it in the spring of 1851, living in it until the year of 1867.

Here Ruth attended school, when there was one, during the winter months and did pretty much as all pioneer children did during the summer months. She helped the mother in the home with the household tasks, caring for the younger children, gathering roots for food and dyes for homespun clothing. Barks were also used for this. Herbs for medicinal purposes had to be gathered and dried for winter use. Gardens had to be planted and tended. In these tasks everyone had to do his or her share and though Ruth was always a tiny little thing, she never weighted 100 in her life, and was only five feet and two inches tall, she worked alongside the huskiest always doing cheerfully what her hands found to do.

She did not marry until she was 22 and she always felt that Alfred Jason Randall was worth waiting for. They were married November 16, 1867, and on December 3 left with him for the southern part of the State to assist in its settlement.

## Eliza Snow Smith Rogers

Interviewer: Roberta Flake Clayton
Navajo County

Eliza Snow Smith Rogers was born in Parowan, Iron County, Utah, February 23, 1859. She was the fourth daughter of Jesse N. and Emma Seraphine West Smith. She early showed a high appreciation for music and singing. As there was no musical instrument in the home, she drew on a board the key board of an organ and would play and sing by the hour.

Her father once said to her, "Eliza, if you'll quit that everlasting singing, I'll buy you a new dress." Often when he could step in the door she would suddenly stop singing and look like she had been caught doing wrong, then he said, "Eliza, if you'll quit looking so sheepish every time I come in and go on signing, I'll buy you another new dress."

The older girls did all of the house work leaving her to do only the odd jobs. This left her too much leisure time. She would often run to the neighbors and help them do their work. They freely showed their appreciation by happy approval of what she had done and often delighted her by letting her play on their organ and practice her songs, which was her greatest delight. Often she was reproved by her mother on returning from running away.

Even though she was sometimes considered a "tom-boy", for she helped her younger brothers to do the chores, ride horses, climb the fences and romp in the shade. The lively little girl found comfort when her father wished a speedy errand run. He would call for Eliza to go quick and come back quick for he must have word soon. Often he said on her trustworthy return, "Thank you, my girl, I can depend on you when I send you." Her childhood was spent attending the district school and music and dancing classes at night.

When she was fourteen there was a ball that everyone was anxious to attend, but each lady must have an escort. As she had none she could not go. She saw her four sisters go off without her and while she sat churning, her tears of disappointment fell freely. Suddenly there came a knock at the door and Smith D. Rogers came in. He had come to see if her sister, Josephine, would go with him. She had already gone, but the mother said, "Eliza is here." To her delight he asked if she would go with him. This was the beginning of their romance. This terminated two years later in their marriage October 12, 1875. From this union there were fifteen children, nine boys and six girls.

## Lydia Ann Herbst Rogers

Interviewer: Roberta Flake Clayton
Navajo County

Her father, John Herbst, was born in Saye, Meiningen, Germany on May 27, 1826. He came with his wife Anna Eva Ditmore to America in 1853 and settled at Quincy, Franklin County, Pennsylvania. There they continued to reside until the spring of 1860 when they moved to Mill Creek, one of the suburbs of Salt Lake City.

Their first home in the west was a one roomed adobe that had previously been used as a stable, but was thoroughly cleaned, white washed, and made habitable, and for a year served as the home of the Herbst family. In it on July 24, 1861, was born Lydia Ann.

She was the fourth child in a family of nine children, 7 girls and 2 boys. Father Herbst was a shoemaker, having learned the trade in his native country and it stood him in very good stead in this new home. He was also a good farmer and provided well for his family, who were never in want for the necessities of life, most of which were produced on his own farm.

Her mother was an invalid for seven years before her death and Annie had to take her share of the responsibility. She assisted, not only in the housework and caring for her invalid mother, but in herding cows, piling hay in the fields, or binding grain into bundles. The farm had to first be cleared and Annie did her share of that, and enjoyed the pungent odor, as well as the bright blazing fire of burning sage. The nearest school was 3 miles away so Annie had little chance of an education, only that which she acquired by her own efforts.

Her parents were hard workers and early taught their children that work was necessary and honorable. Annie remembered very vividly the struggle against grasshoppers when they would be driven into heaps of straw and then burned.

At the age of 13 Annie's was the responsibility of being the cook for the family, and often times performed her task with her baby sister sitting on her hip.

It was on a frequent trip of Mr. Amos Rogers of Snowflake, Arizona, to Salt Lake City that he met Miss Herbst at the house of a business associate. He often said his courtship was "quick and devilish," he didn't want to come back without her so "yes" to him meant now or never. With only one week's preparation they embarked on the sea of matrimony on December 29, 1887.

## Lola Romero

Interviewer: Romelia Gomez
Cochise County

Dona Lola came to Bisbee in 1898 from Sonora, with her mother, a sister and a brother as a young girl of fourteen when another brother, already living in Bisbee and working in the smelter, sent for the rest of the family.

Her other brother started working in the smelter right away, as there was much industry in Bisbee then. Most of those working in the smelter were Mexicans, for the work underground was done only by American miners. The highest wages the Mexican smelter workers were paid wee $2.50 daily. Others were paid $2.00 and less. But even at these low wages it was easy to make a living, for the necessities of life were so much cheaper than they are today. For example materials for dresses cost five and ten cents a yard.

Her younger sister was the only one of the family to attend school in the arrival of the family in Bisbee. She went to Central School, then a little adobe building which was later torn down to make way for the larger brick building of today. There was no compulsion in the attendance of the children sat school, so her sister, like most of the Mexican children going to school then, only went when she felt like it.

Nearly every Sunday the Comachos of Tombstone Canyon gave gay house parties, to which many friends from Bisbee were invited. Dona Lola's family enjoyed walking way up there with the crowd of young people who never missed these good times. They would also walk all the way back home when the parties were over. They couldn't afford a carriage and besides, they would rather walk. Other enjoyable times were had at the dances and plays given at "La Opera" on Opera Drive. The plays were given by actors from Mexico and were very good.

Lola Romero attended the little Catholic Church on Chihuahua Hill, as did most of the Mexicans living here.

## Leonora Allen Russell

Interviewer: G. W. Reeve
Globe

Leonora Allen was born at Lone Mountain, now called Fort Baird near Silver City, New Mexico, November 8th, 1873; when Nora was only three years of age the family moved to Globe, Arizona. Her father, Colonel George A. Allen, later became the first

District Judge of Pinal County, and incidentally was the judge that sentenced Hawley and Grimes, the two outlaws that robbed the mail between Florence and Globe killing the messenger, to be hanged at the big sycamore tree on Broad Street in Globe, 1881.

Leonora came to Globe riding a mule with her mother, all the way from Silver City. The Indians were very bad in this district at that time, and Colonel Allen had guard of three men along to protect his family, and Nora (short for Leonora, who wasn't very tall by the way) says that a large bunch of soldier followed them through looking for bands of raiding Indians. They had to travel nights, and rest in daytime to avoid the Indians as much as possible.

The scouts had a signal that they used to warn the citizens which everyone knew. This signal was a shot followed by two shots space close together; this meant for the settlers to arm themselves and get in the O.K. Corral which they had fortified for defense.

Judge Allen had issued an order that no guns were to be fired in the settlement except as signals when Indians were coming. One night while drinking a little too freely, a couple of the scouts got in a fight over the possession of a burro. One of the scouts shot the burro, and either through force of habit, or because of his befuddled brain, he used the warning signal, one shot followed by two shots spaced close together. All of the inhabitants made haste to the O.K. Corral and prepared for an Indian raid. This happened about midnight and aside from the inconvenience of the populace the only casualty was the death of the burro.

Most of the inhabitants of Globe at that time lived in tents, and the first two room adobe house that was built still stands on Oak Street at the Railroad crossing. Nora's father used to own the entire block in which the Dominion Hotel stands, and at the exact site of this hotel he built a two room house and deeded it to his wife as a present. That was quite a present in those days as most of the "houses" were tents.

In 1882, while visiting the mining camp of McMillan, Leonora's mother was struck on the head by an Indian tomahawk during an Indian raid there. Shortly afterward she died in a hospital in Wilcox from the affects of this blow. Several people were killed in this raid.

Leonora's grandfather ran a freighting boat plying between Madrid, Spain, and other foreign ports and San Francisco, and other west coast ports. On one of these trips he brought a band of Moreno sheep from Spain, unloaded them at San Francisco and drove them across the country to the San Quentin valley where his family was living, and where Leonora's father, who was then a railroad man, met her mother and they were married.

Soon after Leonora's father and mother were married. They left the valley and moved to the neighborhood of Silver City where her father secured employment in the mines and where a few years later Leonora was born.

Leonora's grandfather then brought his sheep to that district. When Nora was three years of age her parents moved to Globe. Her grandfather moved his sheep to McMillan, and this was how the first Moreno sheep were brought into Arizona. But the Indians did not let him raise any sheep there for they soon raided his ranch taking all the sheep and everything else he owned. The grandfather was so thoroughly disgusted that he left the United State and returned to his native land (Italy) where he and his wife spent the reminder of their days.

Colonel Allen, Leonora's father, patented the land on which Roosevelt Dam now stands, and in 1886 sold the dam site to the Government. At that time he had a large ranch there running about 4,000 head of cattle. He was a first cousin to Admiral George Dewey, the "Hero of Manila."

Leonora was in school in California four years, and in 1890 was appointed by the government to teach the Mojave Indians. This position she held for two years when she went to Boston and studied oratory, music and dancing in the New England Conservatory of Music.

After a year of study she secured a position with Alexander Salvane as an understudy for his wife, playing under the name of Maude Dixon in the opera houses in all the large towns and cities in the East and in Canada for two years. Their principal play was known as the "Three Guardsmen." In Nora's spare time she learned fencing, boxing and wrestling and says she often bested some men that were supposed to be very good at these sports.

Senor Alexander Salvane went to Italy on a visit. As he was to meet Leonora on his return, in California, she went to California to await his return. But, the great actor died suddenly while in Italy a comparatively young man, and Leonora was thrown on her own again.

But Leonora said, "Nothing will stop me.", so she organized her own stock company and put on plays and dramatics. She said that she had an unusual memory, and could recite 250 pieces from memory. She took most of her plays from Shakespeare. She says she liked to play Ophelia in Hamlet best of all.

Leonora taught dramatics, but says she soon tired of teaching others how to act. She was playing in the days of Booth, Barrett, McDonald, McClain, Sarah Barnhart, Fannie Davenport, Marie Dressler and Lillian Russell, and says that she met most of these great personages on her travels.

On April 6th, 1917, Leonora married Albert Russell in Globe. Mr. Russell was then assistant engineer of the Old Dominion powerhouse.

**Mary Luella Higbee Schnebly**

Roberta Flake Clayton
Navajo County

Professor Dorsey Ellsworth Schnebly was teaching school in Winchester, Missouri, and he selected Mary Luella Higbee as his brightest pupil, and the one who would make the most of her opportunities. To her was given the distinction of going to college and preparing for a teacher.

It was indeed a blessing to this young girl who was ambitious to make something of herself but whose hopes could not otherwise have been realized because she was the "middle" one in a family of seven children.

Their farm was five miles from their nearest school so the children had to go in a cart, buggy or horseback and many times suffered from high winds and weather. But in spite of all disadvantages, Mary Luella had never faltered not even when she would have to go away to prepare herself for her chosen profession.

Mary Louella spent many happy days during her childhood. There were an abundance of wild plums, cherries, grapes, berries, persimmons, black haws, and hickory, hazel and black walnuts. All of these the children gathered for their winter food. There would be barrels full of nuts, and the father would go to Warsaw, Illinois and trade for a wagon load of apples so that during the long winter evenings there would be refreshments for the family and their frequent visitors. There was always popcorn to pass around.

After two years of teaching in his native state Mr. Schnebly came west, first to Washington where he was Principal of their High School in Pomeroy for a long time. Afterwards he came to Arizona and taught school.

At the age of 35 he decided to marry, and he wrote to his sweetheart who was then 31, to join him in Flagstaff, Arizona, where they were married May 2, 1906.

## Augusta Maria Outsen Smith

Interviewer: Roberta Flake Clayton
Snowflake

On January 14, 1854, in the City of Randers, in far away Denmark was born a baby girl that was destined to play a most important part in the lives of many people in the "Land of Golden dreams", beyond the sea. Her parents, Jens Christian Outsen and Martha Maria Christiansen gave her the name of Augusta Maria.

Before his marriage Jens Christian Outsen served in the war between his native country and Germany that lasted from 1848 to 1850. He was a second lieutenant in rank, and for his bravery was awarded a gold medal signed by the King.

Augusta's father and mother were married in 1852, and it was into a very comfortable home that she was born. Her parents belonged to the Lutheran Church. Her mother had received some money from her parents, and before she was married her father and grandfather Christiansen bought a city lot and built a good home for her.

Grandfather Christiansen was a good carpenter, and grandfather Outsen an excellent cabinet maker, who had receive many prizes and medals for his work. The home was complete even to the furniture ready for the newlyweds to move into.

Augusta started school when she was seven years old, attending eleven months each year with only one month in the summers for vacation. She was taught reading, writing, arithmetic, geography, history and from the Bible. But, no spelling which was always a handicap to her especially when she tried to spell in English. She was sent to a private school when she was twelve. Here she was taught English, and the higher things in art and fancy work. Her mother had long ago given her lessons in knitting and sewing, mending, etc.

During one of her summer vacations, after Augusta became quite a young lady, she went to the City of Vyborg to visit her aunt for whom she was named. This Aunt had a beautiful home and servants, and she owned the only theatre in the city, and took Augusta to see all of the plays, and the interesting sights of the city.

In the year 1850, Apostle Erastus Snow and company brought the restored gospel across the sea to Denmark. The parents of Augusta went to some of the meetings and in a short time they believed the principles to be true. This was in 1854, but it was a year or more before they were baptized and in doing so they lost all of their friends. Her father was dismissed from his carpenter work and found himself without an opening for a job.

Jesse N. Smith was a missionary from America, and on the 3rd of June, 1869 he and Augusta were married at the Mission House. This was just a year and a month before they sailed for America. In 1870 she and her husband, her father and mother and their seven children, left Denmark with the immigrant company which her husband had charge of. They left Randers, 15th of July, going in a steamer across the North Sea as far as Hull. Augusta's little sister Ida, took very sick on the trip and died on the train from Hull to Liverpool. She was buried in that city; 'twas a great sorrow to them all.

They left Liverpool on the ship Minnesota. The journey across the ocean was 18 days in duration, during which time Augusta was very sick, seldom leaving her berth. The captain of the vessel was very kind to them, often sending her fresh fruits and delicacies.

Her husband had been entrusted with several thousand dollars in gold representing the tithings of the saints in Denmark. This he wore in a belt around his body, but when it became too heavy he would leave it with her in her berth. They arrived in New York in safety and went on the train to Salt Lake City.

## Janet Mauretta Johnson Smith

Interviewer: Roberta Flake Clayton
Navajo County

On her paternal line Janet claims such men as Ezekiel Johnson, who lost his life in the Battle of Bunker Hill, her Great Grandfather. Her Grandfather also Ezekiel, was a western frontiersman and pioneer, turning the first soil where Chicago now stands. Her father, Joel Hills Johnson, was one of Utah's most prominent colonizers and pioneers who helped to build up eleven different settlements.

Her Grandparents on her Mother's side were Margaret Mathason and James Fife, who came from Edinburg, Scotland when her Mother Janet was 13 years of age, a six week's voyage.

In a log cabin, in Salt Lake City, Utah, she first saw the light of day. This was on the 17th of December 1848; six weeks after her parents had crossed the plains.

When she was two years old her father moved his family to the southern part of the State of Utah, and started to build up the town of Parowan. Later he moved 12 miles south, to a large spring and here he built a fort, which was known as Fort Johnson. This was necessary on account of Indian depredations.

Janet says in her diary, "It was here that I spent my happiest childhood days. The valley was about six miles long, was surrounded by hills. On the brow of a hill at one end was built the fort, overlooking the whole valley. It was a big meadow, and the cattle and sheep could be seen all day. I liked to go with my brothers when they went with the sheep. My sister Julia usually went along too and we would gather wild flowers and pick berries and currants growing plentifully everywhere. We children used to play "hide and go seek" in the big fort, which was two stories high with a big bastion in the corner with port holes in it where the men could look out and if necessary shot through. In the center of the fort was a well. There were two big gates which were closed and locked at night."

As Janet's father always lived on the frontier, his children did well if they got as much as three months schooling a year. But, she did not depend on book learning alone, but with quick adaptability she early became very efficient in the arts of carding, spinning, weaving, dyeing and knitting as well as the household duties every girl should learn.

There were many suitors for the hand of Janet, but she considered none seriously until Jesse N. Smith became interested in her. They were married October 9, 1866 and lived at Parowan, Utah.

## Lannie Mitchell Smith

Interviewer: Roberta Flake Clayton
Navajo County

Mary Ann was born February 10, 1863, the third of seven children. She first saw the light of day in one of those famous Mormon forts, a series of houses built around an open square, all the door opening into the center, thus forming a solid wall on the outside. The entrance into this enclosed city was through a strong gate.

In addition to this protection the people had to be continually on the lookout for Indians bent on depredations. This condition could not help creating a sense of wariness in the children of the fort. But the vagueness was crystallized by the repeated forays of the Indians which called her Father out with other militiamen to recover cattle and otherwise repel their attacks.

Mary Ann coined for herself a new name early in childhood. She was called "Little Annie", but when she tried to say her name there were too many syllables and she could only articulate "Lannie." The childish effort was so cute that the family quickly adopted the contraction and it remained with her through life.

Her second and third years were spent in the home of her grandfather Bosnell who lived at Nephi, Utah. The family moved there to look after the father who was laid up with rheumatism. She still has vivid memories of the courage her father had in taking the "cupping" treatment for his rheumatism without anesthetic. An instrument called scarfire was placed on his hip or thigh and held firm while the knives slashed the flesh. Then an alcohol cup was filled and emptied; the remaining fumes were set afire and the cup pressed tightly over the perforated flesh. When the flames went out, a vacuum was created which drew stagnant blood from the wound.

When she was nine years old the tragedy of a lifetime came into their home. Her mother had a still born babe and never knew health again. For five years she was home bound, most of the time bed-ridden. Only once in that period was she able to walk out of the house. Her little children danced in glee that their mother could actually come into the garden.

Lannie became the little mother of the family. Even when she went to school she did the breakfast work before going and other work after school. Toward the end, the fourteen year old girl was her mother's principal nurse.

## Nellie M. Smith

Interviewer: Roberta Flake Clayton
Contributed by her daughter Leonora Smith Rogers
Snowflake

Nellie M. Smith was born December 16, 1860 at Provo, Utah, where her family had settled after the journey across the plains in 1855. Her father, William Marsden was an emigrant from England in 1840, landing in New York and later living for a time in Nauvoo, Illinois.

Nellie Marsden Smith
Age 16
*(St. Johns LDS Family History Files)*

William was a cotton spinner by trade. For this reason he was called by the Latter-day Saint leader, Brigham Young, to move to Parowan, Utah and establish a cotton factory. The machinery was constructed from iron material left by John's army at Camp Floyd. Thus it was that Parowan became Nellie's childhood hometown.

Her mother Sarah Scofil, died when Nellie was only seven years old, but the kind hands of a stepmother, Aunt Alice, who was soon brought into the family, she was taught thrift, besides the arts of homemaking.

So it was in Nellie's education the practical training was emphasized more than the scholastic. And, though she attended school three months each winter, at a cost of $8.00 per term, yet the multiplication and figures were learned in practical use in her father's store.

Nellie married Joseph W. Smith, November 5, 1879, in St. George, Utah, just six days before leaving for Snowflake, Arizona, where she was to make her future home.

### Adelinah Taylor

Interviewer: Helen M. Smith
Cochise County

I was born in Spartanburg, South Carolina, in 1847. There were seven children in our family, six girls and one boy. I was the oldest girl and had a great deal of work to do on that account. I began sewing at five years of age, and got so much pleasure from it that I have kept it up ever since when possible. I completed my first quilt at just past six years. I spun and wove, made men's shirts and pants and vests, as well as garments for women and children.

None of us were ever sick, and I didn't know what a doctor was for until after my twelfth year. I might not have known then, but that one of my uncles was a doctor and he visited us at that time.

My father, John Jackson Quinn, was an ardent Democrat, but as ardently against secession. When the Civil War broke out he was quite disgusted. I remember that soon after the war began soldiers from Little Rock marched past our place. They overflowed the yard, drew water from the well until there was none left and we had not so much as a drop with which to quench our thirst, killed our chickens, and even a prize sow Father was keeping for a brood sow. One of the Guinea fowls flew up into a tall tree and I can still see the soldiers trying to drive her down to make a meal for them. They didn't get her and we had one Guinea fowl to start with after they left.

The worse of it was that our fine sow they killed, they had used only a part of one ham, while the remaining meat was left on the ground. We found a nice beef, too, killed, but not so much as a skinning knife put to the carcass. Father was so disgusted that he determined then and there to get out of the likely war area.

We went into eastern Texas, returning after the close of the war. We settled again in the same locality. I was then about fifteen years old. Soon after some Mormon missionaries came to our neighborhood, and many there were converted to their faith. Our family, among others, returned with the missionaries to Arizona.

**Belle Maley Tully**
Interviewer: Jose del Castillo
Tucson

Mother said I was born in Winslow; some said in Colorado. I was born in 1884, some say May, some April. Do you know if you can get a copy of birth certificates that old?

Mrs. Lizzie Steele said that when they seen me they brought me from Colorado. (Mrs. Steele was the first white child born in Arizona.) She and my mother were pals—the one who raised me. Mrs. Jesus Estrada, her name was. They both went to dances together.

My mother's husband was James Henry Maley. As long as I can remember by father's family name is only one spelled that way. My father came to Arizona in 1840 or before that I can't remember. In 1894 James Maley went to Mexico to work in the Grand Central Railroad. He took us down there when I was eight years old. I was raised in Mexico more than here. Stayed in Mexico City mostly. Stayed in Salazar eleven years off and on. Went to Durango, Monterey. In 1919 I came to Arizona. Went back to Hermosillo, stayed there but a month or so and came back to Arizona. A month later I was married to Charles (Carlos) H. Tully. (This is Carlos Tully's second wife.)

First I went to Lolita Prieto's school to learn my first grade of Spanish. Went to Mrs. Miller's. I attended grammar school in Mexico. Then Selisian School convent. When I left school I went into teaching—taught in Salazar, Hacienda de Prieto and Tarasquio.

In Mexico I helped the poor, nursed the sick, taught Catechism in Salazar. I was president of the Sociedad de Maria Auxiliadora. I was the madrena when she was crowned.

**Mary Agnes Flake Turley**
Interviewer: Roberta Flake Clayton
Snowflake

Her father began his career in North Carolina, July 3, 1839, and at the age of two was taken to Mississippi, from there the family went to Illinois. When 8 years old walked across "the Plains" from the Missouri River to Utah driving cows all the way. In 1851 he went with his widowed mother to California, where she helped in the purchase of the San Bernardino Ranch. He with a younger brother and a neighbor man built for her the first adobe house in what is now the city of that name. He made several exploring trips into Arizona, and in 1877 moved here, buying the Stinson Ranch in 1878, founding the town that bears his name and that of a friend, Snowflake, Arizona. Her mother has also been a pioneer of Utah and three of the settlements in that state.

Born February 16, 1866 in Beaver City, Utah, the fifth child and first daughter of William Jordan and Lucy Hannah White Flake, and christened for her two Grandmothers, Mary Agnes. Her father was a full-fledged Southerner and her Mother a dyed-in-the wool Yankee, so to preserve peace the war between the states was never discussed in their home.

Mary's summers were mostly spent on one or another of her Father's ranches and as soon as she was old enough she did her part in milking cows, making butter and cheese, assisting with the housework and younger brothers and sisters as she was one of thirteen children.

Her winters were busy ones, too, for besides her school and the lessons to be studied at home, she must learn to knit her own stockings, her wristlets, mittens, and a nubia for her neck, crochet lace for her underwear, including the half dozen white petticoats each well dressed girl wore, and to do her own sewing.

## Ida Frances Hunt Udall

Interviewer: Roberta Flake Clayton
Contributed by her daughter Pauline H. Smith
Navajo County

Ida Frances Hunt first saw the light of day on the 8th of March 1858. She was laid in her mother's arms in a covered wagon. On account of her unexpected arrival the company was compelled to remain at the crude fort, known to this day as Hamilton Fort, Utah, for some time while mother and babe grew strong enough to travel on to Beaver, some fifty miles to the north.

Ida Hunt Udall
*(St. Johns Historical Society)*

John Hunt and his young wife, Lois Pratt, just turned twenty-one, were moving from San Bernardino, California to Utah. They were traveling with John's father, Captain Jefferson Hunt, of the Mormon Battalion fame, and his family, and others who were returning to Utah to make their home.

John and Lois made their home in Beaver, near Grandmother Pratt, while Captain Hunt and party went on to Ogden Valley to locate. It was here that Ida had lived until she was eighteen when her father decided to move his family over the mountain into Sevier County, on the east where he took out a ditch and raised a crop.

She became very outstanding in Beaver's social life where high standards of education and music were early established under the leadership of her beloved old teacher, Richard S. Horne. He called his pupils by numbers. Ida's was seven.

Ida's voice was early recognized and she was given the leading parts in the choir- was chosen, when but a very young girl, to sing "The Star Spangled Banner" in the big Fourth of July celebration. This being the highest musical honor the community could bestow.

While Beaver became a cultural center, it had also attracted a very rough element due to the miens on the west and the government Soldier Post established there. It became necessary for the citizens of the town to have a peace officer possessed of a rare courage, tact and discernment. In John Hunt they found just such a man. For fifteen years he held this trying position. Ida soon learned to do his office work for him. What pride he took in the education and aptness of his eldest daughter. His entire schooling had consisted of a three months term when but a small lad in Nauvoo, Illinois. Ida also grew into a bosom companion of her dear, patient mother, mother whose poise, dignity, and understanding of the human heart was so rare.

When Ida was but fourteen years old she held the position of bookkeeper for the Beaver Woolen Mills, because of the neatness and legibility of her hand writing she had been offered this position. She drew her pay in Lindsey, Woolsey cloth, knitting yarn, cheese, etc., which helped the family budget as the Sheriff's salary in those days was very meager.

John and Lois now had a family of eight, six daughters and two sons. It fell to Ida's lot to make up the cloth into dresses, not only for herself and little sisters, but even her mother, as she soon became adapt at sewing. Her grandmother had been trained as a tailoress back in New England. She must have taken great pride in Ida's taste and skill and became her little granddaughter's great inspiration both in regards to sewing and scholarship. Grandma Pratt was one of the early school teachers of Utah.

Near their home on the Sevier was a little village named Joseph City, where she taught at the little log cabin school. She was a diligent reader, with a taste for classic literature. Her greatest solace, however, was her guitar and large repertoire of songs. Brothers and sisters also had fine voices. Their regard for their elder sister was almost akin to adoration. In the evenings they would all gather round her and sing, while father and mother listened with the keenest appreciation.

It was in 1877, John was not satisfied with is new home on the Sevier. Colonists were moving into Arizona. John and Lois had been in childhood and youth among the first settlers in the State of Utah and California and so a burning urge took hold of John to attack a new frontier. Lois was always willing to follow and sustain her helpmate, spoke no word of discouragement. On February 21, 1877 they were outfitted and got as far on their journey as Beaver.

In the Sevoia Valley they resided for a little more than a year. William J. Flake had recently purchased the Stinson ranch. He and John Hunt had played together as boys, and lived neighbors as men in San Bernardino, and also Beaver. Inducements were made, by the Flakes for the Hunts to leave New Mexico and locate in the

fertile little Silver Creek Valley. In this trip, when he brought Ida, John felt impressed to come and live near this friend of former years. With Ida's help he selected the site for a home. A month later he brought his family to Snowflake.

Each winter that Ida passed in Beaver she taught school. It would only be natural that when she returned to Snowflake and her family, there would be a sweetheart left behind, and so there was. The following two winters she taught school in the little log school houses at Taylor and then at Snowflake.

It was at this time when David K. Udall came to Snowflake and visited the Hunt home. He was in search of a clerk for their newly established store in St. Johns who could speak the Spanish language. He had been informed that Miss Ida Hunt was capable. The agreement was made and Ida took the two day journey to St. Johns.

The Beaver sweetheart did not measure with this fine cultured man from St. Johns. They were married May 26, 1882.

## Eliza Luella Stewart Udall

Interviewer: unknown
Contributed by her daughter Pearl Udall Nelson

Eliza Luella Stewart Udall was born in Salt Lake City, Utah, May 21st, 1855, a little less than eight years after the first pioneers arrived there. She was the daughter of Levi and Margery Wilkerson Stewart. In her youth she attended private schools in Salt

Lake. Among her tutors wee Sarah E. Carmichael, one of Utah's gifted poets; T. B. Lewis, a veteran teacher who was great inspiration in her life; and a Mrs. Brown, who gave the Steward girls formal instructions in the art of sewing. In her early girlhood she helped her mother in the making of tallow candles and homemade soap and she learned in many ways to meet the needs of a pioneer home.

In the spring of 1870, when she was fifteen years old her father was called to Kanab and told to take his large family. Her father was to be the first Bishop of that town. The colony was small and for awhile the people lived within a fort built as a protection against marauding Indians. In December of that year her mother and five brothers perished in a terrible fire that broke out in the fort, and her own life was providentially preserved at that time.

Before the Stuart family left Salt Lake City President Young requested that one of the girls stay at Tocqueville en route to Kanab to study telegraphy for the line out of Kanab. Ella was left in Tocqueville with Sarah Ann Spillbury as her teacher. In great homesickness she studied almost day and night for six weeks and was then qualified to go into the new telegraph office when it should be opened.

In December, 1871, she was stationed for a time in the telegraph office at Pipe Springs, Arizona, located a few miles from Kanab. Thus she became one of the first telegraph operators in Arizona. During the time of Major Powell's expeditions to the Grand Canyon she telegraphed his reports from the Kanab office to the government in Washington, D. C.

On February 1st, 1875, in Salt Lake City, she was married to David K. Udall of Nephi, Utah.

### Barbara Franco Westfall

Interviewer: Jose del Castillo
Tucson

She was born in Tucson, Arizona in 1885. She is a widow with no children and two brothers and a sister. She lived near Sabino Canyon at Forest Ranger Lookout, her husband being an early ranger. She was raised in the convent of St. Joseph Academy, and stayed there for eight years. She taught school in Redington and in Happy Valley, and conducted summer camps for tourists.

Harold Bell Wright had heard that Mrs. Westfall had a story she told her guests that Mr. Wright was interested in. He went to her summer camp as a guest. Mrs. Westfall told him that she knew what he had come for. Mr. Wright did not get the story.

"I heard grandfather often say that the first of our line to come to America was Don Alejandro Franco, a duke, sent by Kind Phillip II to Mexico as his representative. General Francisco Franco, the chief of the insurgents in Spain fighting for the control of the country at present is a member of the Franco family remaining in Spain.

Don Alejandro married here. Out of this union there sprang Francos that fought at one time or another in the numerous wars in Mexico. There was a Franco that fought with Maximilian. Killed. I had three great Uncles, named Juan Franco that had made something of a name for themselves or another.

The Francos had married within the family from time to time. The last Johns (Juans) went to California during the gold rush. He had a beautiful voice and sang to miners. He returned to Mexico with a big fortune.

My grandfather and grandmother Barbara brought from California a trunk of camphor wood filled with jewels. She was a very lovely lady. Grandfather established himself at Rio Yaqui and had many Yaqui peons in his hacienda. His lady was so beautiful that the Yaquis called her the Virgin of the Yaquis.

Grandfather died of yellow fever. He owned the haciendas of Santa Marta, Santa Clara and Las Muchias—close to Rio Yaqui. Grandmother too was taken by the same disease.

A priest gave masses for the dead and made a lot of money doing so. He claimed the haciendas, he said, for the heirs. The heirs never got anything. But the haciendas became the property of the church.

Mother descended from the Serna family. Francisco Serna, an early governor of Sonora was a relative of mother."

## Joanna Matilda Ericson Westover

Interviewer: Roberta Flake Clayton
Navajo County

In the far off land of Sweden, in the city of Gutenberg on June 4, 1854, Joanna Matild Ericson was born. Her parents were honest, hard working people. Her father was a carpenter by trade and always remembered how she held torches for him to see to work by when she was but a small child. In the winters the days were so short, the sun did not come up until one o'clock in the mornings and set so soon at night that there were not enough intervening hours of daylight in which to earn a living for a large family.

The snow would fall so deep the house would be almost covered and deep trenches would have to be made from the house to the cow barn. With faces pressed against the window panes the children would watch their mother go out of sight in the bend of the path and then wait to see who could be the first to spy her as she came back with her bucket of foamy milk. They would scramble down and run to get their pewter cups and have a drink of the milk fresh from the cow. Ice cream was plentiful; all you had to do was to get some of the white drifted snow and add to your milk, put in a tiny bit of sugar, there never was much to spare, and there you were.

Bread making was an event in their home as it only came twice a year. Large round loaves with holes in the middle were baked that looked not unlike cut doughnuts. These were hung in the attic to dry for future consumption. It took two days to do this. The time of course depending on the size of the family, but when it was done nothing more had to be done about it for six months.

The laundry was done in the same way and one would think the mother would have much leisure time, but that was not the case because there was the spinning of yarn, the weaving of cloth, knitting the stockings and making every article of clothing that the family wore.

The Ericksons were a very devout family as is illustrated by the following incident a new baby had arrived and when the proper time came was taken a few miles away to the minister to be baptized. The sprinkling ceremony was too severe and the baby died on the way home.

## Ellen Oakley William

Interviewer: Roberta Flake Clayton
Snowflake

Pioneering at best is no easy task, but when the husband and father is totally blind, it is a hardship. Such was the case with John Oakley, who with his wife, five little daughters, one grown, married with her husband, and an afflicted brother-in-law, came to Arizona in 1880. They had two yoke of oxen, one span of mules, one of mares and a few head of loose cattle. Settling first at Woodruff where they remained only a short time they came on to Snowflake, and lived for awhile in one of the adobe stables belonging to the ranch which had been fitted up for a residence, as several of the others, one even serving as the first school house.

Ellen was used to privations as her birthplace was a wagon box in the small town of Kanab, Utah. But as she chose the summer time, August 25, 1873, it was not so bad as had the snow been flying.

Her father was a successful nurseryman, and that was one occupation he could pursue, even in his blindness. He would send to Illinois, get root grafts twelve inches long, keep them until they were three years old, and then supply the local people. Many of the roots were only seedlings and they would have to be grafted budded.

Ellen had a great love for her father and was his helper in his business and soon learned all there was to know about trees, shrubs and flowers. All her life she was surrounded by choice plants. In the summers her flowers were the envy of her neighbors, and then when frost came her windows were full of bright cherry blossoms.

Mr. Oakley was a man of education and intelligence, and selected people of culture as his associates. Ellen might be seen leading him by the hand going to homes where he was always a welcome visitor. The hostess would never be too busy to listen to his store of wisdom, or read to him from choice selections, or the meager news that came at rare intervals.

In this way Ellen became a well informed child. When, however, the subject became too deep for her, or there were children in the family to play with, that would be her diversion, but always within sound of his voice.

Her father and her mother, Louisa Jones Oakley, were both born in England. Mrs. Oakley was an invalid for many years, and early in life Ellen learned to take her place with her sisters in the household tasks when not employed with her father. The excellent gardens they always raised, and the vegetables planted for winter use, not only supplied the Oakley family but was an added inducement to the children of the town who knew they would have all the carrots they could eat when they went to play. In those early days when fruit was out of the question carrots tasted mighty good.

Ellen grew into attractive womanhood, and at the age of seventeen took on the duties of wifehood, marrying October 9, 1890, Ira Reeves Willis. They were the parents of six children, two girls and four boys.

## Fannie Jane Roundy Willis

Interviewer: Roberta Flake Clayton
Snowflake

Her father made the supreme sacrifice in exploring this land when in the winter of 1873 he, with thirteen other men, was called by Brigham Young to hunt out a route into Arizona and report on the possibility of establishing homes here. He lost his life in the swollen waters of the treacherous Colorado River. She was born in Centerville, Davis County, Utah, December 21, 1858.

Her father's land bordered the Salt Lake and she had much fun swimming and wading in its briny waters. There were many wild geese and ducks on the lake so they had plenty of meat. Fannie Jane's task was to pick these birds and save the down for feather beds and pillows.

She and her sisters gleaned the whet that was missed by the Cradlers and with a portion of their gleanings, each bought herself a new red calico dress with white dots in them. No coronation gown was ever so prized.

Fannie Jane, at an early age learned to spin and weave, and assisted her mother in making jeans, linseys and coverlets. As all the food was cooked over the fireplace and what they had was that raised at much cost of labor or gathered from the hills, delicacies in the family diet were rare. On special occasions pie of cake was baked in the bake skillet.

One of the first things all pioneers in Utah and Arizona did was to build a meeting house, a sort of Community Center where church, school, theaters and dances could be held. Quadrilles and reels ere the dances most indulged in. Waltzes and "round dances" were frowned upon by the Church leaders. She was very fond of dancing, especially upper reel and was considered a very fine partner.

## Emma Eliza Bryon Wyatte

Interviewer: Kathlyn M. Lathrop
Duncan

I was born in Pike County Alabama, August 6, 1860. I was three years old when my father joined the Confederate Army in the Civil War. I was the second of Mother's three children when Father went to war. I remember the day he left, quite as well as if it was only yesterday. In memory I can see Mother's face, pasty-white, without a trace of a tear, as she kissed him goodbye. Mother was one of the bravest of Pioneer women; she never learned the meaning of the word "fear."

While Father was away to war, Mother planted a small patch of cotton, planted it with a hoe, in hills, and tended it with a hoe. The South didn't have much in way of farm equipment at that time.

We didn't have a gin in our settlement, so when the cotton was picked, we picked the seeds out with our fingers. Then Mother carded the lent into bats, (small rolls) and spun it into thread, then it was dyed. We had only two colors of dye, copper (brown), and indigo (dark blue). The thread was then woven into cloth on a hand loom, and most all our clothing was made by hand, from hand woven material. At an early age I learned to knit my own stockings, and later learned to spin and weave.

Father served less than a year in the army. He was sent home a very sick man, and was allowed to remain at home during the rest of the war. His family needed him and the entire community needed him a great deal more than the army did.

I was about seven years old when we moved to Covenington County, Alabama. My brother older than I died at the age of 12, and by that time there were other smaller children in the family. I started school at about nine years of age. I had to walk four miles to school and take my five year old brother along for company. He was really too young to be going to school, but he learned his A.B.C.s and soon learned to spell and write.

The school house, a one room log hut, had no chinking between the logs and the wind, snow and rain blew in at the cracks sometimes; but there was a large fireplace at one end of the room and the older boys kept up a roaring fire all day.

We school children had to carry our own drinking water from a spring about a quarter of a mile from the school house. Oh yes! We carried our lunch from home; corn bread, baked sweet potatoes, boiled eggs and salt pork, done up in a flour sack, or a tin bucket. We also carried along a small bucket of milk.

I had to start from home at daylight, and it was always getting dark by the time I got home. The road to school was through a deep woods and I would sing to the top of my voice nearly all the way to keep my brother from crying with fright. I never thought of being afraid myself.

We never hurried through the woods, we would watch the birds, and listen to them sing on our way in the morning, and the fire-flies were out for us on our way home in the evening.

When I was seventeen I married George Washington Wyatte, in Covenington County, Alabama. I already knew all the duties of a housewife, but I must admit there was certainly a lot about marriage that I didn't know. Why any ten year old girl now-a-days knows more about marriage than I did at seventeen. Mothers taught their daughters to work, keep house, cook and sew, but they considered it not only a disgrace, but dangerous to the morals of young womanhood to teach them anything about marriage. I raised a family of ten children; nine of them were born in Alabama and one in Arizona.

## Susan Hamilton Youngblood

Interviewer: Roberta Flake Clayton
Navajo County

Down in the far famed sunny South in the little town of Dallas, Monroe County, Mississippi was born on December 15, 1844, a beautiful black haired, black eyed, baby girl. She came to the home of Isaiah and Evaline Baily Walpole Hamilton, and the little Susan was their twelfth child. She was royally welcomed. Living on a plantation these children had an outdoor carefree life, and though her father died when Susan was only nine years of age, he left his family well provided for.

Susan was blessed with many talents, among them that of music which she expressed in her every moment, learning the dances of the darkies on the plantation especially the Double Shuffle, Back Step, Cake Walk and all the other fancy steps she saw. She possessed a beautiful voice, and charmed with her singing and playing of the violin. It was very unusual for a girl to "fiddle" and some of the older, more sanctimonious people thought she was very wicked, and when they heard her clear birdlike whistle they knew she would come to some bad end.

The mode of travel in those pre-war days was on horseback and Susan became famous for her good riding. In those Southern Climes people developed earlier, and it was not usual for girls to marry when 15 years old. Susan was married at that age. Her young husband, Charles C. Whitworth, was stricken with Typhoid Fever and died before they were married a year. The grief of this beautiful young bride was intensified by the knowledge that she was to become a mother, and in five months after his father died, baby Charles was born. Now there was his baby to care for and he must have every attention. Susan went home to live with her widowed mother, who could give her the kind of sympathy she needed.

During these trying times of their widowhood the Civil War broke out, the horror of which can never be written. Living in the extreme southern part of Mississippi they were not near the battle front, nor firing line, but there was the grief of widows, fatherless and sweethearts whose loved ones had given their lives in defense of their homes and families.

During the four years the women had to do the work formerly done by the slaves, and Susan willingly did her part. She would yoke her oxen and with them plow all day, then plant the corn and cotton, then the crop had to be gathered, the only help obtainable was men who were too old or boys to young for war service. These were not very efficient and so the women went to the fields to pick the cotton and take it to the gin, and when it was in the bale sell it.

When the blockade was up at Oxford the price of cotton was very high there, but it was dangerous to try to run the blockade. Susan was afraid of nothing so took her cotton and with her some of her friends decided to run the risk. They reached their destination safely and sold their cotton sat $1.00 a pound. All went well until the first night out of Oxford. They had made camp when a bunch of pickets rode up. This filled the group with fear as they knew the seriousness of their condition.

Susan had a solution, as she usually had, and told one of her friends to join her in giving supper and breakfast to the soldiers. In return for this kindness the two women were told to be the last to leave camp and when they came to a left hand road, to leave the main highway and take this route and to drive as fast as their oxen could go, and they would not be molested. They followed these directions and reached home safely while the others were captured and taken back to Oxford, and their money confiscated. There was too much danger so they did not try this again.

Finally the war was over and six years of widowhood for Susan when she met, loved, and married James Irvin Youngblood in 1868, and they had five children. This marriage like her first was a very happy one, but again it was too good to last and when her youngest child was only four years old her second husband passed away on January 13, 1885.

Again Susan returned with her children to her old home in Mississippi. Here she remained until February 14, 1885, when with four of her children she bid goodbye to her dear old Southern home and came to Snowflake, Arizona. One child had died and her eldest son remained in the South.

# CHAPTER THREE
## Traveling the Hard Trail

*The courage of the camp seemed exhausted and it looked as if they must resign themselves to actual death from starvation out in the midst of a heartless desert where howling wolves would rejoice over their awful fate, and glut their snarling selves upon the famished flesh of their hapless victims.*

*Cathern Overton Emmett*

*The trip back to Arizona was long and tedious for the horses must travel over weary stretches of desert, up steep mountains and on into the barren lowlands again, cross the Big Colorado River at Lee's Ferry, over the desolate wastes and then stop in the vastness of these wastes at a mere fort where a few brave souls were striving to maintain a colony.*

*Emma S. Hansen*

They found themselves struggling on a trail that delivered hardships and promised nothing, not even an easy life at journey's end. Very few of these early pioneer women chose to head into the unknown, the wilderness of the west. The Mormon wives went because their husbands elected to answer "the call" to settle unchartered lands for the Church. Children went because their families did, and a few went on their own volition to find a better life, or seek a personal goal. While their reasons for making the journey and their backgrounds were different, they all experienced and endured the sufferings and deprivation of the journey and frontier life.

Some of these journeyers started their travels in Europe facing first the hazards of the sea. Ann Casbourne Williams Dalton and her family suffered a collision at sea. Although they all survived the hardships of that journey it took its toll. Not all Ann's family members lived to fulfill their dreams in the west.

Getting to the eastern shores of America was only the first leg on a long journey for these travelers. It took Ellen Jane Parks Johnstun thirteen years to arrive in Arizona from her original home in Sheffield, Yorkshire, England.

Americans were also migrating west. During the Civil War years Southerners made their way west to Texas, Oklahoma and Utah. From there many eventually found their way to Arizona.

Some women were vague about dates; others knew precisely when they had traveled. In all cases the trips took place from the mid-eighteen-eighties to the very early nineteen hundreds.

Originally they traveled across country by many means, the most noteworthy and historically remembered was the "Prairie Schooner" or covered wagon which was drawn by horses, mules, oxen, or even in some cases by cows. That was the most convenient means of transportation for the immigrants from the east as many already had the cattle on their farms. For those coming from overseas, or for the land poor travelers, their mode of transportation was the handcart. Many were built by the immigrants making the trip. Loaded with their personal belongings these carts were pulled, or pushed by two people.

For the migrants coming from Utah the conveyance of choice was the wagon box. A high-sided wagon, covered with canvas, the bottom of which was a large base that could be detached from the wheels. When the pioneers ended their journey the wagon base was removed from the rest of the wagon and the "box" became their bedrooms.

The journeys were started in easy stages. But, for those who traveled with handcarts it was a painful beginning as they suffered from leg cramps and aching bodies until they became conditioned to the walking. Although it was an easier journey for those in the wagons, drivers were responsible for the condition of their cattle and soon found that water and feed scarcity limited their traveling ability.

Nineteen year old Ida Frances Hunt Udall kept a diary of the daily travels of her wagon train from their departure in Beaver, Utah in February, 1877 to their arrival at Sunset, Arizona on April 29th. The travelogue is more a chronology in the search for water, the fear of not finding it, and the consequences when they did not. The route was from water hole to water hole, spring to spring, and water tank to water tank. Nothing else was of importance in the lives of the members of the wagon train. No other concerns consumed them as much as the search for water.

There were other problems the emigrants faced in their westward journey. Sometimes the road did not exist and was dug while traveling, and sometimes the route was there, a treacherous route, a death defying road. One such route was across Lee's Backbone. Lydia Ann Herbst Rogers labeled it the roughest place called a road on the whole trip. It was a ridge of solid rock, with a drop of over 1,000 feet on one side. Its top was strewn with one big boulder after another. The roadway was a steep and winding dug way. It took hours to get up one side and down the other. Great dexterity and complete control of the teams were needed to successfully transverse this dangerous segment. It seemed almost impossible to get over without tipping the wagon, yet many did.

Alzada Sophia Kartchner Palmer also acknowledged the serious dangers awaiting the traveler on the route from Utah to Arizona. The Colorado River presented its own type of danger, but it was Lee's Backbone that frightened her the most. While crossing the Backbone one of the wagons was thrown on the two outside wheels almost causing the wagon, oxen, woman and child to tumble over the embankment down hundreds of feet below.

And yet they endured the almost roads, the weather that ranged from sweltering heat to bitter cold, the lack of food and scarcity of water, the dangers from man and nature. Along the journey they struggled through the birth of babies and the death of children, husbands and friends.

It did not help that the Mormon's started their journeys in the winter so that they would arrive in time to plant their crops. The trip was not easy at any time of the year, but the treacherous snow storms and high winter winds made them a living nightmare. There is similarity in many of the Mormon stories. They traveled as a family, and in their individual interviews the more horrific experiences are told by many family members. However how a woman perceived the experience makes for an interesting comparison. Some dwell on an incident, others do not relate it, but tell another version of their trip.

There were some pioneer women who did not have to conquer nature and trails. They were the ones that traveled up from Texas or Mexico, or from the eastern states. They arrived by more sophisticated means such as trains or stage coaches. But their trips held other dangers and discomforts and required the stamina, determination, and courage to challenge the unknown. Regardless of the demands these pioneer women met them and survived to arrive in Arizona to establish a way of life.

The interviewers who wrote in the third person tried to capture the facts and emotions of the pioneer women as they related their experiences. Those who wrote in the first person delivered a piece with more drama and excitement for the reader. Here are their actual words and stories as captured by the Federal Writers' Project interviewers.

### Julia Johnson Smith Ballard

Interviewer: Roberta Flake Clayton
Snowflake

*Utah to Arizona Territory 1879*

When she was three years old, her parents left their home in Utah and started to Arizona where they had been called by President Brigham Young.

She traveled for six weeks in company with thirty others and arrived in Snowflake January 16, 1879. Although young she remembers many things which happened on the way. At night around the campfire the women folks would wash and bake bread for the following day, while the men folks held the articles of clothing before the fire to dry.

Some of the children in the company had the whooping cough and the little son of Smith D. and Elisa Rogers died and was buried at sunset. This cast gloom over the entire company.

### Ann Casbourne Williams Dalton

Interviewer: Roberta Flake Clayton
Navajo County

*Southery, Norfolk, England to Arizona 1850*

At the age of 18 she came to America (from Southery, Norfolk, England) with her parents. While at sea they encountered a terrific storm that lasted twenty four hours, during which their vessel, the *Hibernium*, was rammed and a large hole made in her side by a merchant ship. The vessel was badly disabled, but through the courageous effort of the noble captain and brave crew, the *Hibernium* with all her passengers was saved while the other ship went down with all on board.

After landing safely in New York Harbor, the Casbourne family continued their journey to St. Louis where Ann's two eldest brothers had gone several years previously, and had sent to England sufficient funds to emigrate the remainder of the family.

Shortly after their arrival the father died. Their sorrow at his departure was augmented by the fact they were in a foreign land among strangers.

For two years Ann worked very hard to help support the family. In the meantime she had joined the Church of Jesus Christ of Latter-day Saints and as a company was forming to go west in April 1854 she joined them. She had no money to pay transportation so she did cooking a laundry for the teamsters.

**Cathern Overton Emmet**
Interviewer: Roberta Flake Clayton
Navajo County

*Nauvoo, Illinois to Utah, No Date*

A recital of the hardships of this couple and their two small children endured, in the exodus from Illinois and their journey to the West is almost as miraculous as the famous one of the Israelites from Egypt.

They left a comfortable home in Nauvoo, and crossed the Mississippi River on the ice and camped on the Iowa side at a small Indian village called Punkan, near Davenport. The Indians were very friendly to them, vacating one of their wigwams for them, also at time dividing their food with them.

They had taken one step toward the Rocky Mountains; had been driven from their homes at the point of the bayonet in midwinter by the hostile state of Illinois. They found friends on the Iowa side and as spring opened they made all preparations possible and journey on westward.

At winter quarters they were compelled to stop and rest and make some repairs for the onward march. Here they endured some of the most severe hardships that could be. In their crossing the plains, at one time, food became so scarce in their camp that they were compelled to take portions of a mule which had given out in its travel. No amount of cooking could make this meat tender but it and the broth were eaten by these poor hungry travelers.

One of the daughters was but a nursing babe and during this scarcity of food the mother had no nurse for her babe, and to add to the agony of her own hunger, she was forced to watch her starving baby grow weaker and weaker until one day, the courage of the camp was exhausted and it looked as if they must resign themselves to actual death from starvation out in the midst of a heartless desert where howling wolves would rejoice over their awful fate and glut their snarling selves upon the famished flesh of their hapless victims.

At this trying time their leader went from wagon to wagon for the purpose of comforting and encouraging them, but when he learned fully the sad conditions, he shed tears and exclaimed, "How shall I comfort a starving people when I have no bread to give them?"

The quails came in hundreds, lighting upon the ground among their wagons. All the people gathered quail. They dressed, cooked and ate until all were satisfied. Even the starving babe ate of the broth, revived and lived. They renewed their journey with joy and thanksgiving.

## Lucy H. White Flake

Interviewer: Roberta Flake Clayton
Navajo County

*Utah to Arizona Territory 1877*

For three days the wind had been terrific. The sand and small stones had beaten into the faces of the horses. They would lunge and turn and almost upset the wagons. The wagon covers had been wired down leaving only a small opening in front through which the driver could see and hold the lines that guided the teams. The women and children were huddled inside on the beds which were made on rope corded from side to side and end to end, of the double wagon-boxes. A small stove was placed just back of the spring set to give warmth. The fire was kept burning by gnarled roots of sage and rabbit-brush, which the wind had uncovered.

It seemed at times that the wagons would be tipped over when the road would make a turn and throw them broadside to the wind.

The men and larger boys who were driving the loose cattle and horses had a harder time than the teamsters. Clouds of sand made it impossible for them to see more than a few rods ahead, and the animals would not face the gale but would huddle up together behind any little knoll or scrub cedar they could find and had to be beaten out with quirt or lariat.

Sensing the utter impossibility of traveling in the face of such a storm, William J. Flake ordered his outfit to stop in the first place that offered any protection to the poor beasts, and they had come to a halt where there were some low clay and sand dunes although the distance traveled that day was only about a mile and a half.

Mr. Flake with his family and his eldest son and his wife were on their way to find a home in Arizona. They had a dozen wagons fixed as conveniently as they could be at that time for traveling

William Flake
*(LDS Church History Library)*

and had about 200 head of loose stock and hired men to help drive them.

The country was new and this road at best was only a few wagon tracks, which now were entirely covered by drifting sand. They could not lose their direction however as it was to the southwest the way the wind was coming from.

When the storm began, Mrs. Flake had encouraged the men by telling them the "wind would go down with the sun," but it is said all signs fail in Arizona and that one did. Three days of it had worn out their endurance, and their limited amount of prepared food.

For weeks before these pioneers had left their home in Beaver City, Utah, preparations had been going on for this journey. Mrs. Flake was the kind of woman that "Looks well after the needs of her family." Small sacks of parched corn and dried meat that "the boys might have to nibble on as they rode along," together with big sacks of cookies and crackers–the latter kneaded and pounded with the flat side of an ax until they were crisp and hard when baked, had been the main food during these three days of tempest, and they had been eaten inside the wagons because of the choking sand storm outside.

There was no water at all for the animals and the large barrels on the side of the wagons used for carrying water had been drained to the last drop. Had the company been able to go on as they had planned, they would have come to a water hole but now they had to make a dry camp.

Every one had gone to bed early as that was one way out of a trying situation. For a long time sleep seemed an impossibility as the wagon covers flapped and sagged and the bows creaked with the hard onslaught for each gust of wind. Finally about midnight it calmed a little and the tired emigrants slept.

With the falling of the wind came a heavy snow. Like some doomed soul that for three days had gasped, struggled, fought to escape it fate, now at peace it lay calm and serene beneath a billowy blanket of white. The change was a welcome one. The men who had slept on the ground had covered their heads with their tarpaulins to keep out the sand, and now found themselves buried also in snow. Such a scramble and skirmish. Snowballing and face washing and the attendant shouting awoke the family who raised the wagon covers enough to look out and enjoy the fun.

The poor half famished cattle ate of the snow to quench their thirst. A large place was cleared, a fire built over it to thoroughly fry and warm the ground, and then the fire was moved farther along for cooking and when the sun came out as it did in all its brightness, and what warmth it could muster in late December.

Mr. Flake went to the wagon and taking his wife Lucy in his big strong arms, carried her over to the warm dry ground, where the grub boxes had already been placed, and with all his Southern Chivalry, beseeched his lady-fair to make them some hot, sour dough biscuits, the boys would bake them, fry some good juicy home cured ham, boil some spuds and make the gravy.

One by one the other members of the family were carried over the "torrid zone" as they playfully called it, one suggested that it seemed like Heaven to see the sun again and be able to stretch their limbs and get warm. The wit of the family reminded them the hot place was not Heaven but the one in the opposite direction. Everyone laughed, chatted and how they ate!

After breakfast Lucy ordered the boys to fill the tubs with snow which was melted and heated, and as she stood in her nice dry place and with tub and washboard scrubbed the clothes of the ten members of her family and those of half a dozen hired men, her song of gratitude, happiness and cheer rang out far and near over the frosty air.

## Mary Louisa Whitmore Garner

Interviewer: Roberta Flake Clayton

*Texas to Utah 1857*

A company was forming to leave for Utah soon. Because of her love for her family, Mary decided to remain at least another year with the, but as the time came for the company to start, the father and mother consented for Mary and her two brothers, James M. and Franklin to go with it. As they said goodbye, they realized it would probably be the last time they would see each other, and it was, for the parents both died the same day, ten years later, and were both buried in the same grave.

It happened that it was the same time and route taken by Johnston's Army, who were going west to "subdue the Mormons". They often passed and re-passed each other when one or another company would stop a day or two to let their teams rest, or the Mormons would stay in camp on the Sabbath day.

Some of the soldiers had named their oxen for the leaders of the Mormons and would swear at them calling them by name whenever they thought they could be heard by the immigrants.

Instead of making them angry it only amused them and the young people would answer back with something equally as cutting.

The girls were excellent singers and many an hour was whiled away as their young happy voices rang out in song. Sometimes in plaintive mood they would sing:

Yes, my native land, I love thee
All thy scenes, I love so well
Friends, connections, happy country
Can I bid you all farewell?
Can I leave thee, can I leave thee
Far in distant lands to dwell?

Then they would wipe away the tears of homesickness and dash away for a gallop over the plains and back to the road to join their company and go on again.

**Emma Swanson Hansen**
Interviewer: Roberta Flake Clayton
Navajo County

*Utah to Arizona 1881*

The trip to Arizona was long and tedious for the horses must travel over weary stretches of desert, up steep mountains and down into the barren lowlands again, cross the Big Colorado River at Lee's Ferry, over the desolate wastes and then stop in the vastness of these wastes at a mere fort where a few brave souls were striving to maintain a colony.

Fording the Little Colorado
*(Legends of America)*

The Little Colorado River which stealthily wound its way through the lonely forsaken valley was lined here and there with a few unlovely, crooked cottonwoods. No other trees relieved the severe and grim aspect of the scene.

"Would you like to go back?' asked the gallant husband as they neared their desert home. The young bride, lonely for her kin and the flourishing town she had left behind, wept, and in her bitterness she answered a most yearning, "Yes."

But to go back was impossible. Joseph C. Hansen was not a man to go back on his word. He would do his part to make the wilderness a home for succeeding generations he would do his utmost to answer duties' call.

Upon reaching the fort where the colonists lived to insure protection, the Hansen's were loyally received and like another member of a large united family, Emma, amid crushing heartaches entered into the duties of life at the fort.

## Loretta Ellsworth Hansen

Interviewer: Roberta Flake Clayton
Navajo County

*Utah to Arizona 1880*

In August, 1880 the Ellsworth family left Utah. Six wagons were loaded with the family and their belongings, then there were the cattle and horses to drive. Loretta, who was then twelve, and her eldest sister and two brothers took turns, driving the stock. There were no saddles, so they had to ride bareback. Modesty and custom forbade the girls riding astride in those days, and it was sometimes hard for the girls to sit "sideways" when their horses went over high boulders or had to chase out after the herd.

Their destination when they started was Mexico, but after six weeks of travel they reached Show Low Arizona and Mr. Ellsworth saw the beautiful scenery, the tall pines, the clear streams and good soil, he decided to locate there and bought the Cluff Ranch.

## Mary Adsersen Hansen

Interviewer: Roberta Flake Clayton
Navajo County

*Utah to Arizona Date Unknown*

The terrible wind and hail storm that almost tore the wagon covers from the wagons and were only held on by the united efforts of the mother and children who had taken refuge in one of the wagons while the men were in the other.

The storm had come up suddenly and the men thought it would soon be over, but it so increased in fury that they could not go to the relief of the family who screamed in their fright.

The poor horses were tied to the wagons and as the hailstones took off chunks of hide they jumped and jerked until it seemed they would tip the wagon over. It looked as though they would all be killed, but they escaped with the scare and severe wetting.

An early camp was made as soon as wood could be found and their bedding, clothing and themselves dried before a hot fire.

Finally they reached Adair, or "Fools Hollow," as it was then called, where their daughter Annie was, and soon built a log room adjoining hers.

## Louesa Park Harper

Interviewer: Roberta Flake Clayton
Contributed by her daughter Louesa Rogers
Phoenix

*Utah to Arizona 1880*

At this time in 1880, my parents decided to try again and make another home in Salt River Valley. Arizona was their choice and determination. Leaving Utah in the fall of 1880, they made their way to Arizona in company with a brother Edwin, who was about twenty-two years of age, Jessie Moses and his wife Bell Woodruff, a daughter of Wilford Woodruff, and five children, three wagons, eight horses and one cow which was soon disposed of.

One of the wagons, the one that Uncle Edwin rode in, was one that his father, Charles A. Harper had made to cross the plains in 1847. He was a wheelwright by trade. Well when I was twelve years of age we started out with lovely things to eat that my mother had prepared, one thing especially was a two quart jar of ground cherry preserves and homemade molasses. She also baked good yeast bread and sour dough biscuits. I had never heard tell of sour dough before or since, anyway it took the place of sour milk and made delicious hot bread.

I know I was my Mother's little nurse as I had to take care of my little brother, Park, and one just older than the baby. We had some nerve wracking experiences at crossing the grand old Colorado River at the old Pierce or Serantlia Ferry.

We arrived at Hackberry on the 24th of December 1880, Christmas Eve, and ate our Christmas dinner at this place. We had for special dishes molasses cake and homemade candy cooked on the camp fire. We entered Phoenix on the first of January 1881, with skinny horses, the last end of provisions, and some of us shoeless. I know I had on a pair of my Mother's old shoes and I would hide my feet if anyone came. My Father spent his last dollar and fifty cents, except fifty cents, for a sack of flour at the old Smith mill between Tempe and Phoenix.

**Ellen Jane Parks Johnstun**
Interviewer: Roberta Flake Clayton
Phoenix

*Sheffield, Yorkshire, England to Utah 1855, and Arizona 186?*

About September 1854 my Father sailed for America. He was not financially able to bring Mother and us so he went and settled at Alton, Illinois. He was a mechanic, and made iron machinery. Just as soon as he got settled he borrowed money from a wealthy farmer to send for us.

We sailed April 26, 1855 on Thursday. The ship was the William Stetson, with Captain Stetson commanding. We sailed from Liverpool.

There were 293 Saints on board under Aaron Smithurst. We arrived at New York, May 27. Mother was very sick on the trip and gave birth to a son the day we landed. The Captain said he was the first boy to be born on the ship and asked to be allowed to name him. Mother granted his wish and so he was named William Stetson for the ship and Captain Stetson.

I remember on the ship seeing a young Irish girl hemming a black silk handkerchief with her hair from her head. She and the first mate on the ship were married when we landed in New York.

A great sea turtle was caught and put on deck and we children were allowed to ride it. Captain Stetson would put three or four of us on at once. The Captain was very good to us and sometimes he would gather nuts and candy on the deck for us children to scramble after.

After we landed Mother was moved to Williamburg across from New York City. President John Taylor had charge of the emigrants so we were taken from the ship, it being noisy with remodeling and loading.

On Monday June 3, 1855, both Mother and child died. They were buried there. Mother took convulsions the evening before. This left my little sister Clara, three years old, and myself alone. I was eleven. Father sent money to President Taylor and he sent us with a man going to St. Louis, but he did not care for us. The conductor was kind to us. He gave us fruit and cookies and came to see that we were covered at night.

We arrived in Alton July 4, 1855. Father had come to St. Louis to meet us. We went out into the woods and celebrated our first Fourth of July.

Father had a house furnished for Mother, so he took us there and we lived with him. On May 19, 1856 my sister died very suddenly, it was called congestive chills.

It was decided that I should go west to live with my grandmother Parks, so I started. I took a boat at St. Louis and went up the Missouri River to Florence, Nebraska, called Winter Quarters by the Saints. There I stayed three weeks with the keeper of the Church store. While in this place I baked bread in the oven built by the first Mormon emigrants to pass through there.

A cart company was formed. There were three wagons. Elder Bunker was Captain. They were all ferried across the River at Winter Quarters. The three wagons were to carry the company supply of food. I cannot remember what food we carried other than flour, bacon, beans and occasionally some vegetables, which were purchased at settlements passed. These supplies were issued about once a week. Every Sunday was observed as a day of rest except two. These days we had to make short drives to get to water.

One old gentleman named Jones was sick most of the way across the plains. He died at Sweetwater, one hundred miles from Salt Lake, leaving a wife and son. It was the only death as I remember.

One time on the Platt River, two little girls and I took a handcart and filled it with little children, too small to walk. We thought we would help out the company. We started out after dinner. The road was very sandy so we got tired in the heat so pulled off the road in some breaks to rest in the shade, expecting to hear the company when it came up, but we did not. When we came to the road they had gone by. We traveled until dusk alone, then seeing the campfires down near the river found they had had supper and that a few of the men were ready to start out to hunt for us. We were very tired and receive a lecture never to be forgotten.

Occasionally the company had to halt while great herds of buffalo passed, moving to a new feed ground.

President Brigham Young sent a relief company out to meet us but they found us in such good condition they went on to meet the following company.

We arrived in Salt Lake City in the best condition of any company that year it was said. We reached there October 4 just three days before the General Conference.

I was married in January, on the 26, 1868 to William James Johnstun. He was twenty years older than I and had been married before. He worked as a hostler at the stage line in Salt Lake so that was our first home. Later he went to work for Jenson Stoddard. Mr. Stoddard was pretty well fixed. He was called to go and help colonize Arizona but did not want to go, so William volunteered to go in his place.

We had a good covered wagon and span of government mules. With a company consisting of Captain Smith and wife, George Noble, Fred Kesley and wife, we went to St. George and there were advised by President Snow to camp until we had an interpreter to go with us. We camped at Camp Springs for three weeks spending Christmas there. I fixed a nice dinner. Andrew L. Gibbons joined us as an Indian interpreter. We then traveled down the Virgin River to what was called The Muddy.

We were told to get as close as practical to where the Virgin emptied into the Colorado. We were later advised to get on higher ground on account of health. So after raising one crop we moved and laid out a town. We were discussing a name for it and I suggested that it be called St. Thomas for Captain Smith. This was adopted and St. Thomas was settled. Later Overton and St. Joseph were built above us.

## Virlenda Jennings

Interviewer: Kathlyn M. Lathrop
Duncan

*Texas to Arizona 1890*

We lived there (in Texas) until 1890 when we sold out, bag and baggage, as the saying goes, and came to Arizona Territory. All nine of our children were born there in Texas and the youngest was about five years old when we left there.

We landed in Douglas, Arizona, in the fall, I forget the exact date, of 1890. Buck had made a trip out here and located a place on Cave Creek, in Rucker Canyon, and we went straight out to our new home as soon as we could get our wagons ready. We came to Douglas on the train you see.

That was the first train ride I, or any of the children, had ever had in our lives, and it seemed to us that we were going around the world, and the world went around and around. I guess it was just our heads that went round and around. We were, everyone, sick as could be and vomited most all the way.

I recall that a Negro porter came through the coach where we were selling ham sandwiches on buns. The first we had ever seen or heard of. Buck bought each of us one, eleven in all, and as soon as we ate them we wanted another, another, and another, until we ate about six each. That made 66 sandwiches at ten cents apiece.

That porter kept sayin, "Lawdy! You all sh' do like these hyar things don' you all?" And, I'll say we did! But it made every lasting one of us sicker than ever, not to mention the cost. But Buck Jennings never did kick about the cost of anything his family ever wanted as long as he had the money to pay for it, and if he didn't have the money he most generally managed to get it someway or other.

## Annella Hunt Kartchner

Interviewer: Roberta Flake Clayton
Navajo County

*Utah to Arizona 1877*

The long journey was begun the day after Annella's fifteenth birthday, February 16, 1877. The company was composed of twelve covered wagons, some horse teams and some oxen, with a herd of loose animals to be driven. As they journeyed through southern Utah they often suffered from heat and lack of water. At one time their loose animals went without water for fifty-six hours. They crossed the Colorado River on the lower ferry, called Pierce's Ferry. They were familiar with all the fresh watering places and springs from men who had gone ahead to blaze the trail and open the unknown wilderness for the hardy ones brave enough to take their families and build homes in the barren valley were only Indians had ever lived.

By the time they reached the foot of the San Francisco Mountains, they were travel-worn and some of their teams gave out, so they camped for a week. At such times the Mother and older girls would do the family washing, being prepared with tub and washboard for this purpose. Also, they would bake many loaves of bread, having learned to "set sponge" and do all the other necessary processes of bread making around a campfire.

Here John Hunt was able to exchange cows and oxen and loose horses for a fine team of American horses to continue the journey. But again there was a shortage of water and one night in April as they were crossing the long desert between what is now Flagstaff and Winslow, Annella Hunt and her brother Lewis were walking and driving the loose cattle. Suddenly the girl discovered a white object in a tree. She found it to be writing paper and knew that it must be of great importance to them. They stopped their father to tell him of the discovery.

He lighted the lantern and found it to be a notice of two large tanks of water not far from the road. It had been left for their benefit by men who had gone ahead. The company spent two hours getting their thirsty animals down into those rocky tanks to be watered. They were very thankful for the finding of that little piece of paper, for they felt that it was providential guidance to keep them from perishing.

When they reached the town of Sunset on the Little Colorado River they rested for two days. The leaders there urged them to remain and make their home, but John Hunt decided to go on to the settlement in Sevoia Valley, New Mexico. Two missionaries to the Indians were already there with their families, but outside of four or five families the chief settlers of Sevoia were Navajo and Zuni Indians and Mexicans. These native inhabitants, however, proved to be civilized enough to become good friends of the white settlers, especially in times of distress and sickness. In the fall of 1878, John Hunt was called to be the Bishop of the new Snowflake settlement, on Silver Creek. His family hailed the change with delight as the Sevoia settlement had been so isolated and so lonely.

## Margaret Jane Casteel Kartchner

Interviewer: Roberta Flake Clayton
Navajo County

*Nauvoo, Illinois to Utah 1844to Arizona 1877*

She and her husband began a westward journey in company with a pioneer group in September 1844, but traveled only as far as Iowa City that year. They spent the winter there, doing any work possible for means of subsistence, until another start was made in March 1845.

There was much hardship and short rations of food, and Margaret Jane Kartchner walked for many miles of the journey because she was young and able-bodied. At one time during this hard journey when their rations had been reduced to one gill of corn a day to the person, without salt, they walked in water and mud, shoe-mouth deep, up the Iowa River with no road. Then leaving the river, they turned westward across a large prairie toward the Sioux Indian country.

One day some Frenchmen and Indians came to their camp and invited them to come and camp near their fort. They pointed to their thin cheeks, realizing how near starvation they were. The Indians gave them dried buffalo meat, which the pioneers thought to be the best thing they had ever tasted. They also brought them roasting ears of corn and finally a Frenchman, Mr. Henrie, told the young Kartchners that his Indian wife was away and offered them a boarding place if Margaret would do the cooking. They gladly accepted his offer and sincerely appreciated his kindness.

About the middle of July, a chance came to them to go on a steamboat down the Missouri to St. Louis. They decided this was a good move under the circumstances. They had very few possessions to take on board with them but Mr. Henrie and the Indians prepared two large bundles of dried meat for them. The boatmen, seeing their destitute condition was very kind to them and provided them with food and clothing. A rich French gentleman, traveling for his health gave them a pair of blankets and ten dollars in silver, for which they gave him sincere thanks and appreciation.

William D. Kartchner had an older sister living in St. Louis, but she was proud and haughty and considered the young pioneer couple scarcely worth any notice from her. Margaret became seriously ill with intermittent fever, but the sister, Mrs. James Webb, seldom came to see her. However, a Mrs. Powell, wife of a rich southern planter, from whom they had rented a small room, came often and cared for Margaret administering medicine and attending to her needs. When she was finally out of danger her husband crossed the river and went on foot sixty miles to see his brother, John Kartchner. He came in his wagon and the young couple ferried their belongings across the river in a skiff where he gave them a welcome and a comfortable home during the fall and winter of 1845.

William learned of a pioneer company leaving for the Rocky Mountains in the spring of 1846. His determination to join this company greatly annoyed his brother who had made him fine offers of land if he would stay with him for five years. They finally parted in anger, and William and Margaret Kartchner joined the Mississippi Company in March 1846.

They had hired out to drive a wagon loaded with a thousand pounds of provisions for a Mr. Crow. They traveled to Fort Pueblo, on the Arkansas River, by the latter part of July. Here Mr. Crow broke his obligation, fearing his provisions would run short. This left the young Kartchners again stranded, without even a wagon to camp in. The company had halted here to await instructions from their leader, Brigham Young, and the Kartchners made a camp under a large cottonwood tree, and for a time were at the mercy of kind friends for food. Here, under this cottonwood tree, under these destitute conditions, their baby daughter was born on August 17, 1846, the first white child to be born in the state of Colorado, an honor for which many years later that state presented to her, Sarah Emma Kartchner Miller, of Snowflake, Arizona, a gold medal.

Not long after the birth of their daughter the father obtained work as a blacksmith, in which line he was skilled, at Bent's Fort, eighty miles down the river. The young wife and child were left to the kindness or a Mrs. Catherine Holiday, and the journey was made on horseback.

The work was heavy, largely consisting of work for U. S. Army troops under General Kearny, on their way to the Mexican War. William worked there until late in the fall, thankfully receiving two dollars a day for his labor, but was finally stricken with a serious attack of rheumatism and was obliged to return to Pueblo. His wife was often compelled to walk as much as a hundred yards through snow knee deep to get a cottonwood limb for fuel.

Early in the spring of 1847 they began making preparations to resume their westward journey. With some of the money he had earned they bought an old wagon and provisions, another man of the party permitting them to use a pair of his oxen. William was still unable to walk, but did repairing on his one and other men's wagons by means of his blacksmith tools screwed to his wagon tongue, Margaret carrying the pieces to him which were to be repaired.

When they reached Fort Laramie they learned that they were only three days behind the pioneers under Brigham Young. This company traveled that distance behind them all the rest of the journey reaching the Great Salt Lake Valley July 27, 1847.

In the spring of 1877, William D. Kartchner, sons and sons-in-law with their families were called to help in the colonization of the Little Colorado River Settlements. Several months were spent in gathering provisions and stock, teams, wagons, and supplies for two years, and on November 15, 1877 they made a start for Arizona. The journey to Sunset covered two months and three days, and Margaret Kartchner was sick most of the time.

The Kartchners settled eighteen miles above Sunset and called their settlement Taylor. But, during seven months no dam was proof against the floods which swept them away as if they were nothing. After five dams had gone out, the entire settlement of Taylor was abandoned, and the Kartchner families moved to the new settlement of Snowflake on Silver Creek, a tributary of the Little Colorado, in August 1878.

## Rebecca Steward Kartchner

Interviewer: Roberta Flake Clayton

*Alabama to Arizona 1867?*

At last came time to start. All the other families had gathered there the night before so no one slept much. All were up and ready to start at sunrise. When the wagons were loaded they consisted of a box of clothes, five pounds of flour, a side of hog meat, three pounds of coffee, a few sweet potatoes and five hundred pounds of tobacco. Every man, woman and child that was old enough used tobacco. They had two bake ovens, frying pan and a coffee pot.

Two more families rode in our two wagons. One man had a wife and two babies and the other man had five children. There was twenty one in all for Father's wagons.

They tied the feather bed up in a sheet, pushed it back as far as they could under the wagon cover of Father's wagon and put Evaline and me back against the bed, then put two old home made chairs in front of us with our feet stretched out under them. Father and Mother sat in the chairs. Some of the little boys rode in the other wagon with an older boy. Father was to be the leader so they all started, most of the men, women and big children walking ahead, men with guns on their shoulder, women with sun bonnets on and a big child astraddle on their hips. All were happy as could be but poor old souls did they ever dream what was ahead of them?

There were fifty wagons started on the beginning. Some of the oxen were trying to run away, some were lying down with their yoke on and others crowding and trying to tip the wagon over. In the last wagon was an old man with his little old lady and a little adopted boy in her lap. The old man had a long white beard, he had one old steer working him in the shafts, starting a thousand miles for the west.

Can anyone imagine how those poor folks could see their way through? There wasn't fifty dollars among the whole bunch but they went on never dreaming what was ahead. They traveled until sun down the first day going only eight miles, then they pitched their tents for the night. The next day they only went six miles for everyone and the critters were so stiff and sore.

My sister and I sat in one position all day and didn't even have a drink of water and when we tried to walk it was almost impossible. I couldn't see how I could stand it another day. I couldn't go to play like the rest of the children and slept on the ground that was so hard and cold.

We traveled day after day, week after week until months passed. Our money was going so when we got to Memphis we had very little left. We got there about four o'clock in the afternoon. A man came out where we were all dressed up with his black suit and white collar on. Nearly every ox lay down while he was talking to us. Father asked him when we could cross the Mississippi River and he said not before the next day as there was a big rise in it. All the women and children looked at this man as though they had never seen anyone before. Poor souls hadn't seen very many in their life time. What were they born for? Just to live in the back woods.

This man told them to pull in the camp yard and they didn't know what he meant so he had to explain what a camp yard was. Then a bunch of men came into camp. They each took a man, his wife and smallest children to supper leaving the older ones in camp.

Father, Mother, Evaline, as she was sick, and I all went with one man and Mother had to leave the baby in camp with my oldest sister as Father had no use for babies and didn't want to be bothered with them. We had to climb up stairs and I had no one to look after me so I crawled up like a cat. We thought we were so high in the air, but were only ten feet.

They wouldn't let us pitch our tents that night so we all laid on the ground and looked at the stars. To see the electric lights and hear so much noise was a grand thing to see and surely opened our parents' eyes.

All the women stood around with long belt waisted dress and bonnets and men shoes on with a big child on their arm or one hanging to their breast and holding all they could by hand. Then there were the men all in a bunch with their knives out whittling on sticks, their mouths full of tobacco and most of it coming down on their coat when they would spit. They all had long mustaches, only Father and he wore chin whiskers.

When morning came the sky was cloudy and looked like rain. All were up by daylight. The children were all crying for something to eat but they couldn't make a fire and our parents never thought of going to a store to get anything. There was many an old person in the bunch who never had seen inside a store or a loaf of bread or a pound of cheese. God pity such a bunch. I look back in the year of eighteen hundred and sixty seven and can see how our old parents had to live and it was a shame for such people to bring children in the world to be raised in ignorance.

The man that had charge of the steam boat came soon and told them everything was ready to go and he would take two wagons across the Mississippi River at a time. Our two wagons were the first to go so we pulled on the boat, the little ones still begging for something to eat, and the older ones sick with headaches for want of their usual coffee. It was just ten o'clock when we boarded the boat.

The oxen were so frightened they nearly went overboard. The man had to beat them over the head as they had no ropes to hold them with so there was lots of excitement.

Father told Mother and us children to stand up by the wagon and there was almost a foot of water on the floor where we were standing. My baby sister in Mother's arms almost dead, the older sister holding the six months old baby boy standing close enough so he could pull at Mother's sleeve, and George and I holding to Mother's dress. Oh, what a life for that poor old Mother of mine, and I can look back and say, "God bless her and all the rest that had to live with a man and go through what they did and I know he will."

The water kept getting deeper and deeper on the boat so they got six big Negro men to dip the water out with big buckets. Finally the Captain told all the women and children to go upstairs where it was warm and they could sit down. We all went upstairs where we found some of the nicest chairs and a pretty rug on the floor. A lady told Mother to sit down in a rocking chair with the little sick girl and that was the first rocking chair she had ever sat in, and not being used to anything but a straight chair, she nearly fell over.

In one corner sat two ladies and two men playing cards and were dressed so nice. I wondered if I would ever have nice clothes like that. I sat there and could smell good things cooking and was so hungry. My poor little sick sister needed something to eat so bad and a doctor.

All at once a young man came and cried, "There comes a shark after the boat and if it isn't captured it will turn the boat over." There was a dead man on the boat and that is what the shark was after.

The shark got so close they had to throw the dead man overboard. We all rushed to watch the excitement. The dead man tossed on the waves until the shark got to him, then it swallowed him and went on. Soon some men came on a skiff and stuck a long spear in the shark, then it went to a sand bar and died.

We got off the boat at two o'clock and after we got everything together Father called our old dog, Watch, but he didn't come and we could see him following some Negro men a long ways off. Father liked the dog so well he went after him and found him seven miles from where we got off the ship. He was still with these Negroes and they were on the sand bar where the shark went, had taken the dead man out, and was getting ready to bury him.

We didn't wait for Father or the rest of the wagons behind us, but went on trying to find a place to camp as we hadn't had a thing to eat all day. We couldn't find any wood so went on and on. Finally it began to rain and we drove on until dark. We saw the glimpse of a little house and wanted to get there so we could get in out of the rain and it was raining harder every step the oxen took.

My poor little sick sister, how I wished I had a piece of bread for her. The baby was waiting for Mother so he could 'suck' as the Southerners say, and go to sleep. She had no milk as she hadn't eaten in so long.

A last we pulled up in front of this little house. Everyone went in and there on the walls read "Smallpox, don't come on." We got out as quickly as we could, drove on a little farther where the boys pitched our tent, made our bed on the wet ground, turned the oxen out and went to bed without supper. It was raining so hard we could not find any wood.

In the middle of the night Father came with the dog. It was raining so hard the dog had no place to sleep so went back to this little house and crawled under it. There was an earthen plate under there with some kind of poison on it. The dog was so hungry he licked the plate and the next morning he was dead. The long twenty-two miles Father had walked was all in vain. Mother kept that plate for twenty years.

Finally all the families got together again. On and on they went, over mountains, through rivers and through long flats, pushing on towards the west where there was plenty of sunshine. The oxen pushed and crowded along, some with their tongues out but on they went by the help of the whip.

The old tired mothers kept on the go from early until late, with all the care of the children, while the men went on ahead, with their guns on their shoulders and not a care.

It had been many a day since they had left their little old log houses where they could sit by a big fire, chew their tobacco and dream of what was to come. Now they had their wives and children out in the world, no friends, no money and if one should have died they would not have lumber for a coffin; all they could do would be wrap them up in a quilt and dig them a grave. In all that large group there were only two short handled spades.

Our wagon covers wouldn't turn rain and when a big rain storm came we were all soaked through and through. The women had slat bonnets. The slats were made of paper so one good rain would ruin them. They couldn't get any more paper so would turn their bonnets up in front in order to see. The women and girls had no coats, just small shawls.

We made very short distances during the day averaging six and eight miles. The oxen would get so dry. We only had a two gallon jug to carry water in.

After two long months of these hardships we reached Arkansas where twenty five more families were waiting to join us. We stopped there awhile for our oxen to rest and camped in a little one room house. There was lot of cotton to pick so Mother and the bigger boys started picking to get money for shoes. The price was fifty cents a hundred for picking. Mother did all the work, tended baby and picked five hundred pounds of cotton a day. Father would take the gun and hunt squirrels. My big sister would do nothing but talk to an old married man. He had a wife and two children, and ready for another but my sister was crazy about him.

Mother and the boys picked cotton three weeks then Father took the money and bought shoe leather. From this leather she made six pair of shoes. She could make shoes as well as women of today can make a cream cake.

There was one man who wanted to go with us. He had five children and a sick wife. He waited over night for them. It was snowing. They thought she was too cold so they got some rocks very hot and put them around her to get her warm. She was dying and so near gone she could not tell them they were burning her. After she was dead they found big blisters where every rock touched her.

The next morning Father sent George and me to tell Mother to come home as the baby and Evaline wanted her. We put on our new shoes, tied a rug over our heads, took hold of hands and started out before day light. By the dim fire light that shone through a foot square window we found our way. There were five inches of snow on the ground, we had no coats and when our hands would get cold on one side we would change hands. When we got there we could see the dead women lying on a board, which they called a plank, through the window.

We three went back where Father was and after breakfast Mother took sick. Three or four of the children had chills and fever, in fact, most of the family was sick so we had to stay all winter waiting for Mother to get well or die. She kept getting worse until she didn't know any of us and we had to wean the baby. He was only ten months old and she seldom weaned a baby before they were two years old.

There was an old man and woman planting goobers near us so one day George and I hid in the bushes until they went to dinner then we stole all their goobers, ate them, put a rock in the sack and threw it into the river, then ran. The old couple came back and found their peanuts gone. They tracked us right to our house, measured our feet with a string then we sure got a whipping. I will never forget it. We were so sore that night and had cramps from eating so many goobers we nearly died and Mother was too sick to know.

At last we got ready to start on our way again. There was to be seventy five families now in the bunch. One man had four milk cows that he worked. One man had a bull, a cow, a horse and a mule that he worked. A widow with four children drove two old bulls to her wagon. She would walk all day and drive them. An old Negro slave wanted to go with one family but they told her no. She walked behind the wagon until noon. The family gave her dinner and told her to go home. She went down the road a piece and sat down. Some of the men threw rocks at her.

Mother was so sick she never knew when they put her in the wagon. We traveled two weeks before she could get out of the wagon. We crossed many rivers, went over some of the highest mountains, thru pine trees, down steep rocky places and thru big valleys. The valleys were so big we would travel for miles with neither wood nor water, still dragging out the lives of these poor old sore-footed steers. Sometimes it would be three days between watering places and they would be so thirsty they would reel under their yokes.

Most of the women were bareheaded by now. One day we met a lady in a buggy with bonnets and aprons to sell. We had no money so the women and larger girls cut off their hair and bought themselves bonnets. They all wore long hair twisted up and pinned on top their heads. The first rain spoiled the bonnets as they were full of starch and when they go wet there was nothing to them.

We worried through all kinds of weather, rain, mud, half starved with only two scant meals a day, all of us most in rags and bare footed. The road was only a cow trail so rocky and narrow and washed full of gullies that the men would have to put rocks in the holes to keep the wagons from tipping over. Lots of them would get behind and push the wagons up the steep hills. After four or five months like this we came to a ranch forty miles from any place.

The people were very nice. There was just an old lady about seventy five years old, a man near fifty and a little girl ten years old. Their house was built upon a little hill and below was a pretty meadow with the fattest cows in it. In the corral was a bunch of big fat calves. Father asked this man if we could camp and he told him we could and to turn our cattle in the meadow. Then he turned his cows in the corral and told the crowd to come in and milk all they wanted. The old tired mothers grabbed a bucket and run to milk. They would milk first one cow then another and get what while the calves were sucking. We children sure had a fine supper that night.

The man came to our camp and said that the old lady was his wife and that the little girl was their baby; that his wife was rich and that he had married her for her money. He asked us where we were going and Father told him we were going west to get rich. The next morning when we left, our oxen were so full they groaned under the load.

We went until months had passed and no gold had we found, no, no, nothing but hardship and trouble.

There was another young girl in the crowd that was married just as we left our old southern home. She was going to become a mother and now the time had come. She was sick all day and that night they called Father. He claimed to be a doctor but he really did not know anything about it. He just had lots of nerve. When the baby came he let the baby die and they wrapped it up in an old quilt and lay it in a little hole by the roadside. The broken hearted mother raised her head to see the newly made mound that she would never see again. Nine long moths of suffering and expecting just to leave behind many a sad remembrance. I could hear her scream for hours.

At last we came to Kansas and it was getting very hot weather. The women and children pulled off their shoes and went barefooted in order to save them. Sometimes when we came to a stream of water they would stop and wash what dirty clothes we had. They had no tub or washboard, just rubbed the dirty spots with the palm of their hands.

While we were coming through Kansas we stopped at a man's ranch for the night to let our cattle rest. The man said we looked hungry and he would kill a beef for us. He killed a three year old steer and what a blessing it was to us. Some were so hungry they even ate raw meat. Every part was saved even the feet. God surely watched over us. There was one birth, one death, and one wedding on the road, and also several dances as there were large smooth places on the prairie that is where we danced.

We came slowly on stopping to shoe oxen, fixing old broken wagon wheels, hunting through the woods and getting whatever we could to eat. Sometimes it would be prairie chickens, rabbits, squirrels, prairie dogs. Anything tasted good to us as we were half starved, ragged and sad hearted. It looked like our last days had come but we couldn't give up. The men would pray to God at night to protect us until our journey was through and He did.

At last we came to the state of Oklahoma where the buffalo and Chereque Indians were. At night when we were on the plains the buffalo would come so close to the fire we could see their eyes shining. Sometimes there would be sixty or seventy five in a herd.

One of my brothers could shoot them right in their eyes and down they would come. The rest would run, sometimes toward the camp and we would have to jump and run to our tents. We always made a corral at night with our wagons. Many of the Indian girls would stand around camp and watch our mothers get supper. They were very pretty with fair complexions and rosy cheeks. Two of my big brothers fell in love with them and wanted to get one for a wife. When they tried to talk to them they would laugh and turn their heads away.

We went on and on and finally came to Texas. There we could see miles and miles ahead of us. There were no hills, no wood and very little water and a cloud of dust where cattle and sheep were trying to find water and something to eat. The wind was blowing so hard the men had to turn the rim of their hats under. They were queer looking people with long mustaches and their hats peaked in front and back. The women walking with their bonnets tied around their necks and hanging down their backs, a big baby hanging to their breasts and their dresses open from the neck to the waist. It would be a sight to see today.

Finally we came to a hole of water where a sheep herder had a large flock of sheep. When he saw us coming he started his sheep running and he drove them for miles. We thought we could water our cattle so we stopped and they started dipping our sheep pills. They dug down about three feet but the cattle wouldn't even smell the water and they hadn't drunk for three days.

We went on and in the afternoon we could see what looked like a big mountain and it began to get cooler. The wind began to blow harder and harder and soon we discovered there was a big storm coming. We went a mile farther and then camped as we knew it would e many miles to water if God didn't send us some.

We had just gone to bed when the storm came. Mother put us children to bed when the storm came. There was a big flash of lightening. I could see Mother standing at one end of the tent, and Father at the other. Our tent was ripped right thru the middle. The water was half way to their knees all of us were as wet as rats. We were all crying as hard as we could. I was so nearly frozen I didn't look out again until morning.

Everything in the tent was washed away. Mother's feather bed washed a long way away and lodged by a bunch of bushes. Everyone was disheartened and blue the next morning. Everything was wet, their floor, clothes, bedding and everything. There was nothing to burn but cow chips and a man had to fan them with his hat to make them burn and then it was only smoke.

We stayed there two days to dry our bedding and clothes as the sun came out. We cooked our dough such as it was without salt or baking powder. Then we made another start.

## Caroline Marion Williams Kimball

Interviewer: Roberta Flake Clayton
By her daughter Effie Kimball Merrill
Phoenix

*Utah to Arizona 1878*

Mother felt bad when she thought of taking the boys out of school, but Father cheer her up and told her that traveling to Arizona would be an education to them, and they would be pioneering a new country, where the sun shined and they would soon have a good home and schools.

Father sold his home and grist mill to the highest bidder and prepared for his Arizona Missions. Father had been told that cattle were bringing big prices in the new country, so he decided to make the journey with ox teams.

Father bought ten yoke of oxen and twenty head of cows. We bid all our friends farewell, and on the morning of July 14, 1877, Father, Mother, and family with Mr. Solomon, Edward E. Jones and family started to Arizona.

Mother drove a span of horses to the big carriage as Father had to drive one of the ox teams and my brother David drove the other team. As we were coming along the road the other side of St. George the ox team Father was driving ran off the road way and caused Father to jump from the wagon. He sprained his ankle; this almost caused blood poison. Father suffered a great deal and could not take much responsibility so my little brother Tom, who was only thirteen years old had to take Father's place driving the ox team.

When Mother would see the terrible roads ahead, she felt as though she could never drive the team. I remember many times the front wheels of the carriage would be up in the air so high we children would scream. She drove from Nephi to Hackberry over every foot of the road, sometimes the men would have to make the road by cutting down trees and bushes. All the time Father's leg was awful, but had faith that it would be alright, and faith healed it so that he was able to be around again.

It was a time of hardship and trials, as the Indians were on the war path. Mother would sit up at night, watching over the camp while the men would herd and watch the cattle. We had so many hardships as the oxen traveled so slow and we could hardly make the watering places. Sometimes we did not have any water to cook with and Mother would say, "David do you think we can ever make the journey?"

Father would smile and say, "Of course we can Mother, Dear. Have faith and courage and we will fulfill our mission."

Both man and beast had to have courage and faith to journey on. It took six months traveling from the time we left Utah till we reached Hackberry, a little mining town in the northern part of Arizona.

**Ellen Malmstrom Larson**
Interviewer: Roberta Flake Clayton
Contributed by another
Navajo County

*Lund, Sweden to Utah 1859, to Arizona 1878*

On March 5, 1859 with their three children, Betsy, Caroline and Lehi they emigrated on the ship *William Tapscot* to the United States. It took six weeks to reach New York. From there they went by train to Florence, Nebraska where they had to buy supplies and prepare conveyances to carry them over a thousand miles of desert in habited only be the Indian and wild animals.

They were told that several handcart companies had successfully reached Salt Lake City and they thought that surely they could do what others had done. Her husband being a mechanic they would build their own cart and would pull it to the valleys of the mountains. What an example of faith and courage to their descendants.

On June 9, 1859 they started with the hand cart company led by Captain George Rawley. The journey was hard and tedious. The food supply was limited and the captain was harsh. He forbade them to let the oldest child, who was not quite six, ride on the cart. This nearly broke the mother's heart to have to see the little girl walking every step of the way. She always saved as crust of bread out of her own rations with which to encourage the child to keep trudging on. Betsy often said afterward that no food ever tasted so good to her.

Their baby boy became very sick and they had very little hopes of him living so the mother planned how she could prepare him for burial. But to their great joy he recovered and was always a help and comfort to them all their lives.

They reached Salt Lake City September 15, 1859 making the journey in three months and six days. They went west and settled in the little town of Tooele, from Tooele they moved to West Jordan.

In 1878 on October 30th, Mons Larson left Santaquin for Arizona with his wife and five children. They had three wagons and five teams, also eight head of loose stock. As they were starting out and old friend remarked that the family could settle on top of a ridge of rooks and thrive.

While en route they learned of a town that had plotted out by Erastus Snow and William Flake and named Snowflake. The Larsons decided to look the place over and perhaps locate there. So it was that on December 30th, 1878 that they reached Snowflake and one the following day chose two town lots pitched their tent, hauled a load of wood and were ready to begin building another home.

Instead of having their wagons loaded with furniture and other bric-a-brack they had brought axes, plows, shovels, hoes, harrow-teeth, nails and a case of windowpanes. Also a complete set of carpenter tools, wood cards and a spinning wheel. As wool was plentiful and cheap Mrs. Larson made arrangements for 100 pounds so she and her girls would have something to do while the men were getting out logs for a house and for fence posts.

There was a demand for all the yarn they made and they made $1.00 a pound. By the next year they had a loom made on which they wove rag carpets and beautiful coverlets for beds. She advocated the theory that those who could do the most practical things were the best educated.

## Amy McDonald

Interviewer: Helen Smith
Cochise County

*Texas to Arizona, 1887*

Although I have been back and forth between Texas and Arizona twenty-nine times in a covered wagon, it was not until about 1887 that we made a real stop in Arizona. This was on the Gila River near Fort Thomas; and I was a wife and mother with two children at the time, about twenty two or three years old.

Travel in covered wagons was not so romantic as it is considered today. We would stop in the heat of the day, unhitch and loose the team so that they might pick a few mouthfuls of food. We would cook a little for ourselves, as likely as not eating as much sand as food. The evening stops were much better, of course, although the whole thing grew quite monotonous. The teams hit a long, swinging walk which was itself tiresome after so long a time, as were also the long halts necessary for the animals to feed.

**Sophia De La Mare McLaws**
Interviewer: Rae Rose Kirkham
Joseph City
*Utah to Arizona, 1876*

In January, 1876, we were among those called from various counties of Utah by Brigham Young to colonize the Little Colorado River in Arizona. We were commanded to leave nothing behind to call us back, to stay at the place we were sent, and to feed the Indians—not fight them.

We began the trek February 8, 1876, two weeks later. Each went with those from his own town, and met with the other groups along the trail in Southern Utah. We joined our party in Richfield. Although we came with horses and mules, many came with oxen. The wagons were very comfortable.

Just before we came to Orderville, Utah the snow was six feet deep. The roads had to be shoveled. People from the town brought food to us and helped us over the mountain.

We traveled down the Sevier River, thru the Mount Carmel country, and over to Kanab by March 9, 1876. From there we crossed into Arizona. We arrived at the Kaibab Forest and proceeded to follow the low part of the Buckskin Mountains. There were many hardships. I drove a team over these mountains while my husband dug through bog for a road. Not only did we do this, but all had to do the same. Through this bog we travelled only fifteen miles in three days. I wonder what people would say to that now in 1933?

We next came to Houserock Valley where we began to follow the big Colorado River until we came to Lee's Ferry. Emma Lee, the wife of John D. Lee, and Brother Johnson, a Kanab man, were there. Brother Johnson had been sent to Lee's Ferry to help the pioneers across.

Lee's Ferry - Colorado River - 1870
*(LDS Church History Library)*

We were at Lee's Ferry two or three days. It took that time to swim the cattle through the narrows and to get the wagons to the opposite shore. During our stay at this point we danced by night out on the big river boat which was enclosed with a railing. Fires were kept on the banks of the river to direct us back to shore so that we would not get caught in the rapids. A month later in May, Brigham Young, Jr., Daniel H. Wells, and a Brother Roundy were drawn into the wild vortex of these waters resulting in the death of Brother Roundy by drowning. These men came to organize the companies in Arizona.

Our goal after leaving Lee's Ferry was the Little Colorado. Our first view of this river was indeed a grand sight at Black Point. I was told at that time that John W. Young was building a woolen factory at Moenkopi not far away.

Before long we went on to Black Falls and then to Grand Falls. When we camped at the plot where Winslow now is, it was known as Wolf's Crossing. Not far from this location our efforts to reach the opposite shore of the Little Colorado took three days, for we had to build rafts.

The first Mormon colonizers coming from Utah to Arizona preceded us one month. Among them had been sent four captains who awaited our company with the command to disperse us into four colonies with fifty persons in each. The same captains were to occupy the place of authority over the townships formed. Joseph C. Allen was called to preside over Joseph City. The other settlements formed from our company were: Obed, three miles from here, presided over by Brother George Lake; Brother Lot Smith presided over Sunset; and Jessie Ballinger was in authority over Brigham City, twenty miles from Winslow.

Our town is the only one that grew. The others were deserted in three or four years. Few of these first pioneers remain. Seventy-six persons came in the beginning; forty-five men and twelve women.

This place was originally called Allen after a little boy drew that name from tickets in a hat. That is how we decided the issue after some had wanted it called Ramah, some Winslow. Authorities of the Church came later and changed the name to Joseph City.

**Mary Ann Smith McNeil**
Interviewer: Roberta Flake Clayton
Navajo County

*Utah to Arizona, 1878*

On the 18th of the month, 1878 we started for Arizona to make a new home. I was sick most of the time which was caused by the cold weather. I was very sad because I had to leave my beloved parents and relatives to come to a country that was unsettled, without a home or friends, and where the Redman roamed at will.

By this time I had five children to care for. My baby was only nine months old and was sick most of the time. She couldn't stand the jolting of the wagon so the other children and I took turns walking and carrying her in our arms most of the way. Our outfit consisted of a span of horses in the lead, then a yoke of milk cows and the wheelers were a span of mules. We put the milk cows in the team as we had no one to drive them.

Traveling by team was slow and we hadn't gone far when it began to snow. When we got to the canyon 18 miles from Kanab, Utah, my husband had to leave us and go on to that town for help, as our poor team was given out and we could go no farther. There was 18 inches of snow and bitter cold. I am sure we would have all frozen to death before he got back had not two men happened along traveling our way. They asked a lot of questions. As first I was afraid for fear they might harm us, but instead when they learned of our plight they brought wood to make the camp fire and camped close to my wagon that night. They went on next morning and wanted to take the children and me with them to Kanab but all we had was in that wagon and I did not want to leave it, and then my husband had left me there and there I would remain until he came for me, which he did that night, bringing Joseph Noble and a team belonging to John H. Standifird.

On Christmas Day we reached Kanab, glad to be alive. We lived that winter in Mr. Stanified's cellar and next spring rented the house of Jacob Hamblin who was leaving for Arizona. Here we stayed until fall. We raised a good garden and lots of apples. When the crop was gathered we started again for Arizona.

People told us that apples would bring a good price so we left our cook stove and many other things there that we might load our wagon with apples, but long before we reached our destination they were all frozen and we got nothing for them, besides having to cook over a camp fire for a year before we returned to Kanab and got our stove.

Sometime in December 1879 we arrived at what was then called Walker, now Taylor, three miles above Snowflake. We stayed a week with James Pearce then went to a place on Silver Creek known as Solomon's Ranch. Here Mr. McNeil built a fireplace and chimney of rock near the side of a hill and then stretched a tent over it and there we lived until March of the next year.

## Margaret Lovina Brundage Millett

Interviewer: Roberta Flake Clayton
Snowflake

*Utah to Arizona, 1883*

When Margaret Lovina was eighteen years old, her parents moved to Arizona settling at Lehi, Arizona on the Salt River, arriving March 3rd, 1883. They traveled the Southern route, crossing the Colorado at Scanlon Ferry. Her Father started out with a large herd of cattle and horses, but the feed and water was so scarce that the animals got so poor and trails were so rough, and the cattle so foot sore, that he sold all of them but one milk cow. They milked her night and morning and drank the milk. The night's milk was used next morning for breakfast and the morning's milk strained into a crock, and kept for evening. There was always a pat of butter in it that would be churned during the day by the jolting of the wagon.

The cow proved to be very valuable to the family as all of her calves were heifers. These Margaret Lovina's father gave to his children, beginning with the eldest, first, and from these calves each got a start in the cattle business.

## Eleanor C. Roberts Morris

Interviewer: Roberta Flake Clayton
Contributed by her daughter, Dora Morris Pomeroy
Navajo County

*Illinois to Utah, 1860, to Arizona 1883*

In the spring of 1860 they started west in Captain Walling's Company presumably for California, but Eleanor's continual prayer was that they would get no farther than Utah.

Just after beginning the journey, her sister-in-law Nancy's children had measles, and the children were all exposed and took the disease and were very sick. Eleanor's little boy Edwin, known as 'Little Dock', contracted pneumonia and died May 29, 1860.

There was no help to be had, except in the traveling company. They were far from any towns, but one man who had been over the route before knew where there was a graveyard of 5 graves, so after Hyrum had made a little casket out of a table top, they loaded the things into the other wagon and taking the spring wagon, with the little casket, Hyrum, Eleanor, their little girl and a man named Kenner drove till late at night to reach this spot.

Picture if you will the sadness of this scene that night Digging a little grave in a strange land, so dark, so alone, with danger from Indians, wolves howling, not far away, the little casket lowered and all heaping rocks on top to keep out marauding wolves. No songs, no sermon, just a short simple prayer, leaving their beloved baby in God's keeping—then the long drive ahead, to catch the company, and not knowing if they ever would reach the company or not.

He was buried on the banks of the Platte River near what is now Columbus or Genoa in Nebraska with just 5 other graves for company.

A few days after this there was a terrible stampede of buffaloes, which came very near rushing all of them over the bluff above the

Platt River, but by firing a gun at the leader of the herd, they succeeded in turning them the other way and the company was saved.

Arriving in Salt Lake City in August 1860 they had to wait over as they were out of supplies and Hyrum went to work at once for Bishop Archibald Gardner.

Eleanor begged Bishop Gardner to persuade her husband to not go on, which he did to such good purpose that in October 1861 he was baptized into the Mormon Church.

They made a trip to Mesa, Arizona in the Spring of 1882 and liked the country so well that they each purchased a 40 acre farm and returning to Utah as soon as possible they sold their lands and all properties. January 27, 1883 Hyrum started with his family to return to Arizona.

Hyrum had an outfit of 5 wagons, six teams, 25 head of loose horses and 50 head of cattle. He was accompanied by William Brundoge and family, William Lang and family, Paul Huber and family, Charles Slaughter and son, Frank, Hyrum Smith, Joseph Hirschey and James Wilkins. At St. George, the Company was organized by Erastus Snow, with Morris, Captain Brundage, as Chaplain.

At Hackberry many of the horses and cows had become tender-footed and had to be sold, but the rest were brought on through. On the Hualapai Desert, while journeying on, the children had been allowed to walk beside the wagons, for a change, when all at once from over near the foot hills a band of Indians were seen riding swiftly toward the company.

Hyrum was riding a horse that day and all children were quickly piled into wagons. The train was closed up nearer and every man was told to have his guns ready if needed, but not to plainly in evidence.

Hyrum's early day training stood him in good need now, and as the Indians approached, he rode out to meet them waving a white kerchief as a signal of peace, when to the great joy of all it was found to be a friendly band of Hualapai's selling pine nuts, and you can believe they soon disposed of all they had, trading them for flour and other things.

The Company came by Pierces Ferry where near tragedy was narrowly averted. The ferry had been sold by Mr. Pierce to a man who had had little experienced with the ferry, which was a flat-boat driven by oars. After being loaded, the boat was hauled some distance up-stream, then allowed to follow the current down to the landing on the other side.

After taking three wagons across and ready to start with the fourth, which by the way was the one in which were Mrs. Morris and the girls, they saw a man coming down the hill toward the ferry, very fast and waving his white shirt, and shouting for them to wait for his arrival, as though greatly excited.

It was Mr. Pierce riding a horse, bareback and on arriving he ordered places in the floor of the boat to be uncovered, and it was found to be full of water, which he had bailed out at once declaring that the boat would have sunk in mid-stream.

On reaching Phoenix, it was found to be a very lively place, but a great many saloons and feed stables. Here teams of freighters stood, some with thirty-two horses drawing the wagons, and all driven by one "jerk-line." Also the burro pack trains were much in evidence. When Salt River was reached there was quite a raise in the river, but after a little quicksand was encountered, all crossed in safety.

They arrived in Mesa, March 3, 1883 and put up tents for a few days until they could look around. The second day, one of those "sea breeze or zephyrs" came up and lowered every tent in camp. Quite an introduction to the place.

**Anne Peel Noble**
Interviewer: Roberta Flake Clayton
Contributed by her daughter Jane Noble
Snowflake

*To Utah 1862*

What tragedies and comedies used to commingle in the long immigrant treks over the plains! In the company destined to reach Salt Lake City in November, 1962, was one outfit with the not usual combination of a yoke of oxen and a yoke of cows hitched to a wagon so loaded with household gear that the father, mother, and one child had walked most of the way.

The child would get so tired at times that she dared occasionally to park herself on the handy back steps of the next wagon, until one day, the driver's ox-whip laid cruel welts across her back.

He had not intended that his wife and daughter should walk, but when only a few days out one of his oxen died. This animal he could have replaced but it happened coincidentally that an old lady was stranded for a similar reason. There seemed therefore nothing else to do but take on her and her traps, for the use of her remaining ox. Nancy Peel was thus confronted with the grim necessity of dumping on the open plains goods, in the category of luxuries, to make room for their helpless, but doubtless very worthy passenger, and to walk a thousand miles instead of ride. She rose to the occasion, however, then and ever after, without complaint, as did also her husband and daughter. Jane's parents settled in Bountiful, Utah.

Noble family
*(St. Johns LDS Family History Files)*

**Louisa Jones Oakley**
Interviewer: Roberta Flake Clayton
Snowflake

*To Arizona, 1880*

Among the 1880 pioneers into Snowflake, Arizona, was the Oakley family—the blind husband, John, his wife, Louisa, and their six daughters; the eldest was married and her husband accompanied them, also Robert Jones, an afflicted brother of Louisa. Four tiny graves were left behind them in Utah.

It took a great amount of courage to make the trip, even when everything was in one's favor, but handicapped as this family was, it looked like an impossibility.

In writing of the journey to Arizona, Mrs. Violate Oakley Pearce, then 11 years of age says, "I will remember when we came to the Colorado River. It was running very high. The men had a hard time to keep the animals in the boat. Some of the cattle jumped overboard and the stream took them down so far it was hard for them to find a landing place on the other side. How happy we children were to see them safe.

Two Indians attempted to swim the swollen stream and one of them was drowned. I fancy I can hear the moaning and wailing of the family and friends. They killed his horse and shoved it into the seething water, along with his personal belonging and enough food to last the Indian to the "Happy Hunting Ground." After they crossed the river, the worst was yet to come, the dangerous dug way over "Lee's Backbone."

It was Vilate's task to lead her blind father every step of the way over it and again we take her version of it. "I remember clinging to the side of the road where the cliffs were hung, the mad river below. How my heart beat with fear at the sound of that wild rushing torrent, many, many feet below."

The hardships of that journey was augmented by the fact that two of the three men making it were practically unable to assist, and so to the girls were added the responsibility to assist with camp duties, gathering scanty fuel to prepare the meals. It was an experience, too, for Louisa who left a very devoted lover in England when she joined the Mormons and came to America. Because of the blindness of her husband, and the childish mind of her poor brother, she had to plan and assist with all the labor necessary to making a new home.

**Alzada Sophia Kartchner Palmer**
Interviewer: Roberta Flake Clayton
Navajo County

*Utah to Arizona 1877*

In 1877 they came to Arizona. Her husband drove three yoke of oxen and two wagons, walking all the way from Panguitch, Utah to Arizona. They encountered serious dangers while coming. One was in crossing the Colorado River, another when coming over what they called "Lee's Backbone." At one point the wagon was thrown on the two outside wheels almost throwing wagons, oxen, wife and child, and all the rest over the embankment to hundreds of feet below. But with his skillful control of the oxen, they were spared. They were only two of the many experiences.

For a time they located on the Little Colorado River making farms and building dams. The floods were so bad that her husband became discouraged. One day as he was saddling his horse, William Flake asked him where he was going. When he told him, Mr. Flake said he wanted to go with him. They went east and then south looking for a place where they would like to locate. As they were returning they passed Stinson's ranch, thirty miles south of the Little Colorado, or Silver Creek. Mr. Flake made a trade for the land and several families moved up and began again the work of pioneers, building up the waste place.

## Mary Langdon Pitt

Interviewer: Kathlyn M. Lathrop
Duncan

*New York City to Arizona 1893*

I decided to come to Clifton, June 5, 1893. Life really began for me that day. I had boarded the copper company's special narrow-gage railroad at Lordsburg, New Mexico, early that morning with a sort of premonition that I was doomed to disappointment in finding Father, and it left a sickening feeling in the pit of my stomach.

I tried to interest myself in the scenery along the route, just miles and miles of barren desert, while the mixed freight and passenger train poked along at a snail's pace. Where? I thought, were those towering cliffs and beautiful scenery that Father had mentioned.

My mind changed suddenly about the scenery when we reached the little town of Duncan, and the train plunged into a tunnel of overlapping, green, cottonwoods and the fragrance of flowers, green fields and gardens greeted us.

The town was just a shamble of a few shacks, rough and unpainted, all except the depot, which was painted a bright yellow---and I doubt if that building has ever been painted since. The citizens who were gathered around the depot obviously for the purpose of watching the train come through, were typical westerners as Father had described them; garbed in rough clothing, big hats, boots and spurs and some of them actually wearing guns. I momentarily expected someone to start shooting up the town, or attempt to hold up the train, just beyond the depot to the right two men chained to posts, the only jail the town had so I was informed.

Those prisoner posts, and a line of hitching posts along in front of the stores and saloons had sprouted green leaves, and today they are immense shade trees—what few of them that have been spared to make way for paved sidewalks and streets.

As the train pulled out of Duncan, along down the Gila River, I got another surprise. I had the impression that we were traveling up grade, but if so, that river was certainly flowing the wrong way.

A winding twisting, muddy little stream that reminded me of the rattlers which Father had mentioned in New Mexico; a creepy, crawly, stuffy, jolty little train that most certainly must be going up grade—judging from the way it was panting and puffing along, like fat old man trying to run a foot race.

The river darted out and under, out and under the track like a playful imp playing tag with us, or a puppy chasing its tail, until at last it turned off to the left and disappeared from view. By that time my head was going around in circles and I wasn't sure whether the river had disappeared or not.

The train grunted and groaned on toward the towering cliffs that had suddenly come in view—tinged with a million colors as Father had described them—but I was to ill by that time to enjoy the beauty of them or scarcely notice them.

Then, just as the city of Clifton came in sight--we could see a few houses around the bend in the canyon that we had come into--the train came to a sudden stop that almost threw the passengers out of their seats; and then I seen the river again.

But the strangest thing had happened to that river. It was crystal clear, and actually flowing back along the way we had come! Impossible! But true. I stared and stared, and wondered too, what we had stopped for.

I soon learned why we had stopped. A dead man had been found lying across the track on the railroad bridge. I was having all I could do to keep from vomiting, and the mention of that dead man done the rest—I simply heaved 'em up, as the westerner puts it.

Such a country! Such a people! I thought, rivers flowing in all directions, men chained to posts in the streets, and dead men on railroad tracks, crumbling mountains that were just waiting to topple down upon one. Was I insane, or was I just train sick.

We finally pulled on into the depot, where I boarded a hack that said "Abraham Hotel" in glaring red and black letters painted on white canvases that almost covered the side of the hack, which was drawn by a span of runty, mangy bays.

The hack crossed that river again, and I was positive this time that the stream was flowing southward. Puzzled beyond words to express it, I registered at the Abraham Hotel, and after dinner that evening, Jake Abraham, the proprietor, settled the question of the wrong-way river. In fact there were two rivers; The Gila, flowing northwestward from Duncan, and the San Francisco, flowing southwestward through the center of Clifton; the two rivers joining and flowing on southward to the Gulf of Mexico.

## Ruth Campkin Randall

Interviewer: Roberta Clayton
Navajo County

*Utah To Arizona 1881*

In September, 1881, Ruth, her husband and five small children started for Arizona settling at Tonto Basin. Her husband had previously explored this Basin, which is about 100 miles in length and 80 in width, and lying at the foot of the Mogollon Rim.

Great difficulty was encountered in getting down to the Basin as it is a sheer drop of 1000 feet, but the valley was considered so valuable as a stock raising district that a passable road was made down into it. Over this the emigrants had to pass, the wagons dropping from one boulder to the one below. Into the wild, Indian infested country, it took courage to go, but Ruth did not lack that qualification and uncomplainingly accepted her lot.

## Mary Willis Richards

Interviewer: Roberta Flake Clayton
Snowflake

*Utah To Arizona 1876*

One day, like lightening from a clear sky, came the a call for the little family to leave their happy home, their kindred and friends and go out into the wilds of Arizona to help colonies. No matter what the sacrifice, nothing but death could prevent Joseph H. Richards and his wife, Mary, from answering the call.

Now all was hurry and bustle. The little home must be sold for whatever it would bring. Cash was scarce so grain, flour, corn, anything in the way of provisions could be taken, as each family was advised to have enough on hand to do them two years.

By the fifth of February, 1876, they were ready and made a start on that long perilous journey in the middle of the winter, leaving behind all that was dearest to them on earth.

When they reached the Panguich Divide, they found the snow two feet deep. They could travel only a few miles a day, then after the snow, it was deep mud.

When the feed they brought was gone, their poor tired animals gave out and the travelers must stop every little while for them to rest. For more than three months they toiled on their way, but felt they were greatly blest for the Lord spared all their lives.

On April 20, 1876, they arrived at the settlements on the Little Colorado River, the first companies having arrived the March before. Such a barren desert-looking country they found! Not a tree for miles except an occasional cottonwood on the river.

Rowing Ferry

## Eliza Snow Smith Rogers
Interviewer: Roberta Flake Clayton
Navajo County

*Utah to Arizona 1875*

In the fall of 1875 they were called to go settle in Arizona with the company that was leaving for that place. Although Eliza and her two children had whopping cough they prepared to go. The exposure was too much for little Smith, just four months old, and they laid him to rest at Sunset, Arizona, and then went sadly on to Snowflake which was just being settled.

## Lousea Bee Harper Rogers
Interviewer: Roberta Flake Clayton
Phoenix

*Utah to Arizona 1880*

My parents were pioneers coming to Utah in 1847, leaving Utah for Arizona in 1880. Now from 1847 to 1880 would give Salt Lake City a chance to become quite a city. Then to take a family of small children into an unknown desert, the oldest child being twelve and the youngest one year would raise up another bunch of pioneers. And, that is what my father Harvey John Harper did.

Although I was but twelve years of age, just old enough to know and realize all of the hardships and trials, I think for a long time I worried more than anyone else because I mourned for a long time for my old home and playmates and schoolmates of Big Cottonwood, Utah.

I thought often of my old Grandmother standing in the doorway with her arms up saying "My God, my children all are gone. I'll never see them again." But never once did I hear my Mother complain or regret their coming to Arizona. My Mother would mourn for her dear parents, brothers and sisters and friends sometimes, and wind up singing with tears streaming down her cheeks "Do they think of me at home?"

In my happy early days
Do they ever think of me,
I who shared their every grief,
I who mingles in their glee,
Have their hearts grown old and strange
For the one now creased to roam,
Do they ever think of me
Do they think of me at home?

## Minnie Alice Wooley Rogers

Interviewer: Roberta Flake Clayton
Navajo County

*Utah to Arizona 1879*

She was married October 30th, 1879, when she was seventeen years of age. On November 6, 1879, her wedding journey began, and a long, hard, perilous one it was, lasting three months. In company with the family of her husband's father, Samuel H. Rogers, and two other families, the West's and Wardell's, Minnie left a good home, loving parents, brothers, sisters, and friends, for Arizona to join the pioneers who had gone previously to make a home in that desolate waste inhabited by Indians and outlaws.

During this journey they encountered much snow, and Minnie says she has walked many a mile in snow up to her knees helping to drive the cows. One of the most trying experiences of any, if one can be singled out as worse than any other, is when they came over Lee's Backbone, the terrible mountain encountered immediately after being ferried across the Colorado River, and which was the dread of every traveler who came from Utah to Arizona.

Over this precipice, she and another woman walked and carried a stand of bees. These were probably brought along to provide sweetness later for that lacking in this honeymoon.

Although the memories of those heartbreaking days still bring a shudder to her who so bravely passed through them, she also recalls the nights when the bed was made down on the ground where the snow or rocks had been cleared, where they could lay their poor tired, undernourished bodies down to rest. It was the only time these two lovers could be alone.

Several times on this trip Minnie fainted from exhaustion and lack of food. Their teams and stock also suffered, and some of them were so foot sore and poor that they were left behind in the care of her husband and some of the other men and did not arrive at the settlement known as Sunset until two days after the teams.

The weary emigrants remained in Sunset two days visiting former neighbors and friends who were located there, arriving in Snowflake January 8th, 1880.

## Lydia Ann Herbst Rogers

Interviewer: Roberta Flake Clayton
Navajo County

*Utah to Arizona 1887*

"Tome and tide wait for no man," and Dan Cupid had a cruel rival in King Winter. While Dan kept the fires of love kindled and burning brightly within the hearts of the lovers, old Winter sifted his sparkling whiteness over hill and dale, and heaped the snow so high in the Buckskin Mountains that there was no chance of anyone getting through, so Mr. Rogers and his bride had to bide their time and visited along the way with friends until the snow had melted sufficiently for them to reach Lee's Ferry.

But the Colorado River was frozen over and here they had to remain nearly two weeks, while the ice was chopped loose and floated down stream. When they had safely crossed this treacherous river there was still Lee's Back Bone to be crossed. The roughest place called a road on the whole trip was this. It seemed almost impossible to drive over it without the wagon tipping over, just one big boulder after another and a dug way so steep and winding it took hours to get up one side and down the other.

From the apex of this terrible precipice there was a sheer drop of 1000 feet on one side and only with the greatest dexterity and complete control of the team could the descent be made.

## Virginia Smith Scheerer

Interviewer: Helen Smith
Cochise County

*To Arizona 1881*

I first came to Arizona in 1881, with my Mother and brothers from California, at about sixteen years of age. My father, who became known as "Coyote Smith" had arrived the year before. The railroad came only to Benson, and from there, to reach our place in Turkey Creek, we had to travel in a wagon.

Father met us at Benson, and we spent our night in Tombstone, having reached that place about nightfall. It was a wild place indeed. We shrank from any more contact with its inhabitants than was absolutely necessary.

Father found us some place to stay, I have forgotten where, as I was quite confused and not a little frightened. I do remember that it was quite uncomfortable. We left the next morning without breakfasting, such was Mother's fear of the place. In the future I was kept as far from Tombstone as Mother could manage. I suppose she feared that I might fall in love with some of the many outlaws with which the town was infested.

Our next stop was the roadhouse at Soldier Holes, which we reached about dusk. Some people named Sanders were running the place, and I presume were the owners at the time. I remember that Mrs. Sanders used snuff continuously. There was a barroom and a dining room, but no sleeping quarters; the Sanders apparently kept no roomers, or at least not such a large party as was ours. It was finally decided that we should sleep in the dining room with the Chinaman. It was in late October and quite cold. There were no beds. We used our inadequate bedding for both beds and covers, and kept the Chinaman up all night to feed the fire. In spite of that we were cold. I was indeed glad when morning came and a hot breakfast warmed us up. Late that evening we reached our own home in Turkey Creek.

## Marie Annanettie Hatch Shumway

Interviewer: Roberta Flake Clayton
Navajo County

*Idaho to Arizona 1870*

When I was seven years old my parents Lorenzo H. Hatch and Alice Hanson Hatch came to Arizona settling in the northern part of the Territory at that time long before statehood was granted. The trip was made by wagons drawn by ox and mule teams. There was my father, mother, five brothers, two sisters and myself, one sister being a babe in arms.

We left our home and traveled by team as far as Salt Lake City. Then when we were ready to leave the city, my Father bought tickets so we could have our first train ride. We visited at Lehi a number of days. Then our train riding ended at a small place called York. By that time the boys with the wagons had caught up so on we came.

To me all this was glorious. To my precious Mother I think it must have been a feeling of awe and wonder to know just how she would manage through another siege of pioneering with her family in a new and unsettled land. She had already pioneered in early Utah days also in Idaho before this venture into Arizona. She was really and truly a pioneer woman.

For some time we visited at St. George, Utah, then on to Johnson, Utah where we made another stop, waiting for other emigrants as we felt the need of company. A family by the name of Dean joined us, also an old gentleman whose name was Liston.

We traveled the old wagon road from Kanab, Utah to Lee's Ferry. By this time the weather became cold enough so the teams and cattle could be taken across the Little Colorado on the ice. The wagons and house furniture and the family were ferried across on the big boat. In due time we reached the settlement of Woodruff and here we resided for about two years. Then we moved further up the country finding only one small home in the place in which I have made my home. It wasn't long then other settlers came and our town began to grow and was given the name of Taylor.

## Emma Larson Smith

Interviewer: Roberta Flake Clayton
Contributed by her daughter Lorana Smith Broadbent
Navajo County

*Utah to Arizona 1863*

Considerable preparation was required for the desert journey. The outfit consisted of two wagons, trailed together, drawn with horses, then one heavier wagon, drawn by two yoke of oxen and one yoke of cows. The oldest brother drove the horse team and the next brother, Alof, only 18 years drove the oxen with Emma, fifteen years, to manage the brakes for him which was quite a job on crude rough roads. The oxen teams had to go on ahead because they traveled slower and many times were out of sight of the others in the Indian inhabited desert, which was a test of their courage.

After several weeks they arrived in what is now Snowflake, Arizona in December 23rd, and on account of a new storm the sun was not visible. When the sun rose the next day Emma was turned in directions and she always said the sun seemed to rise up in the south.

## Lannie Mitchell Smith

Interviewer: Roberta Flake Clayton
Navajo County

She consented to become the bride of Jesse Nathanial Smith, Jr. Thus at the early age of seventeen her beautiful.

Childhood life came abruptly to an end. Her husband was only nineteen. They were married October 14, 1880. Three weeks after their marriage this young couple loaded what belongings they had and the remaining effects of his Father into a couple of wagons and followed his family to Arizona.

Their route led them around through Bear Flat, Panguich, Kanab and over the Buckskin Mountain to Lee's Ferry. Jesse's 13 year old brother, Silas and a boy, Johnny Lister, drove the second wagon. For three weeks these youngsters traveled alone over the five hundred mile wasteland to their new home.

At Lee's Ferry they crossed the mighty Colorado. It was a thrill to the young wife, but she could not stand to let her husband cross without her. They arrived at Snowflake, Arizona just as winter set in.

## Eliza Ellen Parkinson Tanner

Interviewer: Roberta Flake Clayton
Snowflake

*Utah to Arizona 1877*

During these days of '76 and '77, many of the strong able bodied well-to-do men were being called to settle Arizona, Nevada and Idaho, by the Leaders of the Mormon Church, and Henry was called to Arizona, so with his bride made preparations for the journey into the barren wastes of Arizona. This trip lasted eleven weeks and was filled with hardship.

Henry having a good saddle horse was delegated to look after the loose stock of the company with which they traveled. This left Eliza to drive their four horse team a great deal of the way. One morning they saw horses coming back and found that they belonged to a company that was a few days ahead. It was decided that Henry should take the horses ahead to the owners, so Eliza had to drive the team that day, though the wind was blowing a perfect gale.

This greatly frightened the horses but she managed to control them and drove out round the tree and back into the road. When she reached camp she had to go to bed at once with a sick headache, and said that was the hardest day she had ever spent.

Scarcity of water was the greatest problem on the route. When found it sometimes took two days for the little springs to supply enough to water the animals, and fill up the large water barrels that were carried on the outside of every emigrant's wagon.

At one time they had been without water until the animals were exhausted; so Henry sent out to find water. He traveled for hours and at length turned back disheartened. On nearing the camp he looked up and saw some green trees and felt impressed to go there. On reaching the trees he found a small spring with plenty of water. He called to the company, "Here is water." But they did not believe him until he dipped his hat brimful and threw it into the air.

They came to the Colorado River and crossed by Pearce's Ferry. They floated their wagons across and Eliza much afraid rode in theirs. They swam their livestock. From there they came to Flagstaff.

Finally on May 1, 1887, the Tanners settled in the old fort at St. Joseph, (now Joseph City) built as a protection against the Indians, however the people believed it was better to feed the Indians rather than fight them.

## Adelinah Quinn Taylor

Interviewer: Helen M. Smith

*South Carolina to Arizona, 1863*

Our family, among others, returned with the missionaries to Arizona. This group traveled in covered wagons with ox teams, and were six month on the way. We crossed the Mississippi River at Memphis, I recall. Soon after this crossing, after traversing low, slough land, we camped at another river whose name I have forgotten.

There were fishermen camped below our camp at some small distance, and Father sent my brother down to their camp to see if he could buy some fish. They offered him an enormous fish weighing around seventy-five pounds, for which they wanted "two bits". My brother had never before heard the expression, and he returned all the way to camp to ask Father what was meant by "two bits", and whether or not he should buy the fish. He bought it and it was delicious, making an excellent meal for the whole camp.

We cooked in Dutch ovens or on sticks in the ground beside the fire, depending upon what the food in question was like. Somewhere at the latter end of the trip, provisions ran low, and we were really hungry. There had been no game sighted for several days. Suddenly someone nudged me, Father had drawn a bead on a large jackrabbit. We all shut our eyes and drew ourselves up tensely until a shout told us that Father had got the rabbit. Such a feast we had that night at the campfire where the rabbit was boiled in a large pot and dumplings added. It was the best food I have ever tasted.

It was somewhere near the end of our journey, too, that we came very close to being swept away by a flood. We had come to a very deep and wide wash, dry, of course. This was in the evening, and as soon as we had gone down the steep bank of the wash and across it, we made camp. The other side of the wash was not so steep, and we stopped in its shelter rather than to go on to the top.

The evening meal was over, and all in the camp had long since gone to sleep, except for the guards, when there was a sudden loud hallowing from the top of our bank. Father started from the tent in alarm, as did the others, thinking we were attacked by Indians. Someone then shouted from the darkness above that a flood was coming down the wash and for us to get out at once. We lost no time in hitching up the wagons and pulling out, and none too soon, for the wash was soon full of swiftly running water. We never discovered who had roused us in the middle of the night and warned us, for the person who had shouted from the bank was never seen by any of us.

We were almost the first settlers in what is now Safford. The Quinns and their relatives formed much of the wagon train, and since all settled nearby, we were related in some way to the whole settlement in the course of a few years.

## Rebecca Reed Hancock Tenney

Interviewer: Roberta Flake Clayton
Snowflake

*Utah to Arizona 1879*

When less than two years old she was brought to Arizona by her Mother and the older members of the family. One evening, after they had made an early camp, Rebecca and one of her older sisters went out to hunt cedar berries and pine gum. She got tired and thought to return to camp alone. When she came to the road they had left, she started back over the road they had traveled that day, and trudged on and on looking for the camp. When the sister returned and Rebecca was not with her great excitement reigned. Everyone set out on the search. Finally her little footprints were found in the dusty wagon tracks, but her brother Joseph followed her for two miles before he overtook her. When she returned to camp she was seated upon his shoulders, and greeted all with a happy smile. The family reached Taylor, Arizona on New Year's Day, 1870.

## Sarah Ann Salina Smithson Turley

Interviewer: Roberta Clayton
Navajo County

*Utah to Arizona 1881*

Before the beginning of the Mormon colonization in Arizona Jacob Hamblin with a party of selected men made the trip to this section of the country to confer with the Indians to try and make peace with them, and succeeded so well that shortly after Mormons were called by Brigham Young to bring their families and settle here.

James D. Smithson was one who was sent with Jacob Hamblin on this perilous journey. They crossed the Colorado River on a reef of rooks known as Ute Crossing. Two horses were tied together so that if one slipped off into the deep water, or lost his balance and fell the other horse and rider could pull him back.

The company had a safe landing, and held a council with the Chiefs of the Navajos, with whom they made peace and obtained permission to pass through their territory unmolested. After visiting some of the Navajo and Hopi villages and doing a little exploring in the vicinity of northern Arizona the company returned and reported. Many hardships were encountered but the trip was made in safety and a favorable report made to President Young.

On the first day of February 1881 the Smithson family started out alone, Arizona bound, to find a new home. By this time a fairly good wagon road had been made by the hundreds of emigrants who had gone on before and the trip was a short one.

On the first of March they reached a place on the Little Colorado where the camp of John W. Young, a contractor for the railroad was located. This was between Joseph City and Holbrook. Here Mr. Smithson obtained employment for himself and older boys, while Mrs. Smithson and her daughters cooked for about one hundred men. Here they remained four months.

At the end of four months they moved along up the Little Colorado to the settlement of Woodruff where seven families had already located. When they reached there the mother said, "This place is good enough for me." So, here they began making their home and that was their last pioneering.

## Delilah Willis Turley

Interviewer: Roberta Flake Clayton
Snowflake

*Utah to Arizona 1879*

Delilah was six years of age when her parent moved to Arizona, settling first at Brigham City, on the Little Colorado, near where Winslow now is located. They only remained there one winter going on to Tonto Basin, in the spring, with one of her father's brothers, John Willis and his family. They spent the summer at Tonto Basin, and then moved to Johnson, Utah. The family was not satisfied there so after a year returned to Arizona, this time locating in Snowflake.

The last move to Arizona was one in which Delilah had a miraculous escape from death. The roads were almost impassable and in the most dangerous places, and the hardest pulls for the horses, all who could got out and walked. On one of these terrible places, where the wagons bounced from one boulder to another, the Willis wagon tipped over, bottom side up. Delilah had been left in the wagon, peacefully asleep. She was the only occupant, and all thought she would be crushed, but she was taken out unharmed in any way.

## Mary Agnes Flake Turley

Interviewer: Roberta Flake Clayton
Snowflake

*Utah to Arizona 1877*

When she was eleven years old her Father moved his family to Arizona. The boys and five hired men were needed to drive the cattle, so Mary became one of the teamsters, and drove over some of the most terrible places that were ever called roads. When coming over "Lee's Backbone", her wagon was directly behind her Father's. He heard her call "whoa" to her horses, and looking back he saw that she had been pulled from her wagon and was clinging to the brake. He stopped his team to go to her rescue, but she shouted "I'm all right, Father, go on."

For this trip her Father had got her some high topped boots, just like the ones he had for her brothers. Her Mother seriously objected to having her daughter's feet thus shod, but the Father was vindicated when the snow became so deep it almost came to the tops of the boots.

The winter was bitter cold, and though everything was done for the comfort of the family that could be, the suffering was very great. To add to the seriousness of the situation, Mary and her sister Jane both took Diphtheria. The Mother had never seen a case of it before, and but for the services of a dear old blind nurse, both girls might have died, and other members of the family as well.

In December the family reached the settlements on the Little Colorado River.

## Ida Frances Hunt Udall

Interviewer: Roberta Flake Clayton
Navajo County

*Utah to Arizona 1877*

One can only imagine Ida's feeling—a cultured, refined girl of nineteen years, facing the primitive and wild of the Arizona wilderness. On the stub of a receipt book, done in lead pencil, she kept a daily record of that journey, it reads as follows:

"Left Beaver, Utah, February 21st, 1877. Camped at Buckhorn Springs 22nd, came to Parowan and stayed with Edward Dalton and spent a very pleasant evening with them. 23rd, came to Hamilton's got there in a rainstorm. 24th, camped on Blackridge, rained all night. 25th, got to Harrisburg after dark, raining still. Stayed at Aunt Peggy's, Eliza and Henry went to Toquer. 28th, came to Washington and stayed there four days. Went to St. George in the meantime. Left Washington on the 3rd day of March, came out a mile and a half from town and camped, several of our relatives and friends coming with us, among them Sam Porter and Jimmie Hunt. The next morning we were drummed out of camp by the Marshall band of Washington.

It was Sunday morning, March 4th that we started out into the wilderness, not expecting to see any human inhabitants again until we reached the Colorado River. There were five wagons and four men in the train. We had a very hard day of it having to travel in the track of one wagon most of the day, but succeeded in reaching the Macao Springs about dark, where we camped for the night. These springs are 20 miles from Washington, Utah. Crossed the Arizona line March 4th. March 5th we came about two miles from the springs and there camped to wait for John Bushman and others who were to overtake us. March 6th found the families of John Bushman and Mr. Westover, also Messer Bentley and Cunningham in camp, the latter were going as pilots and road surveyors. We came that night within two miles of the Coyote Holes and next morning, March 7$^{th}$ came on to the Holes, which are nine miles from Macao Springs and camped there for the day.

March 8$^{th}$, my nineteenth birthday, we came 20 miles to one of the Hidden Springs called the Sink Spring, very good road with the exception of the last four miles which is down a steep rooky canyon. March 9$^{th}$, Messer Bentley and Cunningham accompanied by my father went ahead to explore the road. We here overtook four wagons that were ahead of us. This made ten wagons besides Mr. Bentley's carriage.

March 10$^{th}$, came up the canyon four miles to another of the Hidden Springs, where we camped to await the report of the explorers. My father returned the evening of March 11$^{th}$, stating that we could not possibly get through to the river that route so we must turn around and go back eight miles of the road we had come and take the road leading by the Kane Springs.

On the Trail
(Wagon Train, Legends of America)

March 12$^{th}$, came back eight miles and took the road turning Northwest. Traveled eight miles to Pangram Pockets. Nooned there and came on down the canyon and made a dry camp. The next day, found water about noon at a small spring called Peep Pockets, two and half miles off the road, watered the animals and came on and made a dry camp.

March 15$^{th}$, started at daylight and traveled till sundown before we found water and that was one and half miles from the road. The animals suffered very much for want of water, some of the horn stock having gone 53 hours without and all of them 30, but one of the oxen gave clear out. This water is about 26 miles from Pangram Pockets and there is plenty of it but no grass. The next water called Tasha Spring was eight miles from there.

The train started early, March 16, and some of the wagons were till after dark getting into camp, the animals being weak and most of the road very rough. Tasha Spring is a very pretty place, there being plenty of water and green vegetation, which was very refreshing to us. The ground seemed to be under cultivation by the Indians, and I will mention that two were there, which were the first we had seen after leaving the settlements in Utah. It really seemed pleasant to see them and to know that some living beings besides us were in this barren desert country.

March 17 we laid by at the spring, where we could enjoy all the water we wished for a short time. March 18, we started early in hopes to reach the Big Colorado River which was said to be eight miles from that spring. It was very sandy the first part of the day and in the afternoon we came down a wash where the wagon jumped one boulder to another most of the way, but luckily we got through without any accident only the breaking of one plough by a projecting rock. About sundown we came out of the wash onto a hill a mile long where we had to double two or three teams onto one wagon to get them up at all. It was after 10 o'clock when we got the last wagon up the hill and the ferry man who was there said it was two miles farther to the river, so they determined to camp there till morning through the night though there was not any water in the train.

March 19, we came in sight of the long looked for river about eight o'clock. I wondered when I looked at the great body of water why it had to be all in one place when it would make the country so much more desirable all round to have it divided around. We had been dreading the crossing of the river all the way, but we found it by far the pleasantest thing of our journey. The ferry was in a splendid place. The water being very smooth, the wagons went across without the least trouble.

March 20, we laid by at the river, as they had to ferry and swim all the animals across and after we were all safely landed, we took all the music we had in the train, (which was one guitar), and went out for a sail by moonlight. March 21, we left the river and came up a wash six miles to a small spring where we camped for the night. 22, started for a spring 16 miles from there, and traveled till late in the evening, some of the teams reached the water, and others were left behind to come in the next day where we stayed for the day.

March 24, came up a wash six miles to a small spring where we camped for the night. The country and climate seemed to be changing rapidly. It was cooler and more fertile after we left the river. We camped at this spring till the 26th when we mobbed up one and half miles farther to Iron Spring where we were to camp several days while the men worked the road down a steep mountain into Wallop Valley. As the grass and water were tolerable plenty here, they thought it would be quite advantageous to the teams, which were very jaded after their hard journey. Here one of Henry's mares died of distemper.

After the road down the mountain was completed, the men thinking the company was too large, on account of the water, divided the train into three parts. Messer Bushman and Blackburn started ahead and the Westover Company second, and our team and Henry's started Sunday, April 1, and came about 12 miles; the next morning started before daylight and got to water, which was four miles off the road, before sunrise. Stayed there all that day.

Tuesday, April 3, started to cross Wallop Valley which is a 35 mile desert. Traveled most of the night and reached Steven's ranch about 10 o'clock the next day. April 4, this water is also two and half miles from the road. April 5, came seven miles and camped. During the day we came into Old Beal and Butterfield route on which we were to travel the remainder of our journey. This was a good hard road which looked so nice to us that we felt as though we did not want to stop at all. A mile of Hackberry, a little mining camp, they took the stock to water.

Friday, April 6, came on seven miles to another Steven's ranch and camped for noon. This is Fortoonx Spring and 1 1/2 farther on is another spring where we had to leave our near lead ox (Duke) who had been nearly "given out" for some time. There was a very little grass here so we did not expect to ever see him alive again. We came about five miles from there and camped for the night.

The next day, April 7, came about 10 miles to Young Spring where there were a great many Indians and very little water. There were only two little springs. Had it not been for a ranch about three miles from the road on the left where the men went to water the stock and fill the barrels preparatory to starting on the desert, the animals would have suffered greatly for want of water. Here old Bread, our best ox, got down on a rocky hill and was not able to get up so we sold him to the Indians who killed him to eat. This left only two oxen in the team and we had to work the cows in place of the other. Monday afternoon we started from Young Springs and came five miles where the men found a small tank a mile from the road that watered the ox team. Stayed there all night because we could not find the loose cattle in the dark.

Tuesday, April 10, started at daylight and traveled a few miles at a time, giving the animals what water we thought we could spare and when daylight came upon us there was no sign of water. We traveled a few miles or as long as the teams would hold out and then camped for the night. April 11, started at daylight, came upon the road and traveled till 10 o'clock, we were now about 25 miles from the small tank. Here we met a horseman who said we were within eight miles of plenty of water so we gave the animals all the water we had, rested a while and went on feeling quite hopeful. Found several small tanks within five miles instead of eight so we camped there for the night and the next day, April 12, went on one mile farther and found Kerline well where we camped.

Making Camp On the Trail

April 13, left the spring and struck Patridge Run, which is ten miles, about 2 o'clock and went a little farther and camped. The next day came to the last water on the run, about 4 o'clock. Here we filled the barrels and started on to the desert. Made a dry camp. Sunday, April 15, came to Dan V. Lee Avijo Camp almost noon, found no water. This is 15 miles from the run. Traveled until after dark and while waiting for the teams to get up a steep hill we found a little notice stating there was a little water to the left of the road. This proved to be enough to water all the stock that were badly in need of it, so we camped there for the night.

Monday, April 16, we awoke and found it snowing. We started about 10 o'clock and reached Law's Springs about 3 o'clock pm. During the day we came in sight of the San Francisco Mountain, which is a beautiful white peak noted for the large forest of Pine trees surrounding it which is inhibited by all kinds of game. Law's Spring is 15 miles from O'Leavey's camp which makes the distance 35 miles in all.

April 17$^{th}$, left the spring and traveled through the forest of beautiful pines (the grandest I have ever seen.) It stormed on us nearly all day. About 4 o'clock in the afternoon we came in sight of a log cabin in a little opening in the timber. We were delighted to see any kind of a house in such a storm. On arriving there we found it empty and unlocked, so we took refuge in it. The owners came in the evening and made us very welcome. This, they said, was Spring Valley which was eight miles from Laws Spring.

Stayed there two days in hopes the roads would be better and on April 20, started from there quite early and before we had come very far we found Messers Bushman, Blackburn and Nichols horses which had strayed away from them. We caught them and put in two of the mules in place of the weak animals in our teams. Henry drove the rest while his wife drove his team. So we reached San Francisco Spring before dark. Here we found our friends all well, waiting for us. This is a nice valley at the foot of the S.F. Mountain. While we camped in this valley our brindle ox died from eating some poison weed, we supposed.

We now found it impossible to take the ox team further for it left only one ox out of the four. So my Father was obliged to exchange the light wagon and five horn stock we had left for a large span of horses and harness and put all the loading into the other two wagons. After this my Father exchanged Kit and Florey, the two poorest mares for a good fat mare and horse.

We now had a pretty good team and we left San Francisco Peaks April 24, came to the four mile water and camped. Next day came two miles and filled our barrels and came about 12 miles and camped.

April 26 reached Turkey Tanks about eight miles by 10 o'clock Here Messers Bushman and Cervy's horses strayed from them and we did not get them till sundown when we came down one mile to a large tank and camped for the night.

April 27, we reached the Little Colorado River which is two miles. We were happily disappointed in the country. Traveled up the river one day and a half, 25 miles, and arrived at Lot Smith's camp at Sunset, April 29, about noon.

**Casimira Valenzuela**
Interviewer: Romelia Gomez
Cochise County

*Mexico to Arizona Date Unknown*

She has lived in Bisbee quite a long time, coming here from Durango, Sonora, her birthplace, during the revelation of Madero, whose followers were called Moderistas. That is the best she can do in regard to saying in what year she crossed to the U.S. At that time her son was working in Bisbee for Billy Brophy doing some sort of work in his store and Mr. Brophy is supposed to have sent for Casimira to come to Bisbee to live with her son.

On their way over here, near Torreon, the train on which Casimira and her daughter were passengers was ambushed by Moderista revolutionists and riddled by bullets. It was the most terrifying experience in their lives. The train was held up for three hours, while revolutionists and pacifists exchanged gunfire.

The smoke-filled passenger cars, the shattering of glass windows, the yelling and curses from both parties, and the wailings of the terrified men, women and children will live always in her memory.

Many of her fellow passengers were killed right before her eyes, while she and her daughter cowered under the benches. They were miraculously saved from being shot only, she says, because during those awful hours she continuously prayed La Magnifica, a prayer in which she had the deepest faith.

When the revolutionists were out of ammunition they fled leaving the dead to be taken to Torreon. No further encounter with the revolutionists marked their journey from there on.

**Mary Jane Robinson West**
Interviewer: Roberta Clayton
Snowflake - Navajo County

*Utah to Arizona 1879*

Arizona must be settled. Others of John's family had already gone, consisting of his father and mother and his sister, Emma West Smith, her husband and family. It was in 1879 that they drove their weary teams into the little town of Snowflake. John's brother in law, Jesse N. Smith had selected a site which he thought might please them, the block just west of his own, with only a street between them.

The journey had been a very hard one. First they had chosen a bad time of the year. They lost a greater part of the cattle they were bringing. At Lee's Ferry, on the Colorado River, Mary Jane was stricken with a severe illness. All the way over those terrible roads she seemed to lie in an almost unconscious condition. Part of the time she was almost standing on her head because of the steepness of the road in places.

John often said the worry of that trip was very hard for him to endure. Said at first he worried greatly over the loss of their cattle but when his brave wife was stricken down he felt his other worries were as nothing compared with the thought of losing her.

She was still very weak when they reached their destination. John with the help of their four young boys set up the tent on their new location, fixed up the stove and a homemade bedstead.

"Put down the strips of rag carpet we brought, John and our little organ. I want it to look like home." When this was done Mary Jane was helped out of the wagon. She was still very weak, helped inside the tent. She sat down at the organ and said to her family, "Come, lets sing a hymn."

She played and the boys gathered around and sang, but said John, in telling of it, "I'm afraid I wasn't much help--I felt all choked up."

## Annie Woods Westover

Interviewer: Roberta flake Clayton
Navajo County

*Utah to Arizona 1876*

When I was seven years old my Father, James T. Woods, was called to Arizona to help establish the United Order on the Little Colorado River. We bade goodbye to home and friends and sallied forth in the midst of a heavy snow storm, February 7, 1876. The journey of three months and ten days was fraught with perils and hardships similar to those who made the trip across the plains to Utah.

When we crossed the Buckskin Mountain the road had to be worked with picks and shovels through nine feet of snow in places. Many of our party suffered from frost bitten hands, feet and ears. After sitting in a cramped position all day, we had to line up for the night in a sitting posture crosswise of the wagon box like sardines in a can, too cold to remove wraps, overshoes, our breath forming into frost around our faces. One wagon had to accommodate one family together with all its worldly belonging, such as food supplies, farming implements, and seeds.

As canned milk, vegetables and all canned goods were then unknown, our bill-of-fare consisted of dry beans, bacon, flour, rice and dried fruits; campfire bread baked over any kind of a fire we could get. Bread burned if wind was heavy and doughy if wood supply was scarce.

Water supply-any kind we could find, muddy, brackish, or even stagnant. After we struck the Little Colorado River our only supply was in holes along the river bottom, and in places so stagnant that fish were dead and floating among the green slime; but was water and had to be used by man as well as beast. This was boiled over a sage brush fire to sterilize it, then strained into barrels and used very sparingly.

Before we reached our destination, while we plodded our weary way across those wastes of glistening sand, (on foot, to lighten the load of our jaded teams), the mercury registered 114 degrees and our tongues were swollen from thirst. Oh, for a drink of pure cold water from our wells in Utah.

We arrived at our destination the fore part of May, making the journey in about three months and ten days.

## Nancy Cedenia Bagley Willis

Interviewer: Roberts Flake Clayton
Phoenix

*Utah to Arizona 1878*

In 1877, a call came to my father to go to Arizona to help build that new country. I pleaded with my husband to go that I might be with my mother. What loving daughter does not know my feelings? Merrill sold our home and farm. With two new wagons, a white-topped carriage, fine teams, one year's provisions, ten cows and calves, we started on this journey on April 12, 1878.

The trees were in full bloom, the perfume was wafted in the air. It was with sad hearts that we bade good-bye to our first home. I drove a team all the way over some of the most terrible roads that a wagon could be taken over. We would travel sometimes all day and night to get water, then make another forced drive. We drank from bitter, brackish pools of water as there was nothing better.

The first day of May we nooned on the desert among beautiful wild flowers. My sister, Melissa, with her three children, had separated from her husband and was with us. To cheer her up and also to observe an old custom, she was crowned the Queen of May.

When we reached the Colorado River, which we had been dreading ever since we started, the water was so high the ferry men hesitated in crossing us over. After we were safely across, we rested for some days. We pitched our tents and unfurled the American flag that Merrill and I had made before leaving home. Took the organ and violin from the wagon and as our pioneer mothers and fathers had done before, we danced on the big flat rocks.

**Lucy Jane Flake Wood**
Interviewer: Roberta Flake Clayton
Snowflake

*Utah to Arizona 1877*

When Jane was seven years old her father was called to assist in the settlement of Arizona, and in the fall of the year 1877, with his family, household belongings, provisions, cattle and horses started on the long perilous journey into Indian infested desert, over a road that could scarcely be called a trail.

They were leaving behind hosts of friends, relatives and three little graves. The youngest member of the family was only two months old, but another joined them at Grand Falls on the Little Colorado, while they were on their way out, this one, a fine baby boy born to Jane's oldest brother and his wife.

Several hired men were employed to help with the driving. The winter was very severe, some days only a few miles could be made for fear the men would freeze to death and one day they only went a mile and a half, as the snow and sleet was so strong the animals refused to face it. Jane's father had fixed the covered wagons as comfortable as possible, and a stove in each one, but wood was scarce, and when found was hauled along as there might not be any where they would be forced to camp. That trip lasted three months, and the memory of it is a nightmare to all of the family who were old enough to share in its hardships.

After a couple of weeks the Flake train overtook that of Isaac Turley. One of the Turley children was very sick, and at the top of Buckskin Mountain, it died. One of the men who had been over the road knew there was a grave at the foot of the mountain, and so they took the baby's body and buried it there by the side of that beautiful May Whiting, and the grief stricken drove her team on as she had all of the way. This incident cast a gloom over the entire company, but especially over Jane as she was young and very impressionable.

Soon after leaving the last settlement in Utah, Kanab, the eldest daughter of the Flake family, Mary took sick with a very sore throat. Several days late they overtook another wagon train, and with them was "Aunt Abbie" a nurse, whose equal has never been found in Northern Arizona. Mary's father told Aunt Abbie that he had a very sick girl and would like for her to come to the wagon and see what was the matter. She was totally blind, but as soon as she reached the wagon where the sick girl lay she exclaimed, "Oh, it is Diphtheria, I can smell it."

Aunt Abbie immediately set to work doctoring Mary and everything possible was done for her, all were so solicitous for her welfare that Jane became envious, and hoped she would get the disease. She not only hoped, but she too became very attentive to her sister, so much so, that she would expose herself, unnecessarily with the result that she "got it" and had it so much worse than Mary did that her life was despaired of, and only for the constant and tender care of her Mother and the nurse she would have died.

One of the children, an eight year old boy belonging to the other company did die, and his body frozen and taken on to the first settlement in Arizona, en route, where he was buried. This time, Jane herself was too ill to realize it.

Finally the family reached the Little Colorado River in January and settled at a place they called Taylor, across the river about five miles west of the present Joseph City.

They remained here only seven months, then her father bought the Stinson Ranch on Silver Creek and founded the town of Snowflake. Jane says the first clear water they had to drink since they came to Arizona was when they reached Silver Creek.

## Annie Chandler Woods

Interviewer: Roberta Flake Clayton
By her daughter Annie Woods Westover
Navajo County

*England to Utah 1852*

Emigrated in 1852, with her mother and brothers and sisters. Her Father a wealthy English nobleman, who did not accept the

Gospel, but intended to follow them to Utah for the sake of being with the family as soon as he put his extensive financial interest in shape.

They were on the ocean nine weeks, had rough seas, and during the voyage small pox broke out on board the vessel, her sister being one victim, but finally recovered.

Her Mother and the youngest brother, Andrew, died at New Orleans of Cholera leaving the three orphan children to come on to the Valley alone. They had been born and reared in the lap of luxury. Their being left orphans and in poverty and homeless in a new country such as Utah was at the early day meant sufferings and hardship such as mortal tongue cannot describe.

After the mother's death they soon lost track of the Father. He never came to Utah, nor did the children ever receive one dollar of their vast wealth.

**Emma Eliza Bryon Wyatte**
Interviewer: Kathlyn M. Lathrop
Duncan

*Alabama to Arizona 1901*

We started west in 1899. We came by train to Stanford, Colorado. We were not very well satisfied in Alabama, and although we had a little money, it seemed hard to get another "start" like we had at home.

When we lost our seventeen-year-old daughter in Colorado, we just couldn't stay there any longer. So in the winter of 1901 we headed for Arizona Territory.

This time we traveled by wagon, in order to bring what stock, pigs and chickens, and household goods we had accumulated again. We were on the road one month and five days, in the dead of winter. I dipped up snow and melted it to wash our clothes along the road. It was a miserable trip, with eight youngsters to look after, besides the stock to tend, and weather was so cold. We landed at Fort Thomas, Arizona, in time to put in a crop.

# CHAPTER FOUR
## Life on the Frontier

*I have lived for months where my only neighbors were Indians and my one music the howl of the coyote.*

*Charlotte Tanner Nelson*

Mormon women found themselves living in the raw frontier. They did not settle into established towns but in small beginning villages which had been created by earlier Mormon settlers, or in the prime wilderness where their duty was to set up a settlement. For them it wasn't a matter of going from one home into another; it was going from a home to nothing. No house awaited these women and their families at the end of the journey. All they would have would be what they carried with them and what they would create with their own hands.

Non-Mormon women headed to the small towns and cities of Arizona. Mining towns such as Bisbee and Tombstone attracted Mexican women and easterners. Tucson, with its large Mexican population was a magnet for those who joined their families and friends in the semi-tame Arizona. For the Anglos Arizona offered the lure of land and many set up ranches which were isolated but within a day's drive, with a good team, to the nearest town.

Yet all of them, in some way or another, were setting presidents, defining ways of doing things, and establishing methods for living successfully in a wild land. And, they all suffered deprivations and hardships. Their coping skills are at times creative, other times based on sheer determination though their goals may have been different.

The members of the Church of Latter-day Saints were not just migrants, they were colonizers. Their mission was to find land potentially capable of sustaining towns and villages and build them. Then create a way of life that reflected their religion, its values and its ways of life. Their mission required they go into unsettled land, or at the least, land that was sparsely settled.

These pioneer women coming into the untamed west planned their baggage carefully taking only the most essential items. However, unforeseen dangers on the road often caused them to jettison some of their prized items. Many arrived far poorer than when they left.

The first pioneers to establish the small villages had an absolute blank slate to work with. The responsibility was tremendous; they were not only physically setting up a town, they were creating a lifestyle and establishing a social structure.

Many of the Mormon wives shared their husbands, and in some cases their homes with their husband's other wives. The "plural wives" referred to each other as Sister, and the children called them Aunts. Polygamy was a practice of the members of the Church of Latter Day Saints at this time, and was the fuel for much of the discrimination both by the Government and non-Mormons.

The heaps of praise piled on the wives by the interviewer, or even referred to by the wives themselves, the litany of their skills and accomplishments might be an effort to establish and recognize their individuality or position in the family.

The other group of women pioneers belonged to various other religions, or no religion, but their religion played a minor role in their lives. They came to Arizona for a variety of reasons. Perhaps it was to join family members that had proceeded them, or to follow a dream, or simply because they hoped to escape a paralyzing poverty. Some of them went not into the wilderness, but into established towns. Sometimes the towns were no more than a few adobe buildings, a muddy square, and a population of Mexicans with a few Anglos and a few Indians who were passing through.

Yet even for them the frontier towns supplied them with less than what many were used to, and made demands on their endurance and determination. The lives of these women, more so than the Mormon pioneers, are filled with the adventures that meet our expectations of what the west was back in the late eighteen hundreds and early nineteen hundreds.

Both pioneer women's groups shared some commonality. While the men planned towns and planted crops, dug irrigation ditches, raised cattle, and built adobes, the women saw to the running of the households, the education of the children, and some simple pleasures of life. Although the home and child rearing was their primary responsibility they were also found working out in the fields and with the cattle.

The task of making a home and a life on the frontier did not allow for categorized gender work for the men were not always around to do their chores. When they left to fight the Indians, chase outlaws, go on a Mormon mission, or leave for extended periods to work elsewhere, the women stepped in and did the men's work.

Although floods, cruel weather, and lack of food and water plagued them it didn't take away their determination. It was this determination and their ingenuity that enabled them to create a livable life for their families in an untamed land. While life on the frontier was hard, it was not bleak. People came together for entertainment such as dances, and songfests. Church was another way of bringing people together and for some religious responsibilities were socially fulfilling.

These frontier life experiences are in the words of the woman or in the words heard and recorded by the interviewer. Electronic recording devices were rare in 1935 and most of the interviews were captured with paper pen and pencil by the interviewer.

In these stories of frontier living there is adventure and humor... good old western humor. There is also tragedy, heartbreak, and heroism.

## Elizabeth Adelaide Hoopes Allen

Interviewer: Roberta Flake Clayton
Phoenix

Her ability to do things was displayed in her youth and it did not desert her in later life. Situations often rose which gave her ample opportunity to use that ability. On one occasion when her husband and her brother were on a freighting trip, leaving her and her sister-in-law to keep up the home, the women decided they must have some meat to eat. Mary said she would knock the pig in the head if Elizabeth Adelaide would cut its throat. They agreed.

When the water was hot and everything was ready Mary took the axe and entered the pig pen. She raised the axe and let it fall upon the head of the pig. But, her strength was not great and she had failed to extinguish the life of the animal which ran around the pen squealing. Elizabeth Adelaide saw Mary hurriedly climbing from the pen and heard her screaming. She came running to the rescue carrying with her a butcher knife. She heroically entered the pen and cut the pig's throat.

Washing Women
*(St. Johns Historical Society)*

We women of our modern day cannot seem to understand just how our Mothers and Grandmothers played the part of manufacturers in addition to their every day household duties and the rearing and caring for their large families. Elizabeth was one of the characters who was not a stranger to work. Late hours on many a night found her seated at the machine, spinning wheel, or loom engaged in preparing raiment for her children, herself, or her husband while the family was peacefully sleeping.

Often she would "kill two birds with one stone." If she found a few minutes to rest her weary limbs, her fingers were busy with the knitting needles shaping the yarn into stockings for the winter's use. There was no time to be wasted so she knit as she went to Relief Society meeting or to visit her friends.

Arizona was being settled the latter part of the 70's but it was not until 1882 that the Allen family decided to go. On the 13th of November, 1882, they entered what is now Mesa City. Here they were met by some of their former friends who had come previously and who gave them a hearty welcome. After a few days they acquired a quarter section of land on which was already built a two-room house.

The following summer in July, another baby girl was born. She was but a few weeks old when a plague of smallpox increased the trials of the faithful pioneers in Mesa. Both Elizabeth and her husband were ever ready to go to those who were sick and minister to their wants. Although they were exposed, neither of them nor any of their children took the dreaded disease.

In one home both parents died and she took their three small children and cared for them. That summer was a very sad one for each week found the little colony decreased by two or more of its inhabitants? Trying as they were this affliction seemed to draw the people nearer together.

## Clara Styron Armstrong

Interviewer: G.W. Reeve
Globe

In 1882 Mr. Styron moved his family to George's Creek, where he ran a large farm and ranch. While living on this ranch Miss Clara made the acquaintance of a young man by the name of Marion Frances Armstrong, who was the manager of a large ranch known as The Border Ranch located on the border.

Mr. Armstrong decided he needed a cowgirl wife, so in October 1884, when Clara was twenty years of age, she became Mrs. M. F. Armstrong, and went to the Border Ranch to take her place as the manager's wife.

Mr. Armstrong had a contract with the Government to raise, bale and deliver to Fort Stanton, alfalfa hay for the cavalry stationed there. Mr. Armstrong had nine brothers who served in the Civil War on the Confederate side.

Then, in 1898, Mr. J. N. Porter, manager of the First National Bank at Globe, and who was a cousin of Mr. Armstrong's, induced Mr. Armstrong to move to Globe to engage in business.

The First National Bank then stood on part of the ground now covered by the Colonial Hotel Building on Broad Street. There was no other bank there at that time. Mr. George W. P. Hunt, ex Governor of Arizona was then the manager of the Old Dominion store, which was situated on the site that the Valley National bank now occupies.

Mr. Armstrong started a business of house-wrecking and house-moving in Globe. Mrs. Armstrong opened up a boarding house to help the family finances along. When the town of Miami was opened up in 1909, Mr. Armstrong increased his business to include that town in his operations, and would ride to Miami on the motor bus that ran on rails to Miami in the mornings, and return the same way at night.

In 1910 the town of Miami was growing so rapidly that Mr. Armstrong moved to Miami to ply his business, and Mrs. Armstrong operated a large boarding house in Miami, sometimes having as many as 150 borders. Her boarding house was situated where the Chief Hotel now stands, on Live Oak Street. As the town continued to boom a Street Superintendent was needed, and Mr. Armstrong was elected to that office.

The Post Office at Miami was a small frame building, and as the town grew and spread over the valley it was decided at a Citizen's Meeting that the Post Office should be moved to a more suitable location. The Post Office was jacked up and put on wheels, preparatory to being moved, when some of the citizens put in objections and raised so much sand about having the Post Office moved out of their immediate neighborhood that the actual moving was put off until the arguments could be settled.

Some heavy timbers were placed in front for steps, and the Post Office continued to operate, a Post Office on Wheels, for several weeks before the argument was finally settled and the building was moved to the new location. This was in the year of 1912.

In the years following the Post Office was moved again, and it became a joke with the citizens about having a portable post office. Once a man said to a friend, "Well I must go to the Post Office and get my mail", and his friend said, "Just wait a while and they will likely move the Post Office right by here."

In those days most of the arguments were settled out of court, and every man carried at least one gun; some carried two. One evening while the crowd was passing the Post Office, going to a dance at the Old Dreamland, they heard a shot in the Post Office and upon investigating found that a young man had shot and killed old man Danner.

It developed that Mr. Danner had warned the young man to stay away from his daughters. The young man denied that he had forced his attentions on the girls, and proceeded to tell the old man what kind of a snake he was, to be so mean to his girls, and not allow them to have company. The argument waxed hot, and the old man pulled his gun, but the younger man beat him to the shot and killed him.

## Dona Eulalia Arana

Interviewer: Rozella Gomez
Cochise County

Donna Eulalia Arana came to Bisbee from Guanajuato, Mexico, in 1901 with her husband and two children, both boys. Upon arriving here they went to live "en el monte". El Monte being the hills beyond Zacatecas where Mr. Arana built a rude "Jacalito" for his family. Here they lived for about three years, Mr. Arana doing his work of being a "lenero", wood-seller, clearing the hills surrounding his home of all the wood with which they were covered.

At first he had only two little burros to haul his wood, and then he kept on buying more by ones and twos until he had eight of them.

He worked independently, going from house to house to sell the wood. At first he sold a "cargo", or load of chopped firewood tied with a cord, for fifty cents; later he sold it by the sack-full at twenty five cents a sack.

The boys never attended school as they were always busy working with their father, besides being too far off from the school building. When Zacatecas began to be populated they moved down there.

The Arana family, doing quite well in their wood selling business, started buying houses put up for sale in Zacatecas until they had ten of these, which they rented cheaply at two, three and four dollars a month. They were always occupied. These houses were later sold, one by one, because the taxes on them cost more than they were worth.

Mr. Arana used to go down to a hotel on Brewery Gulch every day to get garbage foods for his chickens and burros. The hotel was always crowded and very busy. The clattering of dishes in the kitchen, the passing to and fro of hurrying waiters and waitresses, the amount of food thrown away daily, and the renting for $10.00 a month of rooms so tiny that one had scarcely fitted in them...all signifying to the fact that Bisbee had much business downtown.

Donna Eulalia never attended dances or fiestas in Bisbee or in Mexico. She was brought up very strictly in Mexico by stern, church-going parents who allowed her to go only "from her home to the church, and from church, home again". Not having been allowed to have good times when she was a young girl she didn't care for them later. Besides she had always lived more or less away from the center of town where most of the community affairs are staged.

Even when her son built the "Cinco de Mayo" dancehall in Zacatecas and made dances here she never attended them. She knew that many persons attended them, however and that her son always made money on these dances.

One time a man named Rice was shot here by a drunkard, but not much interest was given to the affair and the murderer fled from Bisbee.

Dona Eulalia doesn't go to church any more, as she is troubled by rheumatism, but she does enough praying at home for all the people in Bisbee.

Mrs. Arena keeps a few chickens and so, in taking care of them, in doing the housework, or going down to the store for groceries, and in doing one thing and another, she manages to keep busy all day long. She goes to bed quite tired at night. She gets water from a well right below her house and likes this water better than that which is piped.

## Julia Johnson Smith Ballard

Interviewer: Roberta Flake Clayton
Snowflake

When she was three years old, her parent left their home in Utah and started to Arizona where they had been called by President Brigham Young. On arriving at their destination the Pioneers lived in their wagon boxes until they could have logs made from the timber to build their houses.

The men folk worked together helping one another and whenever it came time to raise a roof they had quite a celebration; the women folks helping by cooking as fine a dinner as was possible for those days. Jesse N. Smith's house was the first to have a shingled roof in what was then Apache County.

In the fall after the crop was harvested, Julia's father went back to Salt Lake City to finish out his term at the Utah Legislature and left Aunt Janet and her five little girls here. In the spring he returned and brought Aunt Emma and Aunt Augusta with their families.

Homestead with Outhouse
*(St. Johns Historical Society)*

These were the days when little girls wore their hair braided and Aunt Janet had so many duties and so many little girls that it was hard for her to comb each little head and braid it up properly each day, so Sister Larson, their good Swedish neighbor just across the street, offered to assist.

Little Julia would go over each morning and after Emma, who afterwards became Aunt Em, had nicely combed and braided her hair, Sister Larson would say, "Put her up in her high chair and give her a cup of coffee (barley coffee.)"

The first crop of wheat was greatly appreciated and was ground by hand in coffee mills. Julia took her turn with the other members of the family grinding. Sometimes it took too long to make a batch of bread so they would make what they called minute pudding, making a dip of milk with sugar and nutmeg to pour over it. Someone asked why they called it minute pudding and was told, "Because it takes a minute to make and a minute to eat it.

Before the railroad came through Holbrook all the flour and sugar was hauled from Albuquerque by team. Salt was hauled from the Salt Beds in New Mexico.

As a child she and the other children used to go to the field and glean the wheat. They sold the wheat heads to make hats. She learned to braid the 4 strand, or notched braid, braiding yards and yards for her mother who made hats for the whole neighborhood. Men's, women's and children's home-made hats were all they had in those days.

One of her main tasks was to tend the baby and she faithfully rocked the cradle and tended five of the younger children while her mother (who was a nurse) went out to aid the sick. Often on returning in the dead of night or early morning she found faithful little Julia with her foot still in the rocker pad and her head drooped over the cradle in sleep.

As a child she used to enjoy the family outings. Going graping and doing her full part in the potato field, helping with planting and digging that vegetable so important to her father's large family.

**May Arthur Bates**
Interviewer: Helen M. Smith
Cochise County

My father was sent for by the Old Dominion Mining Company of Globe. He was a machinist and blacksmith and he was to oversee the installation of the machinery at the O. D. Mine. The company built us a little house of logs.

I was about six years old when we moved to Globe. One of my early memories is of Mother calling me excitedly one day to see a strange sight. We were not at home, but I do not remember where we were or what the occasion was. I do remember that there was a small grove of trees near. An ox was suspended from two of these trees by wide bands around his belly. "Oh Mother," I cried, "what a funny way to milk a cow." Mother explained to me that it was not a cow, but an ox, and that they were to put shoes on it. I thought it quite funny that an ox was to wear shoes. About that time one of the men took a leg of the ox, held it between his knees, and put on a shoe.

Another of my early memories is of a cyclone. I know that many people will not believe that there could be a cyclone in such a mountainous place as Globe, or that there has even been a cyclone in Arizona. However, I am sure that our experience would make anyone believe it possible.

In Globe at this time there was a school and a few scholars. It must have been shortly after our arrival, for I was still considered too young to attend school. The teacher was a woman who had two children, a girl of about thirteen, named Blanche, and a boy too small to go to school. Mother cared for this boy, younger than I, during the day while his mother taught, and after school Blanche would come for him and take him home.

One evening Blanche came for her brother and lingered to talk a few minutes with Mother before starting home. She and Blanche were on the front porch talking, the little boy was asleep on the bed, and I was lying beside him, having just awakened from my nap.

Blanche started in the house saying she must get her brother and go, but Mother called her attention to a dark, queer looking cloud which was approaching rapidly and said that she had better not start out until they saw what was going to happen. Mother feared a heavy windstorm, through which Blanch would not be able to struggle with her little brother. They watched the cloud for a few minutes.

Mother told me afterward that it was funnel shaped in the sky, with a long tail like an elephant's trunk reaching from the sky to the ground, and writhing about like a snake. The wind began to rise, and suddenly the storm hit the cabin. The little boy was still asleep, but I began to get scared. Mother told Blanche that they must get the children immediately and go to the dugout. Father was away, but he had told Mother many times that the dugout was safer than the house in case of a storm. Blanche wanted to go out the front door, but Mother thought it safer to go out the window by the bed because there were no objects on that side of the cabin which would be likely to hit us and the dugout was closer.

Mother raised the window, told Blanche to crawl out and she would hand her one of the children. By this time the wind was a howling fury, rain was pouring down, and it was completely dark. This all took place quicker than I can tell it.

Blanche crawled out and stood shivering in the rain and darkness. Mother grasped me under one arm, the boy under the other, stood on the bed prepared to jump out. There was a flash of lightening, a crash, and a large tree fell heavily across that corner of the house, smashing in the roof and walls.

Blanched screamed, but I do not remember that Mother made a sound. I was too frightened to scream. The roof and walls broke the force of the tree, but it fell heavily enough across the bed to pin Mother down, one of us still under each arm.

The rest of the cabin was shaking violently in the wind.

"Stand back!" Mother screamed at Blanche. "The rest of the cabin will go in a minute and when it falls its weight will probably bring up the tree at this end and I may be able to get from under it."

About that time there was another blinding crash, another heavy wind, and the other end of the cabin fell inward. The weight of the logs caused the end of the tree, which was across the bed, to spring up suddenly. Mother crawled or wriggled or somehow got through the window quicker than thought, scraping much of the skin of my face on a log as she went. There was another crash behind us and the rest of the cabin was leveled.

Mother somehow got the few necessary steps to the dugout, still with a child under each arm, and Blanche clinging to her skirts. We were all safe and unhurt with the exception of a few scratches. We were wet to the skin, or indeed I believe I was even wet inside, shivering with cold.

There was food in the dugout, and gunny sacks with which Mother wrapped us the best she could. We sat still shivering, with gunny sacks around us, and waited for the storm to subside. All our chickens were drowned and swept away by the water which ran down the mountain side in a deluge, and all our belongings were also washed away.

We had a big Shepherd dog of which we were very proud, and of course we resigned ourselves to his loss. However, we found him after the storm under the bed, of which some part still remained. He was unhurt, but rather badly frightened.

Eventually the mine closed down and the Arthur family decided to return to California. We were warned that a river we must cross had been rising rapidly, and that heavy rain might make us some trouble along some distance of the way. We soon found this true. I remember in crossing the river that we saw vegetables, chickens, and various and sundry articles of food as well as other things floating down the river. Mother rescued several hens from the water and we took them with us in a box fastened under the wagon.

We had not traveled any great distance from Globe when we came to a small cabin. Father stopped to water the team. This cabin was tenanted by an old man whose actions seemed queer to Father. However, he allowed Father to water the team, and even allowed us to go inside the cabin,

We soon noticed that an Indian's feet were sticking out from under the bed. When the man was satisfied that Father was not an officer, he told us that his wife and children had been killed by Indians, and that he killed Indians whenever opportunity offered, in retaliation.

He had just killed two who came to the cabin when Father came up, and he had shoved them hastily under the bed. He enticed all passing Indians into the cabin, up to the number of two or even three, and he said that at that time he had not been discovered, nor had he allowed any to escape. We were glad to get away from that cabin.

## Ella Emily Burk Merrill Brown

Interviewer: Roberta Clayton
Navajo County

When she became a widow her youngest was a baby boy about two years old. She would have to leave him and the other children to the care of the eldest daughter, then thirteen years of age, while she walked a mile away where she would work as hard as she could all day at housework, then come at night to help do the big washing on a washboard, iron, make their clothes, and prepare food for the next two days. For this work she received $1.00 per day. One day's wages would be spent for food for the seven of them, and the next for a chair, other furniture or clothing for the family.

Her first washer was a hand power one that she paid for by doing the owner's washing, but no one with the latest improved electric was prouder than she. A bedstead was earned by cleaning house and thus her home was furnished.

Though she had been the owner of many homes, she now had none except a rented one. One time that Ella recalls was when the rent was due but she hadn't a dust of flour in the house. She asked the landlord if he would wait a few days for $3.00 of the rent so she could buy some flour. He told her he had to have it all and right then. She paid him and then went to each of the three stores of the town to try to get a sack of flour but no one would give her credit. What could she do?

The children were hungry and she had no bread and no way of getting any. Then Ella had a chance to prove that a friend in need is a friend indeed for a neighbor sent for her to come over and get a sack of flour and work for the pay.

For sixteen years Ella struggled against poverty. Her children grew up and married and made homes of their own, all but her youngest son. She had chances to marry again but did not on account of the children. After all were married but the baby she accepted the hand of a neighbor, Benjamin Brown, whose wife had died and left only one unmarried daughter. She was away to Salt Lake City when her father and Ella were married. When she later came home she and Ella's son followed the example of their parents and married each other.

Old St. Johns
*(LDS Church History Library)*

## Catherine Barlow Burton

Interviewer: Roberta Flake Clayton
Phoenix

Kate and her friend Emma Daley Ellsworth had the first ice cream parlor in Mesa. That was about 1887. It was locate in the Sam Cowen Building. The ice had to be shipped from Phoenix. They had their own cows, and had plenty of milk and cream. They baked their own cakes and gave a generous helping of cake and a big dish of ice cream for a quarter. They did very well and had lots of fun doing it; but competition came in and spoiled their business.

Her husband William established the first undertaking business in Mesa. She was a great help to him. Sometimes when he had to go out of town for a corpse Kate would go with him. One night he was called to the Mental Hospital. She decided to go along. He put the long basket in the hearse and they started out. The night was a dark one. As they rode along she heard voices from the rear. She grabbed her husband and screamed with fright. It proved to be a couple of messengers riding along on their bikes holding to the back corners of their hearse. When they heard the blood curdling yell it was hard to tell who were the most frightened.

William had the reputation of being without fear, and he could not realize that others are not as brave. Once when he and Kate were out in their car among the hills they saw three Mexicans a short distance away. As they came nearer he recognized the middle one as a criminal who had broken jail while he was a peace officer. Without a minutes hesitation William stopped the car, told Kate to get in the back seat and ordered the Mexican into the seat beside him.

Neither the Mexican nor his companions made any resistance. Perhaps they knew too well the Marshall's reputation. After the prisoner was in the car William handed his pistol back to Kate and told her not to be afraid to use it if the prisoner made a crooked move. There is no telling what she would have done, at least she says she doesn't know, but it worked and they delivered their prisoner again to Phoenix. Kate had many anxious moments while Bill was sheriff because there were many reckless and desperate characters come to Mesa in those days.

## Ilaria Valenzuela Casillas

Interviewer: Romelia Gomez
Cochise County

Ilaria has lived in Bisbee practically all her life, having been brought over from Sonora, Mexico when she was about seven or eight months old sometime round 1885.

Her father, Mr. Valenzuela was nearly always working out of town, with cattle, or in ranches in Gleason, Tombstone, or in the Sulphur Springs Valley, which is why his family stayed at Bisbee. He never did actual mine or lease work, but for a while he hauled wood for the smelter, which was then in Bisbee. He was under contract to do this work and she remembers his mentioning Pete

Johnson, who was well liked among the Mexican wood haulers, so he might have worked for Mr. Johnson.

Their first home in Bisbee was near the Central School, and it was this school which she attended for five years, during which time she learned a little English. Central School was then a four-room adobe building where six grades were taught.

The family moved to a house situated below the Franklin School building, which was then not a school but "La Opera" or Opera House recreation hall of all nationalities. Here were enjoyed by Mexicans, Americans, Italians, Spaniards, frequent dances and also skating parties. This two-story building consisted of two very large halls, one upstairs and the other downstairs. The dance music was provided by local Mexican orchestras which usually consisted of a clarinet player, a violinist, a bass viola player and one or more guitar players. These guitar players really could sing too.

Ilaria was then too small to attend these dances until later on. She and her pals would much rather play at hide-and-go-seek among the graves at the cemetery, which was then situated where the City Park now stands. Once in a while one of them would carelessly pick a flower from some grave, whereupon an old lady would tell them that the ghosts of those buried there would come and get them in the night time. That never seemed to scare the children at all.

The Valenzuela's next residence was at upper Tombstone Canyon. Here they build their own house of wood, of which there was plenty in the surrounding hills. Ilaria walked with other children to Central School every morning, in good and bad weather alike and enjoyed it all very much, especially when it snowed a lot. She recalls that during one heavy snowstorm an intoxicated Mexican fellow was found frozen to death, lying in the snow in Tombstone canyon. All the children who lived here were greatly awed and excited at this unusual happening and could talk of nothing else for several days.

She remembers coming down from Tombstone Canyon to funerals in town, riding in carriages drawn by two horses. On either side of the road trees and bushes swished the sides of the carriages and all one could see on the hillsides were trees and more trees all the way down to Main Street.

Ilaria has always been a Catholic. In those days, there being only one Catholic Church in town, everyone went to the little Sacred Heart Church which is now for the Mexican people. It was even smaller than it is now, but nevertheless all the Catholic officials of the mining companies faithfully attended mass on Sundays and were quite generous with their donations. Priests were changed often and were of different nationalities, sometimes an American priest was officiating, at other times the pastor was a Mexican or of some other nationality. All the children sang in the choir under the direction of Miss Massey quite a robust person, who was inclined to faint frequently in the middle of a hymn, always causing much consternation among the children, who never knew what caused these fainting spells.

### Ann Casbourne Williams Dalton

Interviewer: Roberta Flake Clayton
Navajo County

She was married on Valentine Day, 1855. For seven short months they enjoyed the bliss of perfect happiness. Her husband was working as a sawyer at a mill in Big Cottonwood Canyon. Just one week from the day he left his young bride he was brought back a corpse. In some unaccountable manner he was thrown across the saw and instantly killed on September 7, 1855. On November 19 she gave birth to a baby girl.

Ann endured all the suffering from lack of food and the comforts of life incident to pioneering in several localities in Utah, and to add to her affliction, she was stricken with palsy and for three months was absolutely helpless.

Slowly she recovered partial use of her body and was able to do her housework although her toes and fingers were always drawn.

After a year of widowhood she married John Dalton and had five daughters and one son. Widowed again Ann came to Arizona in 1879 with her son-in-law Charles Brewer and his brothers. For a number of years she lived in Taylor, Arizona and then in Pinedale.

### Achsah May Hatch Decker

Contributed by her daughter Helen E. Decker
Interviewer: Roberta Flake Clayton
Navajo County

One Sunday when Achsah May was a young child and her brother Wilford was still younger, her father went to Lone Pine. He was so absorbed in conversation with a fellow traveler that he forgot to notice where he was driving and he calmly, or it was decided, uncalmly dumped his whole family in the Show Low River. When his wife came up she was screaming voluminously with her baby clutched desperately under one arm, her other hand grasping a wagon wheel and both feet kicking about wildly in search for little Achsah May. "Aha", said the fellow traveler suddenly and reached for a tiny bit of debris floating about. As he pulled, up came Achsah May. She had fallen with her head down so that she had fastened in the single trees of the wagon.

A noble deed was done that day for my mother's life was saved. But more important to the child was the beautiful pair of shoes she had on. The first thing she said after regaining consciousness was, "Are my white kid shoes spoiled?"

Woodruff, in and before the "Gay 90s" was the business center through which all the mails and freight to Fort Apache passed. Then also, the Woodruff dam was in and Woodruff was a very prosperous farming community. Midst the gayety and hilarity then so prevalent in the community Achsah May was a prominent participant. In fact she turned out to be a second Pasteur in the little town, or at least, an advocate of sanitation. She is noted as being the maker of the first screen door ever made in Woodruff. With stimulus other screens were used in doors and windows and thus helped to abolish many contagious summer diseases.

## Victoria Fredona Gooch

Interviewer: Kathlyn M. Lathrop
Duncan

Saloons, restricted red light districts, gambling dens, ramshackle frame buildings, and board sidewalks still typified the western cow towns and mining camps when I opened a boarding house in Duncan twenty-seven years ago.

My husband was a man who never wanted to settle down in one place very long at a time. He made lots of money in his younger days, and we have owned several good houses, but it seemed that we never could "hang on" to them somehow. He was also good and kind, kind to the children and proud of every one of them.

Three of our children died in infancy. When my other four, two boys and two girls, were still small my husband got steel from the blacksmith forge in his eyes and was totally blind for three years.

After that we tried farming and ranching a little, but after several unsuccessful years we went back to city life where he did contract work and eventually back to blacksmithing.

I always did everything I could to help out. I have owned and operated several milliner shops, dressmaking shops, one with eight machines going at once. I have run boarding houses and restaurants, and once worked in a garment factory.

Women at the Mormon Dairy
*(National Archives)*

I have tried to give my children the best education I could, but they have educated themselves mostly.

When we came to Duncan, my husband bought out a blacksmith shop and I opened a boarding house. The late Governor G. W. P. Hunt has eaten many meals in my boarding house. Many

Arizona statesmen and politicians will remember the banquets that I have served them at the Mission Inn in Duncan.

Then came 1917 and the World War. I became a War Mother along with the thousands of other American mothers.

My youngest son, Allen Lee Willard Gooch, was among the first to go from Greenlee County. My oldest son had been called in the last draft, but he never had to go. He wanted to go with the first bunch, but they wouldn't have him, he had a family to take care of and was too old they said.

I prayed constantly for the safe return of my boy. I promised God if he would only let my boy die on his own American soil I wouldn't grieve. What a foolish promise! But God heard my prayers; my boy came safely home at the end of the war.

He was killed September 21 in an accident when a sudden head rise rushed down C-bar-A canyon and swept the car over the cement curbing. He died on his own soil, not twenty miles from his own home in Duncan. But how could I keep that promise not to grieve?

My hero son was an outstanding member of the American Legion, and the beautiful military funeral service of the legion was a just and wonderful tribute to the clean life he led. He is buried beside his father in the American Legion plot in the Duncan Cemetery.

## Miriam Dalton Hancock

Interviewer: Roberta Flake Clayton
Navajo County

When her children were small Miriam washed, carded, and spun yarn and knitted it into socks for her husband and stocking for herself and children. Her husband earned the wool by shearing sheep. As wool was only three cents a pound much of this time she utilized it in the making of yarn, mattresses, and warm wool comforts.

In the year of 1921 Miriam was advised to take her husband to a lower latitude as he was ill of heart trouble. They went to Willcox to the home of their oldest son, and on the 18th of July, 1921 Lyman Hancock passed away.

Many occasions presented themselves to prove that the Hancocks were friends of the Indians, in spite of some of the depredations they had suffered in common with the other early settlers at the hands of the Redskins. Friendships thus formed were enduring.

**Emma Swanson Hansen**
Interviewer: Roberta Flake Clayton
Navajo County

Joseph City is a unique community because it was founded by a group of young people who were sent as colonizers to the bleak Arizona desert by the powerful Mormon leader, Brigham Young.

The settlers for the most part were couples, in their first years of wedded life, who answered the call of a mighty leader, remained true to their trust, established homes, and built up a commonwealth for their children to possess.

While Emma and her husband still lived at the fort her first child, a son, was born. With the added burden she assumed her proper route with other young mothers who took turns going up the river, six miles, to where the men were striving against all sorts of odds to put in a dam whereby water could be sent through a system of canals to their thirsty farming lands. Here the women cooked in a tent for their valiant heroes amid flying dust and other discomforts, did their best to prepare palatable food from the staples, beans and flour.

Because the teams must be fed and cared for during the Sabbath while the men worshipped at the settlement, cuts were drawn each Saturday night to see who must remain on the job over Sunday. It happened that Joseph Hansen drew the fated bean one windy Saturday eve. Sunday came howling in as only an Arizona dust storm can usher in a new day. To add to the disagreeableness of the storm, the horses broke away, thus forcing the husband to leave his wife and two children alone within the shelter of the camp tent while he went on foot in quests of the straying animals.

His search was long and vexing while the wind grew more fierce. During the prolonged absence the camp tent was blown down leaving the bewildered wife to seek the shelter of a wagon box. It was here, pitifully huddled together that the husband found his family after his trying search for the lost horses. It seemed that those dust storms in the uncivilized country presented one of the worst trials that early pioneers had to endure.

The elements were all wide and seemingly beyond the control of a handful of settlers who had nothing but their physical abilities and splendid powers of endurance to cope against the furies of nature.

Fifteen times their dam in the Colorado River was swept away by treacherous floods but still the colonists persevered. They learned from work and bitter experiences how to make the arid alkali lands yield them a comfortable living. The last big dam, a cement structure has withstood the ravages of the worst floods known.

When the families at the fort separated to build homes the Hansons made them a temporary little structure in the fields. From here they moved to a lot in the newly made town site where they built a two-roomed house.

Each morning as soon as breakfast was eaten, whether the weather was warm or cold, blustery or calm, she went with pails of warm milk to feed the little calves and to care for her flock of chickens. She even gathered alfalfa, cutting it with a scythe, to give the swine a goodly daily ration.

She provided her table with eggs and generally had some to sell. She cured her own pork, hardly ever being without fine bacon, shoulders or hams. For more than thirty years her family was never without homemade butter.

It was with a feeling of hurt pride that the mother had to submit to creamery butter after an unparalleled record of providing so nicely for her household use as well as selling many pounds of extra good butter to satisfied customers.

Her cellar has always been stocked with home preserved foods. The jellies were particularly fine as well as the many fruits and vegetables.

For her children and herself she did all the sewing, even making shirts for her grandsons over which they gleefully exclaimed "They look just like boughten ones, don't they!" The family shoes were half soled by her skillful hands.

The Hanson family suffered through the epidemics of measles, whopping cough, scarlet fever, flu and was even in quarantine for small pox and diphtheria with no break in its numbers.

The mother bore grave suffering from toothache having to endure its ruthless pain until her teeth decayed in her mouth leaving dreadful snags and roots. These were finally removed to her great relief when the science of dentistry reached these faraway sections from the centers of civilizations.

**Mary Adsersen Hansen**
Interviewer: Robert Flake Clayton
Navajo County

Finally they reached Adair or "fools Hollow" as it was then called, where their daughter Annie was, and soon built a log room adjoining hers. After the crops were gathered that fall Mr. Hansen got a good job of mason work at Fort Apache. Here he received fair wages but there were no stores near so the family often had to go without the necessities of life. Salt was obtained from the salt beds a couple of days travel away. This was in lumps about the size of a small marble and was rolled with a bottle to make it fine enough for table use.

Mr. Hansen returned from Fort Apache in the spring and he and his sons took up a dry farm about a mile and a half south of their first location and put in a crop.

In the late summer of this year, 1881, the Apaches began causing considerable trouble, and one night about sundown word came that they had gone on the warpath and were headed toward the settlements and that all the people in those parts were to gather at Cooley's Ranch where Mr. Cooley had a large house with as much haste as possible. A fort was built around the house and wagon covers fastened together and stretched over to keep out the sun and rain. It was built out of thick logs with port holes to shoot through in case of an attack.

The men took turns standing guard and the women doing the cooking. Here they remained until peace was again restored. They returned to their farm but there was no water on it and they could not find any by digging wells, they moved again, this time up near a wash where they dug a well and found good water. Here they built another log house. This one served as a Sunday School house and dance hall, by moving the beds and furniture out, as well as a home.

This all made more work for Mary whose health was very poor, and was so overworked anyway. Beside the cooking, washing, ironing and the care of her six children she made everything the family wore, except the shoes. Even these she made for the smaller ones, cutting the uppers from the tops of old shoes, or old felt hats if these could be had, and her husband would put on the soles with wooden pegs he had made. He also carved lasts for the various sizes from wood. Each member of the family was fitted out with two pairs of stockings which was part of her summer work, and were ready when the cold weather would no longer permit bare feet. The boys' hats were from the jeans or denims to match their trousers. The girls had denim bonnets to keep the freckles off. Mary was very proud and very particular. No one else's children should be cleaner or neater than hers. Early in life her children were taught to work and she permitted no slipshod methods.

The stork visited the home of the Hansens with regularity and was always welcome no matter how hard the times were. There was no need for a doctor, a faithful old midwife took care of both mother and child and it didn't matter to her what she was paid in, or if at all, she was but doing her part in colonizing a new country.

Old House with Couple on Porch
*(St. Johns Family History Files)*

**Belle Hefley**
Interviewer: John Vick
Cochise County

Bout 1885, Belle and her husband came to Bisbee, which at that time was only a tent colony. There were no houses or "jacalitos." The present Post Office site was then the center of the colony and eventually a library was built there. Jim Burnet and Jim Carr hauled ore by wagon train to Fairbanks. The stables were located at what is now the town of Don Luis.

Mr. Hefley, a native of Iowa, ran a hotel in Silver City, New Mexico for awhile. In Bisbee he ran a butcher shop with a man named Harrington. It was called the "Family Meat Market."

The officer of the law was a Mr. Williams in the days when Belle first came to Bisbee. He was very clever and once fooled a notorious bandit by hiding the payroll in a tent back of the library. The payroll had been brought down from Tombstone on a Saturday, and on Sunday the bandit came into town. Williams met him, fed him a big chicken dinner, and told him there was no money in the town because there were no banks. The bandit then left without bothering anyone.

When Dan Lewis and Dan Simons were officers, they would take a paternalistic interest in the cowboys who came to town on Saturdays. They had to check their six-shooters when they entered a bar, and the two officers would also take care of their money for them, doling them out only a small amount to be spent on drink.

Then, as now, every nationality except Chinese was represented in Bisbee. Sometimes a hundred men could be seen scrapping ore from the sides of the mountains around Bisbee and carrying it in gunny sacks on their shoulders to the buyer who took it by wagon train to the smelter. Mr. Hefley at one time took care of some property on which gold miles were located by a Mr. Anguis, apparently the Father of the present senator from Cochise County.

Thirty or forty years ago there were lots of streams and springs around Bisbee. Wild cherries, grapes and bananas grew in abundance. There were many oak trees (bellotas) on the slopes of the mountains. In those days there were many bad floods due to cloudbursts. A flood-gate was constructed in Upper Tombstone Canyon for partial control of these sudden floods.

The first school in Bisbee had log benches. The teacher used to come from Tombstone for the five school days and return for the weekend. Oxen were used in the early days for hauling as well as burros.

Frank Dubacher started the first saloon in brewery Gulch, and about the same time, one was started on Chihuahua Hill. In Brewery Gulch there was a place for "Free Coinage" where gold and silver could be minted.

Belle claims that when she first came to Bisbee one man could make ten or fifteen dollars a day jut carrying sacks of on his back to the wagon trains. There was a spirit of cooperation among the early miners. If one of them fell ill his fellows would help him get his ore to the smelter.

## Dona Isabel Juarez Hernandez

Interviewer: Romelia Gomez
Cochise County

Isabel doesn't remember much about Bisbee in 1896, except that it was almost uninhabited except for Chihuahua Hill, Brewery Gulch, and the business section of the town. All the rest was a wilderness, the hills being covered with brush and mesquite and veyota trees.

Isabel's brother worked in the smelter and her Mother took in washing and had borders. They lived on Chihuahua Hill right above a hotel which was named "San Jose."

Her family, as well as every other one in Bisbee, bought their water from "aquadores", who delivered to them a bag of water every other day charging twenty-five cents for it. If you had the ready cash you paid then and there for the water. If you didn't, you paid them at the end of the month.

Isabel Jurez never attended school in Bisbee, and cannot understand or speak any English at all. But, her younger sister went to Central School during the short time they lived here. Central School was then a shabby, one-room little building.

Isabel's family, being of Catholic faith, used to attend services at the little Sacred Heart Church, to which all Catholics went, there not being any other Catholic Church in town. A priest came from Fairbanks about every two or three months to perform the services here and the little church had no regular pastor then. He rarely stayed more than fifteen days in Bisbee on his trips here.

For recreation the only dances she attended were a few at the Opera House, where skating parties were also held sometimes. She was never much of a pleasure seeking person, knowing little of what went on outside her home and having few friends in town because she didn't like to go out much.

When the smelter was moved to Douglas the Jurez family moved to Douglas and from there to Agua Prieta, Sonora. Here Isabel married and had four of her six children. Then in 1911, when Agua Prieta was threatened by the revolutionists, many of the people slipped across to the U. S. Among these were the Hernandezs.

## Carmen Hillman

Interviewer: Romelia Gomez
Cochise County

Her husband, an American, was an aguador (water carrier) and had three Mexicans working for him. Mr. Hillman paid each of these laborers three dollars a day and the people of Bisbee paid four dollars a month for water. The water was delivered to them in canvas water bags which were made by Mrs. Hillman.

She made them by sewing a double piece of canvas on both sides, leaving an opening at the top through which the water was poured. The water was obtained from a tank at Zacatecas Canyon by means of buckets.

The water bags were strung on poles which were then placed crosswise on the burro's backs (there were twenty-five burros to do the work of distributing water to all Bisbee residents.) The task of these water carriers was a difficult one, for much snow fell often in Bisbee in the winter and the steep, slippery hills were hard to climb. Mr. Hillman supervised the work on horseback.

After the water hauling period Mr. Hillman mined a tunnel on Miller Hill with another American for two years. From there he went to work at the Sacramento Pit. The year after the World War work in the mines was very scarce, so he went to Cananea where he worked until his death in 1922.

In 1902 there were no houses in Bisbee, only jacalitos (thatch-covered huts.) The Mexican people were much given to fiestas and mariachia (serenades) and the $15^{th}$ of September was always an occasion for a parade on Main Street, speech-making and dancing at the City Park.

The tejanos used to come from Tombstone to raise disturbances at a dance hall in brewery Gulch and were much disliked by the local residents. Also there were at that time many surramatos here (Spanish speaking people from Spain and different parts of Mexico who spoke in different dialects of Spanish.)

The women of these times wore very long, wide skirts, frilly blouses, high-top shoes, laced or buttoned, and large hats gaily adorned with plumes and flowers.

A big fire occurred in Lowell and many houses burned down, among which was Mr. Hillman's. For awhile, because of the scarcity of houses, all these families without homes were obliged to live in tents close by the place where the fire had occurred until such time when our houses could be erected.

## Virlenda Jennings

Interviewer: Kathlyn M. Lathrop
Duncan

I married Buck Jennings two months after I met him. He had come to Texas from Missouri, less than a year before that. He was just a young adventurer, who nobody seemed to know much about seeking to make a fortune, all his very own, in the wild and wooly west. Yes I reckon he found plenty of adventures all right.

My folks you see were wealthy plantation owners, and Buck, well he was just a nobody, not even a soldier, just working around where ever he could get work. Naturally my folks objected to such a marriage for me. We eloped to the Squire and were married before anybody knew anything about it.

After we were married that's when the fun started. If you call it fun. Elopements were not all that easy in those days. Father always said "If you dance you certainly have to pay the fiddler." Well, that fiddler certainly got his pay. They could, and often did hang a man for stealing a girl in Texas at that time, no matter whether he married her or not.

I was afraid to go home and afraid not to. I was not so much afraid of what they would do to me as I was afraid of what Father would do to Buck. Girls who eloped, or otherwise displeased their parents, were usually just locked up in their rooms until they came to their senses.

We had eloped on horseback over to old Squire Kelly's house, oh bout eight or ten miles I reckon. It was coming daybreak when we got started back. I knew they must have missed me already and were most likely out looking for us with the bloodhounds or a posse of armed men ready to shoot Buck down like a criminal, or take him off and hang him.

We were riding along talking about what was best to do. Buck wanted to take me straight home and just up and tell them that we were married and meant to stay that way. He was brave like that. But I was afraid to go on. I wanted to stay at Squire Kelly's until Father cooled down a little.

Just as we rounded a bend in the trail we came face to face with Father and a posse. I nearly fainted away. Father was as surprised as we were. We all just sat there staring at each other for several minutes before anybody said anything at all.

There had been rumors of an Indian uprising in a community a few miles to the west of us, and Father and his men were on their way to investigate that rumor. I hadn't even been missed from my room. But, of course, I didn't know that right then, and neither did Buck.

Well Father suddenly exploded. Those explosions of his were anything but funny. He thundered out demanding to know just what Buck Jennings might be doing at that hour of the morning with his daughter on the trail. Of course there was not anything to do but face the music then.

Buck didn't act the least bit excited or afraid, I was too scared to know whether I was proud of him or not right then. He began speaking up to Father as bold as brave as you please and told him all about it. In memory I can still see us all sitting there on our horses, me scared so bad I couldn't speak to save me, and the look on the faces of that posse of men that spelled DOOM for Buck in big letters.

The men took Buck away, they said, to jail, and they were not very gentle about it either. Father took me straight home and locked me up in my room. Mother refused to even speak to me or look at me. The last thing I heard Father say to Mother as they locked me in was "The scoundrel's neck will be stretched with rope before another day."

I cried all the rest of that day, but by night I had made up my mind what to do, or try to do at least. To hang a man for merely loving a girl enough to marry her was nothing but coldblooded murder in my sight. Oh, I don't know, I guess I did really love him, but what can a thirteen-year-old girl know about love?

I thought I did anyway. I was determined they should not hang him. I would stop it someway, but I wasn't so sure I had thought of a way that would really stop it.

Right then I wished I could write. I wanted to write him a note and explain my plan. I knew I could trust old Lily, the Negro Mammy, to take it to him, if even at the risk of her own life, but I had to give up that idea as I couldn't write and did not know anyone whom I could trust to write it.

I decided to send Lily that night to the jail where they had taken him, and tell him just what I was going to do. I had no idea what I might do if that plan failed to work. I was going to tell a lie and swear to it on the bible, if they ask me to.

When old Lily brought me my supper I told her what I wanted her to do for me. I can still seem to see her kind old black face and the understanding in her eyes now that I recall it all, as I do almost every day of my life, when she said to me, "Lawayassy! Chile!

They'd kill him sho! They'd kill him chile! You all mustn't do dat! I'll go tell him, and I'll swear its de truth, don' matter what they does to ole Lily." I knew of course, that old Lily would be horse whipped, but Buck had to be saved.

I was going to tell them that I was going to have a baby and Buck had married me to save me from disgrace. I knew Father would rather be dead than face that sort of disgrace. I thought he ought to be grateful to Buck. If I could just get Buck to back me up in that lie.

Well I did not have to tell that lie after all. Yes, girls that age always were and always will be that silly I reckon. Old Lily did not bring my breakfast next morning. She didn't come back as she said she would that night and bring me a message from Buck; she never went to Buck.

Sarah, the young Negro who brought my breakfast told me about it. Old Lily died in her sleep that night. I have often wondered if she took poison, or just died of fright thinking about the whipping she would get. She was too old and feeble to have stood much of a whipping. Of course nobody ever made any investigations in a Negro's death them days.

Mother came in around noon that day and asked me a lot of questions. I was afraid to lie to her, but she must have understood a lot more about love and marriage than I thought she did. Anyway, she had a lot of influence on Father. I was allowed to go down to supper that night and was not locked in again. That puzzled me more than ever. I thought maybe they had already hanged Buck.

I couldn't have trusted Sarah with anything, not even to ask her questions. She was too afraid of that whip. I didn't sleep a wink all that night. Nobody said a word about Buck to me at breakfast, and I was about fit to be tied when Father and Buck came riding in around noon, yes, together, and laughing and talking. Buck kissed me right before everybody.

Well, as I said before, Buck Jennings had nothing to start on, no land, and no money to speak of. Father built us a cabin, a two-room log hut, not much better than the Negro cabins, and gave Buck all the land he wanted to tend. He gave me all my own stock, with my brand on it, and gave Buck a good wagon and span of work mules, and all the farming tools he needed, or all the kind of tools that was available in those days.

My stock consisted of, one saddle horse, 13 fine milk cows, 25 head of beef stock, two sows and 16 pigs. Mother gave me a start of chickens, and I had all my own quilts and linens that I had made myself to start with. I also took the furniture out of my own room, and Buck built our tables and chairs and things like that.

Father built a Negro cabin in my back yard and gave me old Ben and old Nancy to help with the chores. They were too old to do much of anything, but they lived with me until they died. We got along fine until the Civil War broke out and Buck had to go to war.

Mother died the year I was married and Father married again, just a few months before the war broke out. Rachel, my stepmother, was a young widow with two children of her own, and the meanest, most jealous woman God ever allowed to live on this earth.

When Father went away to war she was so mean to my two little brothers, Davy, about nine years old, and Henry, about seven that I took them to live with me. They were company to me anyway and lots of help now that old Ben and old Nancy were both dead and I had my baby to look after besides tending the place.

I was home that Christmas day with the children and by night the earth was covered with a blanket of snow and everything seemed so peaceful. I just had to sing as I sat at my spinning wheel that night, and the children were picking out their boots full of cotton. I was humming "Silent night," when Buck opened the door and stepped in. That was a real Christmas to me!

Oh yes, of course I had the door barred, but when Buck knocked and called to me I got up and opened it for him. I wasn't much surprised to see him as I had been expecting him home on a furlough for some time. I had a new suit, new overcoat, and three pair of new sox ready for him.

He brought news from the battlefront that meant more to me and all the rest of the women in the neighborhood than any kind of a Christmas present could have meant. That was the first furlough Buck Jennings had had since he went away to war in 1861, and it was the last one until the end of the war.

When the war finally ended, Father was dead, killed in battle, and both my little brothers had died of colriehobis during that last winter of the war. The Negroes were free and my stepmother claimed all the plantation, what there was left of it to claim.

The United State government gave me my share of land as the heir of a Civil War Veteran when the time came around, and Buck got his land as a Civil War Veteran over in Sabine County on the Sabine River. We moved to our new home in the fall of 1868. We lived there until 1890 when we sold out, bag and baggage, as the saying goes, and came to Arizona Territory. All nine of our children were born there in Texas, and the youngest was about five years old when we left there.

We landed in Douglas, Arizona, in the fall; I forget the exact date, of 1890. Buck had made a trip out here and located a place on Cave Creek, in Rucker Canyon, and we went straight out to our new home as soon as we could get our wagons ready. We came to Douglas on the train you see.

The ranch house we moved into was just a nigger shack compared to the big comfortable home we left in Texas. If it had of been possible me and every one of the children would have taken the next train right straight back to Texas.

But, Lan' sakes! When we did get used to it out here, why, wild horses couldn't have dragged us back to Texas, or anywhere else. I reckon there is just something about this Arizona country that gets into your blood and stays there.

Buck Jennings died and left me alone on the ranch in Rucker Canyon in 1918, while the last of our sons were away in France in the World War. Our son, William, never came home either. They are all gone now except Luther, he lives in Globe, and my baby daughter Ethel Moore, and I live with her.

Ethel has had bad luck with her men. It seems that she can never get one to live somehow. She has been married five times and has buried every one of her husbands. The longest any of them lived after they married her was seven years. That was Bill Moore, the last one. He got killed by being thrown from a bucking bronco on their ranch up here at the head of the Blue River, around ten years ago.

Her first husband was struck by lightning two days after they were married in Flagstaff. The second died of pneumonia three months after they were married; the third was a gambler and he was shot and killed about a year after they married, the fourth was drowned in the Rio Perko at Holbrook during a flood. So that's the way of it—they just won't live after they marry her.

People seem to think it strange that a woman, or any person, my age could remember things so clearly. Well maybe it is rather unusual in a way, a person who has seen nearly one hundred years of life is bound to get things a little muddled in their minds at times with so terribly much to remember you know.

When I first heard about trains and railroads I couldn't imagine what they were like until I seen one. I remember the first train I ever seen. I don't recall just what year it was, but it was back in the early "80s" I think. Buck took us all in to see the train come in on its first run. That was certainly a red-letter day for all of the Buck Jennings family. We took our dinner and stayed all day then went to a wagon yard and stayed all night, going home the next day.

If anyone had been silly enough to try to tell me, then, that there would even be such a thing as an airplane I reckon I would have called them crazy as a bat. If they had suggested that I would ever ride on one of the things I would have known they were crazy.

The first automobile I ever seen was as we came through the city of Dallas on our way out here. A strange sight to my eyes these horseless buggy things. The first airplanes I recollect was during the World War when we heard them soaring over our ranch through the sky, army planes I guess from the fort at Douglas, or maybe they were just ordinary planes but anyway they were an interesting sight. I never was too sure that one of them wouldn't fall right through the roof sometime.

I went with my daughter to El Paso two years ago (1937) and took my first, and only, ride on an airplane. Yes Siree! I climbed right on, or into, the thing and did not get seasick or the least bit dizzy all the time I was in the thing, but when I got out of it my head whirled around so I couldn't stand up. Of course everybody around the airport laughed at me, and the El Paso paper carried a big front page article about the 92 year old grandmother riding in a plane. Some stunt for me to pull wasn't it?

God has seen fit to let me live on earth this long, I suppose for his own reasons, and he has given me a second eyesight to see with. But, I reckon he thinks these store teeth are good enough and he certainly has found no reason to begin giving me back any youth.

I weigh just two pounds more than my age (96 years old) and I reckon most people think I am a mummy, or something dried on the bones, until I start talking, then I reckon they know I am something that has still got life in it all right.

My hair has been snow white like this since I was a little past fifty, but I never had it cut until two year ago. I never needed one of them permanent things; my hair was always curly like this.

I learned to read when my children began to grow up and go to school. I can't read so very well, but I do enjoy reading anything that I can understand at all, like the newspapers, the bible, little western magazines with those bang, bangity, bang stories in them that keep the old days fresh in my mind.

I have practically quit piecing quilts now as we have so many more than Ethel and I will ever need. Ethel is an old white haired woman herself you see. And, my rhumatiz bothers me so much I don't get out and a round as much as I would like to. I just sit and read most of the time.

Read, dream, and wish! That's about all there is left for one my age to do, and I thank God that he has left me my memory and I do not have to sit in that shadow of half-insanity and wait for the death angel to take me home to be with my loved ones who have gone on before me.

I came to Clifton to live with Ethel when I sold the ranch back in 1920. We lived at her home on the head of Blue River until last winter, or fall rather (1938) when she sold out and moved to town. She got enough out of her ranch to keep her about the rest of her life I reckon, and I draw a Civil War Widow's pension myself, so that takes care of us two very nicely.

I love this part of Arizona very much. You see these old hills are old, old, old, and wrinkled like me and I know they'll still be here after I'm gone.

**Olive Jewell**
Interviewer: Helen M. Smith
Cochise County

The Apache Indians were thick around Snowflake. I saw some of Geronimo's band, but not that famous Indian himself, when they were being shipped to Florida. They were taken through where we lived in their way to Holbrook from where they were to be shipped.

Typhoid broke out in the camp, of a virulent type, and almost all in camp took it. My sister died, and for awhile my Mother's life was despaired of, but I was not even sick. I was quite worn out, though, from nursing so many sick. There were a great many deaths, sometimes three or four from one family. It was a terrible experience.

Soon after that we went to Utah, where I was married in the Temple to Leonard Jewell. Returning to Arizona, we went to Safford, where my husband farmed and raised cattle. While living there three children were born to us, and one died of measles.

At Safford for two or three years we had no flour except what we produced ourselves. Sometimes there was no way to grind our wheat, since the mill didn't work without plenty of water. Later flour began to be freighted in from Wilcox, probably the Eagle Flour Mills at Tucson. I cooked on a fireplace for three years, having no stove. We built our house ourselves, one room with four posts for four corners, walls made of two thicknesses of sheeting sewed together. We put small logs across the posts for a roof, brush on the logs, and a cattail leaf which shed water like shingles, over that. We did have a good floor but that was all.

We raised hay and grain and sold it at Fort Thomas and San Carlos and also kept bees and raised an orchard. As soon as we could afford it we built a house of cottonwood logs. We had just begun to get a good start when malaria got my husband so badly that we had to leave.

We went back to Snowflake where Mr. Jewell freighted for awhile, but the location did not seem favorable for his health, so we went to Woodruff.

Old Snowflake
*(LDS Church History Library)*

At Woodruff we bought a home and another baby come to us there, while we also lost a child. It was the same old story—Mr. Jewell was not well. All the rest of our lives we moved about from place to place trying to find a favorable climate for him.

From Woodruff we went to Pinetop on the line of the Indian reservation. There was no water there, so we stayed only a short time and drifted onto the Blue River toward Clifton.

My husband got work at a saw mill there. While we were there his brother, Herschel Jewell, was severely frozen at Springerville. He was brought to us, and I cared for him for nine months during which he could not walk and could not even feed himself. The balls of his feet and some of his toes had to be removed. He was always afterward crippled and was never able to work after.

We had to move to get somewhere where the elder children could go to school as their education had been neglected long enough. We chose Duncan because we thought the climate might be beneficial to Mr. Jewell, and there was a school there.

He worked for a dollar a day and board, but on that we lived nicely. Soon we were able to buy a little slice of land. We cut cottonwood poles and put up for the sides of the house, these covered with willows woven around and across the poles. The roof was of dirt. There the children got a start in school.

From there our wanderings took us to Huachuca Flats, between Naco and the Huachucas. We lived in a tent while there, not long because of the grasshoppers which were more numerous and more ferocious than any others I have ever seen.

Our next stop was St. David, where Mr. Jewell freighted, farmed, and did anything else he could, his health rapidly growing worse. We drifted to Tombstone and from Tombstone shortly to the Sulphur Springs Valley, where we homesteaded.

At first we lived in tents, but afterward built a mud house which was more comfortable. Soon after it was built the Arizona Eastern started to build a railroad to Naco, and in the survey our house was on the right of way. They paid us for the house and we bought lumber and built another house from the proceeds.

We sold the homestead to buy medicine for my husband, but nothing we did was of any avail. Most of our married life was spent under the shadow of sickness. When he was unable to work I picked cotton, worked in private homes, in the fields, at anything I could to earn enough for the family to live.

## Carmen Renteria Lucero

Interviewer: Jose del Castillo
Tucson

There was sort of a Spanish school of adobe walls and flat roof located near where the courthouse now stands. I was about seven or eight years of age. I did not go to school. I had to help keeping house. They would not let us girls go to school because if we learn to read and write we might write the boys and soon get married.

Our parents taught us to sew, cook, and learn us manners. They were very proper. There was no sewing machine then and we did all sewing by hand as I have been doing many, many years.

I was twelve years old when I saw the first sewing machine in Tucson. It was Charlie Brown's the saloon-keepers. He bought it for his wife. We thought the machine a unique thing. It could sew and embroider; and you did not have to sew by hand anymore, but it must cost a lot of money, we thought.

We ground our wheat and corn in a grinder-mill. It consisted of two flat slabs of round stones. They cut the slabs from the rocks in the mountain. The base stone is fastened to a solid frame of wood. Around this stone was a grooved receptacle of cement to receive the meal. A peg was fastened through a hole in the center of the base slab of stone, and then the top slab with a corresponding hole was placed over the other. Another hole served as the feeding opening in which grains were dropped and the mill ground. Turning the mill was done by a horse or burro. Handle was attached to the top slab, arranged like that of the arrastnas and turned by an animal just like it.

We got grains, Sonora Wheat, from Mexico. The Papagos raised grains too. We traded with them. But, grandfather got lands and planted our own grains, fruit trees (peaches and apricots, pomegranates, etc.) and many kinds of vegetables.

We the children got up at three o'clock in the morning and prayed, even before we had rubbed the sleep from our eyes, and chanted hymns. In the evening we did the same thing—pray and say our rosary. The Vesper peel rang out at eight o'clock.

In the daytime we did our daily household duties. We sew, wash, and many other small things to do. There was always some ironing. As I was the oldest in the family I stayed home to help in the household work. No, I never worked at any other job or occupation.

In the afternoon we had siesta and, when we woke up, we ate pinole, ground corn and sometimes we put ground parched wheat. We used panocha (slabs of brown sugar) for sweetening. We drank something made like pinole—parched corn or wheat and stirred in a lot of water and sweetened.

We seldom drank coffee and that was very much later. There was no coffee in town when I was a little girl. The one I knew of was given by one American lady to a Mexican woman who used to sell fruits and vegetables. She traded it for fruits and told this Mexican that coffee was good.

The Mexican women cooked the green coffee beans like she did with frijoles. As the coffee beans did not get soft after hours of cooking she cooked them all day. She found that she had a very bad bargain.

When the American lady came by another time, the Mexican told her that the coffee was no good; that she cooked it and cooked it all day and still it was not fit to eat. The American lady laughed and laughed. She then explained how coffee was made.

Do they use the promenade in the plaza and listen to the serenta? Young man, there was no plaza. When there was a fiesta, they rented the land. The fiesta was that of San Agustin. It lasted eight days. That was the time too that the priest from Magdalena came to Tucson. He came also to Baptize, perform weddings long overdue, confirm and officiate at the town patron's fiesta.

Lots of people came from Sonora. Pilgrims from California, New Mexico and Texas came, driving in wagons, riding horses, and walking. They came from all over the southwest. They came with things and goods to sell, to trade. They came to dance and to gamble and to pray.

There were going to be armadas around the fiesta ground. Oh, it was like a circus; lots of things to eat and drink in the booths, many games and things to buy. They had card games. My papa got fighting cocks for they had cock fights in those days.

Those fighting cocks my father raised them for the cock fights. He raised the finest birds in these parts. He got the birds from Sinaloa. He took good care of them and gave them training in bravery and technique. He would tie each bird to a stake in the yard like you graze a horse or cow.

At the fights they used to tie sharp glass shards to the foot and let the shard stick behind. Sometimes they cut their necks in the fight. Father used to get twenty five dollars in gold for one bird when he sold them.

During the fiesta there were games of sports. They had greased poles on top of which they put money. Whoever climbed to the top and reached for the money got it. The greased pig was fun. A bag of money was tied to the greased pig and whoever got hold of the pig and undid the bag got the money.

There were bailes and tiswin to drink. We danced on the ground, tapped hard. There were players playing the violin, the banjo, and guitars. They played Mexican music mostly as the musicians were usually Mexicans. We girls were escorted by our Madres and Aunts. Everybody danced and had a good time. At Levin's park there was a lot of amusements, including plays.

I was about three years old I think when they built the San Agustin church. We went to church when there was a priest and that was at the Church of San Cosmo del Tucson at the foot of the Sentinel Peak.

Oh, yes, they got drunk on tiswin when they drank too much.

There was another game we used to have at the fiesta. It was called piñata. There was a decorated olla, a jar. A person carrying a pole was blindfolded and would be turned around to lose his direction and then let loose to find the olla. Where he supposed it to be he would knock the olla by pushing the pole up.

Mormon Family
*(St. John's Family History Files)*

**Amy McDonald**
Interviewer: Helen M. Smith
Cochise County

My husband freighted from Globe to Willcox, and was away from home a good part of the time. At first we lived in the covered wagon, cooked on an open campfire, and raised what corn and vegetables we could. Another child was born to me there, and the children and I did what we could to raise green food while Mr. McDonald was away.

One day I was making bread. I had cooked one "batch" in the Dutch oven over a campfire. The wind was blowing strongly and I had been having a little trouble to keep my fire. I took out the cooked bread and stooped to place another batch in the oven. A strong guest of wind struck just then, scattering the fire until not so much as a coal remained, and filling the oven with sand, right on top of my nice dough. The children dove under the wagon as the sand hit. I stood there and the air was blue around me as I expressed my opinion of the place, the climate, the wind, and particularly of any and all people who would live in such a place. I have never used such strong language before or since.

About that time a stronger gust of wind struck me. I was carried twenty-five or thirty yards by its force. I had absolutely nothing more to say!

Sandstorms were certainly a trial in those days. We built a shack, half house, half dugout. The house came just enough above the ground to allow for a small window in one end. In the other we had a strong plank door. After a sandstorm coming from the direction of the door, we found that we could not get out. The shack was literally buried in sand. My husband was forced to tear out the window at the other end and dig out from that side, after which he shoveled the sand away from the door so that it could again be opened.

For awhile we lived in a tent. In this, too, the wind was a great bother. Anything anywhere near the sides of the tent would be knocked over when the wind came up. Ploughing or outside work was made difficult and uncomfortable by the sand. It was so sharp that it literally cut one's face and hands; and it seemed that sandstorms always came up when work outside was a necessity.

People in that locality lived on what they raised, mostly. Wheat, corn, vegetables, hogs, and milk cows supplied the absolute necessities in most cases. Cloth was freighted in, but money was so scarce that few could buy any quantity. Most of the cloth was hand woven. People had few clothes, and practically none except what was absolutely required.

There was no recreation or pastime worthy of the name. My only pastime was an occasional visit with a neighbor, my knitting needles busy while I talked. I was fifty-one years old when I saw my first picture show.

Every fall I made a barrel of lye, which was afterward used for soap-making, hominy, etc. Mesquite or oak wood was the only thing we could use to produce an ash good for lye; and these woods were often hard to secure. I had an ash hopper, a hollow log above which was two posts with a plank across them, the plank supporting two others which slanted into the log. We dripped the water slowly down these slanting logs and over the ashes in the hopper to make the lye.

Our light was a small, twisted piece of cloth stuck into a tin plate of tallow. A small bowl with a spout in one end to support the "wick" was hailed as a great invention, and was a prized possession among the women. The advent of coal oil lamps (and stoves) was another matter. No one in our neighborhood would consider using either, believing that they were dangerous and likely to blow up, and an "invention of the devil." My first coal oil lamp was a small brass affair with a round wick and no chimney.

We moved to the Chiricahuas above the Sulphur Spring Valley sometime in the early '90s. We lived in a little canyon called Rock Creek. My husband cut and hauled wood to the mining camps. We lived there when the railroad through the valley was surveyed; when the town of Douglas was laid out. We never bothered with Douglas-we considered it too small a town to be a possible market for our wood.

My brother-in-law Mr. Hazelwood came to live with us in the late "90s. He hauled wood also, and met his fate at that occupation. He was accustomed to piling two cords of wood on the wagon bed, above which he placed his seat. This made him ride high in the air with almost no way or securing himself in his seat. One of the wagon wheels struck a stump in the road, tilting the wagon to a considerable angle. Mr. Hazelwood tried to retain his balance as he was thrown violently out of his seat. He succeeded only in falling between the wagon and the mules, and one of the mules gave him such a severe kick in the head that he never recovered. He had a wife and two children in New Mexico, and it was six months before we could get word to them about the accident.

While we lived in the Chiricahuas an epidemic struck the locality. I imagine it was something on the order of influenza, but no one then knew much about it except that it seemed quite virulent in its attacks. We moved temporarily to place near the New Mexico line called "Devil's Sink Hole" to escape the contagion.

## Mary Ann Smith McNeil

Interviewer: Roberta Flake Clayton
Navajo County

"I was very sad because I had to leave my beloved parents and relatives to come to a country that was unsettled, without a home or friends and where the Redman roamed at will.

Sometime in December 1879 we arrived at what was then called Walker, now Taylor, three miles above Snowflake. We stayed a week with James Pearce then went to a place on Silver Creek known as Solomon's Ranch.

Here Mr. McNeil built a fireplace and chimney of rock near the side of a hill and then stretched a tent over it. Here we lived until March of the next year.

Mr. Standifird had previously moved to Arizona and lived about a quarter of a mile south of us. We had to go to his place to grind corn for bread on his coffee mill as we had none of our own.

My husband was a shoemaker and would take his tools and go to Snowflake and Taylor and repair shoes, taking anything we could use in exchange. The people there were little better off than ourselves.

One night we had only enough food in the house for one meal so I coaxed the children to leave it for breakfast, so that night we went to bed without supper. In the night John came home with a little corn that he had traded dried apples for.

We were entirely without soap at one time and no grease to make any. We didn't know what to do, but a fat coyote had been pestering round so John set a trap for it. With the tallow I got out of the coyote and lye made of corn cobs I made some soap. It did not harden like soap made from beef tallow, but it was better than none."

One of Mrs. McNeil's neighbors tells how neatly she always dressed her children. The little girls dresses always had to be laundered just so and "boughten starch" was out of the questions. The McNeils didn't have flour for bread but Mrs. McNeil would take a bowl of corn meal to a neighbor and trade it for flour to make starch for their dresses and aprons.

"That winter we lost our best horse. He starved to death. There was no feed on the range and we had no money to buy feed. Then in the spring we moved over to a place called Forest Dale on the Indian Reservation.

We lived with the Indians all summer. We bought some corn at five cents a pound. We had to shuck, shell, and grind it on a hand mill. We thought that was an awful high price for musty, mildewed corn. The smell of it made me so sick while it was baking; sometimes I wondered how I lived through the summer. All we had to eat was that musty corn bread and molasses with a little milk. All the clothes my boys had to wear was just a shirt, no pants, and the girls a little slip.

After the musty corn was gone all we had to eat was what we had raised in the garden, and that was mostly green corn. Yes! It was green corn for breakfast, corn for dinner and corn for supper with a little Dutch cheese (like cottage cheese) for a change. When the cheese got hard enough to grate, John made me a grater out of a tin pan. So we all had a grating good time to keep ourselves in bread and mush.

The winter of 1880 we moved from Forest Dale to Show Low. There another baby was born to me. It took John nearly all winter to have his corn out of Forest Dale, but that was what we depended on for bread, so we had to have it hauled out.

Many times I got so hungry for flour bread that I felt like I would give all I owned for a cup of tea and a piece of flour bread.

One day my son Dan and I hitched up our ox team and drove out to Robert Scott's sheep camp to get some supplies from a little supply store he kept for his sheep men. Mr. Scott fixed us some dinner consisting of hot biscuits, fried mutton and tea. Just what I had been longing for. It was a feast I never will forget.

After we moved to Show Low Geronimo and his followers gave the people another scare. The people got together in a fort so they could fight if they had to. John wasn't afraid so wouldn't go into the fort. So we moved down to the Lone Pine Crossing.

Old Father Reidhead and two or three more families lived there. We stayed there all winter. We were hungry most of the time as food was scarce. One day John caught a beaver in the creek and we ate that and enjoyed it."

## Emma Perry Merrill

Interviewer: Roberta Flake Clayton
Navajo County

The Merrills left their home early in March and arrived at St. David, on the San Pedro River in Cochise County, June 17, 1881.

They started out with a large band of horses and a hired man to drive them but had to leave him and the horses until later.

Their first home in Arizona was a dug out with poles stuck in the front, a window of white cloth, and a strip of homemade carpet for a door. The floor was a puncheon one, and was scrubbed to such a whiteness, with a mat made of grasses and sewed together, "that you could eat off of it."

As soon as they were settled Mr. Merrill had to go back after the horses. He was gone for three months, and during that time neither heard from the other. That was a long, lonesome time for Emma, away from her people in a new land and living under such conditions. She was too proud to let anyone see her tears, but when at night she was shut in her lowly home and then no one ever knew how many nights she cried herself to sleep.

Wagon train in St. John's
*(Mike Marriott)*

After seven years spent in St. David, the Merrills moved to Safford and then to Thatcher where they build a good home. The supreme test, however, came to this brave little woman on July 26, 1896, when her husband was taken from her.

She was left with ten children, nine boys and a girl, and the youngest a baby three month old. As soon as the shock of her bereavement was over Emma realized, as never before, the blessedness of work. Their precious family had to be provided for, and now it was her responsibility alone.

The trustees of the school came to her and offered her the school. At first she demurred as she thought her methods might be old fashioned, but possibly because of the efficient manner in which she manager her own family, they insisted that she take it. She did and taught for four years.

As soon as her own children were old enough she gave them little duties to perform and they worked together so that their mother, and the ones who were old enough, could be sat school on time. Her daughter stayed at home to take care of the smaller children. She carried the baby to his mother at recesses to get his dinner, and then he would have to be satisfied until she returned at night and noon.

The daughter's education was not neglected. She was given her assignments and at night when the babies were all tucked in, mother and daughter would go over the lessons together before they planned the next day's duties.

Soon Emma learned that the small wages then paid to teachers was not sufficient to meet the demands of the fast growing children, so she learned the dress making trade. She took in sewing for ten years. Then her nimble fingers made and trimmed the hats worn by the discriminating.

When her husband died there was a mortgage on all of their belongings. Emma through her industry and thrift managed to pay it off as well as keeping her family. She says they were never hungry, cold or ragged, and were taught to wear their patches with pride. The home was ruled by kindness.

The boys were easily controlled; she could sit and talk to them and they would do anything she asked. She never had to strike one of her children in their lives.

Santa Claus always visited the children when they were small. This was taken care of by a wealthy aunt who each year sent a crisp ten dollar bill to good old Saint Nick, with instruction that it was to bring all the joy that that amount could buy. It was not hard for this family to believe in old Santa because he never failed to bring just the things that they wanted.

One night when the troubles and cares of the day had been most trying and her loneliness for her beloved husband so great she felt she could not go on, she dreamed of him; a good comforting visit in which he told her that she only had to live one day at a time, and that no matter how hard life was to remember that he would always be near her. For days she almost felt his presence, and has never again felt that utter loneliness.

**Annie Moore**
Interviewer: Helen M. Smith
Cochise County

Our arrival at Tombstone was quite embarrassing to me since the whole town turned out to meet the stage. My folks met me there and we drove out to Rucker. It was a desolate looking country, being the year of the big drought. Cattle were lying everywhere, dead and dying. We used to carry water in our Stetsons to cattle which were down, but it was no use. They seemed to have no heart to try to live, and wouldn't drink or eat when it was offered.

Living conditions were good enough for that time. Everyone had good stoves, although some of the men cooks still liked to cook in their Dutch ovens. I remember the deep apple pies, made from dried apples, and the biscuits one of our cooks used to make in the Dutch oven. I have never tasted so good since. There were only three permanent wells anywhere around us and water was a real problem. We used to have to haul water, and when the men started out away from the place to work they were invariably told "If you want anything to eat when you get back better haul up some water."

We got our mail and our provisions about every six months in Tombstone. Later we got to going to Willcox, which was a center for cattlemen. Still later Pearce opened up and we felt almost cosmopolitan.

The only amusement we had was dancing. We used to ride to Willcox in a big wagon with a high, backless seat. It was forty seven miles and took all day. Our faces would be pretty well baked after a whole day in the hot sun. We would go to some hospitable home and steam our faces in hot water, apply witch hazel, don our best attire, and dance all night. The music was a fiddle; the one tune was a waltz to which we danced over and over. There were no wallflowers among the girls and women, there being too few for the men anyhow. We all danced every set. At daylight the dance would break up, we would go to some house for coffee and breakfast, and then home. On the way back we would tie the reins to the seat, lie down in the bottom of the wagon, and let the horses bring us home. One of these dances was a great event in our lives and we all enjoyed ourselves thoroughly.

I had a friend, a Miss Delaney, who took up a homestead a few miles up from our place. She was quite a self reliant woman, who cut her own posts, dug her post holes, and built her fence. She used to wear a pair of very full bloomers in which to work. This was rather unusual for that time. Women usually dressed quite modestly, even to the full riding habits. We even rode side saddles. Once when I was staying a few days with Miss Delaney as a witness for her to prove up, the government man came out. He was horseback, and it was still quite early in the morning. At the sound of hoofs, Miss Delaney went outside to see who was coming. The government man was riding up at an easy lope, but when he saw her standing in the door in those enormous bloomers he took one startled look and then turned and fled. It struck me so funny that I laughed for half an hour afterward. I told her he would probably come back and that she should put on a dress. She said she had no dresses there and he would just have to talk to her as she was. After awhile he did return, riding cautiously this time, and looking the shack over carefully as he came. I went outside and stood by the door. He said nothing about the costume, but he eyed it askance several times while he was talking to her. Everything was all right in spite of it and the business was soon finished.

I had the first post office near here. The mail was hauled from Pearce three times a week. It arrived about noon, and so did the neighbors for their mail. Every mail day I had about twenty five people for dinner, this for about seven years. I kept trying to find someone else who would handle the mail, but with no success. Finally I simply sent the key to Washington and quit handling it.

## Eleanor C. Roberts Morris

Interviewer: Roberta Flake Clayton
Contributed by their Daughter Dora Morris Pomeroy

In March 1862, as the Southern Utah section was needing Pioneers the old spirit of pushing into new lands became uppermost and the little family journeyed south and after some time located at Springdale, a small town on the Virgin River. It was here on February 14, 1863 that their son Hyrum B. Jr. was born.

The family soon moved a few miles farther down the river to a better location at Rockville and bought a home and planted out a large fruit orchard. They also owned a tract of land up the river, in Zion's Canyon, where the Lodge now stands in Zion's National Park.

May 14, 1866, a baby daughter, Eleanor R. was born, and when only ten days old the settlers all were ordered to move at once to Grafton for protection. The husband being away after renegade Indians, Eleanor hired a man to move her few things and she and her three little ones to this place.

He came with jut the running gears of the wagon on which he placed three boards and she had to sit on this and hold the little ones on while they made the trip in one of those red dust or sand storms so common there.

They moved into a three room house with three other families. Having to live on dirt floors both she and the baby contracted colds that came near being the death of both.

Aunt Annie Millet, a very eccentric old lady, lived in one of the rooms, and little Hyrum had watched her dyeing yarn. One day when her back was turned he put her two white kittens in the dye pot and when she lifted them out they were a beautiful blue.

Once during these perilous times, when Eleanor and her little ones, with her sister-in-law and her little children were living together, as Hyrum was away, their flour got so low that they thought every meal would be the last. They prayed for the Lord to keep them through till their men folks came home, and for ten days that flour never lessened, but the very day the men came home the flour gave out. They had to live on cane seed bread for two weeks until flour could be brought from Beaver. Fruit drying and hauling it north was the main source of revenue.

Some time later, peace being restored, everyone moved home again and in April 10, 1870, Eliza R. was born, and exactly three years later, at the same time of day, the last baby, Sophia Isadora was born.

Now that all was peace and quiet, Hyrum longed for more new country to conquer. In company with George Staples and Frank Rappleye they made a trip to Mesa, Arizona in the spring of 1882 and liked the country so well that they each purchased a 40 acre farm. Returning to Utah as soon as possible Hyrum sold his lands and all properties. January 27, 1883, he started with his family to return to Arizona.

They arrived in Mesa, March 3, 1883, and put up tents for a few days until they could look around. The second day one of those "sea breeze or zephyrs" came up and lowered every tent in camp. Quite an introduction to the place.

Hyrum bought a lot with a one room adobe house on it in the western part of town where they lived and worked the farm. He also hauled produce to the mining camps. This first summer was truly a nightmare as one of the young men who came with them took sick, and in spite of all they could be done, soon died.

Then came the smallpox siege, which was so terrible, taking half of many a family. The town was quarantined in and it was pretty hard living, but Hyrum stayed at the ranch and raised the crop and ran a molasses mill. Eleanor cared for the home and the family. None of their family were stricken.

The land was unusually fertile and many of the melons raised this year weighed fifty pounds each. Hyrum was a great one for an orchard and soon had a fine one growing. Being a Kentuckian he always had a number of fine breed horses on the place and made pets of all of them.

Times were very hard and there being only two girls left in the family they had to help their father on the farm and became adept in all kinds of work. Dora especially who was very hardy went to the field with her father, pitching hay, handling the team, milking cows or chopping wood, as the need was.

Old Bisbee
*(AHS #660)*

## Charlotte Ann Tanner Nelson

Interviewer: Roberta Flake Clayton
Navajo County

For six months they lived at Lee's Ferry on the Big Colorado. In speaking of some of the experiences through which she passed in those early days, Mrs. Nelson say, "I have lived for months where my only neighbors were Indians and my one music the howl of the coyote. We ground our wheat in a coffee mill. Our only food was beans, venison and cow's milk. I tanned our deer skins and from them made shoes. Gleaned wheat from which I saved the straw and braided hats. I colored the straw with orange, brown, and black dyes, taken from the cypress and lye, the brown from sumac, and the black from oak bark."

One of her homes was made with poles stuck upright in the ground, the cracks "chinked" with mud and then Mrs. Nelson declares she whitewashed the inside with a paste made of buttermilk and ashes of cottonwood and oak.

Mrs. Nelson studied nursing, obtaining all the medical knowledge she could and went out as a nurse bringing, according to her count, 1,234 babies into the world, never losing a mother or a child. She took care of cases in a radius of forty miles from her home near Springerville, sometimes having as high as nine patients at once. She never had a doctor in attendance. At one time a Mexican woman gave birth to triplets, and all the help Mrs. Nelson had was a ten year old Mexican boy. She remembers one trip over the mountain from Eager to Alpine when the snow was so deep she had to keep shoveling it out of the front of the buggy she was riding in.

## Ethelinda Murray Osborne

Interviewer: Roberta Flake Clayton
Phoenix

In the month of May 1870 her Father brought his family west en route to California. They were driving oxen and had a large herd of loose cattle. The trip was hard on the stock because of scarcity of grass and water.

Whenever both of these necessities were found in the same locality many days or even weeks were spent there until the supply was exhausted. Hence, it was December before the company reached Maricopa.

Mr. Murray heard of the possibilities of the valley of the Salt River. Leaving his outfit there he came on. He was so delighted with what he found that he let the company go on to California without him.

Ethelinda's father did not live long to enjoy his new home. The following May he passed away leaving his smaller children in the care of a married daughter and older members of the family.

When the Murrays arrived there was only one little store, and only a few houses. The valley was covered with large mesquite trees and Palo Verde. This had to be cleared off and the ground leveled off for farming. Raiding Apache bands robbed the family of most of all their cattle. Land could be preempted and farmed. The Murray boys were hard workers and it was not long before they began to prosper.

The distance from saw mills prevented the use of lumber in the homes. The houses were built of adobe, the roof of ocotillo and palm stems covered with grass, than a layer of dirt, which made them passable cool in summer.

The floors were also dirt. They were patted down until they were almost as hard as the cement floors now so fashionable.

Everything that could not be produced here had to be freighted in from California. Screens for the windows and doors were unknown. The flies were terrible as were the centipedes, scorpions, and tarantulas.

The school was a little one room building where all the pupils sat on split log benches with peg legs to hold them up. There was a long recitation bench where at the top of the little desk bell the next class was seated. If it were reading, then each one opened the book and in rotation read the lesson verse by verse. Sometimes the teacher played a trick by skipping around. That was unfair advantage because it did not give you a chance to figure out which would be your paragraph and study it while the ones ahead of you read theirs aloud.

If the lesson was grammar or arithmetic, then there was the black board where you might be called upon at any time to get up and diagram a sentence, or work an example in long division.

Then, there were the spelling lessons where you had to go down one every time you missed a word until finally you found yourself at the foot of the class. Or, if you were a good speller you might work yourself up to the head. You could only stay there three nights in succession, then you would have to go to the foot. How you studied to get to the top again. The spelling bees were looked forward to with pleasure by the good scholars as it gave them a chance to show off.

Friday afternoons were red letter occasions because then there were songs, recitations and sometimes even playlets of farce."

**Lucy Bedford Phillips**
Interviewer: Kathlyn M. Lathrop
Duncan

Ollie Phillips and me grew up together and went to school together. I think we were always sweethearts. If he ever went with any other girl I never heard about it. We didn't start going together though until we were considered grown up. My parents never believed in child marriage.

I was twenty and Ollie was twenty-one when we were married. We had a simple home wedding with all our friends and relatives present. My brother and his wife "stood up" with us—we didn't have bridesmaids and matrons of honor and best men in my time.

We didn't have much to start on. Father gave me my own saddle horse and a milk cow. I had my own quilts and sheets and things, a whole hope chest full of everything like that that one would need to keep house on. Ollie had his own saddle horse and his father gave him a team of work mules.

Nobody made any money working for wages those days. Wages were not over seventy five cents a day, but everything was much cheaper in the stores then too. We paid five cents a yard for good calico, got five cents a dozen for eggs, ten cents a pound for butter, but boots and shoes were high as a cat's back. Twenty to twenty-five dollars for a pair of men's boots, they'd last a year or maybe several years, and ten dollars and up for women's shoes.

A few months after our marriage we were living in the country and had gone to Llanotown to spend Sunday with my parents. It was the day of the big races between Blevins Thunderbold and Major, two very fast horses. All the men folk had gone to the races. We women could watch them from Mother's front yard.

We were sitting there in the shade talking about the race. They were over and people were leaving. Suddenly we heard shooting and seen people scrambling in every direction. Then all at once a young man jumped our fence and fell right at my feet, or maybe fell over the fence.

I was so scared I couldn't speak. I had never seen the man before in my life. Then just as suddenly he jumped up. Bolted the fence and ran out of sight leaving a pool of blood where he had fallen and a trail of blood behind him.

It was the Williamson-Pearl feud broke out over the races. I reckon that was it. The young man, I learned, was Joe Boyd. They found him dead a full mile from where he had been shot, just over the heart.

Pa (my Ollie) and Father came running home and made us all get in the house and shut the doors. They didn't want any of us to get hurt by flying bullets, and they didn't want to get mixed up in that feud either.

Most everybody in town was fighting before it stopped, people running, horses racing in the streets, and bullets flying in every direction. I think there were fourteen people altogether killed and wounded in that foolish feud battle.

A notorious Madam of a rooming house, called Madam Kate something or other, shot from an upper window and killed two men. I don't recall just who it was she killed, but I think she was fighting on the Pearl side.

After that Jink Williamson, who was being held in an old building used for a jail, was supposed to have burned to death when the building burned down. But it wasn't Jink Williamson, known here as Jim, he dropped dead while out tending a trap line a mile or so from town. He is buried in the Duncan cemetery. He was an old white headed man when he died.

Pa (my Ollie) was always a sort of a dreamer, you might say. He was a natural born prospector too. I've always had a notion that he would find a gold mine that would make him a millionaire someday.

The first pay dirt he ever struck was on a claim over in Gillespie County, Texas. That was really the gold mine that he had been dreaming about all his life, but he didn't realize it when it came, poor dear Pa.

He gave his brother Buff, and a friend Sid Howard, each a third interest in that claim. When they had an offer to sell, why they just sold for a song and sang it themselves. They got just $700. Since then, that same mine had produced several millions of dollars in gold. Just think of it. His dream and it sold for $700.

Pa took his part of the money and bought a new team and wagon. Then, we started out to Arizona, where Pa was so sure he'd find gold that he could shovel up with a spade.

We had two wagons and teams, and there were two families of us, and Sid Howard came along too. We brought three saddle horses. That's all the stock we had then. We brought no chickens, pigs, or milk cows. There never was a prospector who cared to fool with such things much.

We crossed the Staked Plains, but we didn't suffer for water, we brought water in barrels to last from one water hole to another. We were about three or four months on the road. Pa never was in a hurry to get any place. We camped along and rested the teams, and the men scouted around for gold mines that were not there.

No, we did not find any gold in piles when we got there, but Pa did find several mines that would have made him rich if—well there's always an 'if' to everything Pa had anything to do with.

Dear generous hearted Pa. He never could enjoy anything without every one he knew enjoying it with him. Every claim he ever did locate he gave away shares in it to everybody who wanted one.

He located the first claim at the Ash Peak mines here, and some claims over in Apache Box Canyon. Either claim would have made him a fortune, 'if'—well, it didn't matter, we never went cold or hungry.

When Pa first struck 'pay dirt' at Ash Peak people flocked in here from everywhere and located claims. It was something similar to the California Gold Rush, only not quite so many people as that, and not so much gold.

Pa was offered $75,000 for his claim, but he remembered what he had lost on his claims in Texas, or I guess it was me who remember it most. He refused and to his sorrow. Which proves that a man should never, NEVER, listen to his wife's advice about business.

Someone who happened to know more about Arizona mining laws than Pa did jumped his claim and he didn't get a single dollar out of it. Another fortune blowed up.

Then Pa and Mr. Packer located a silver claim in the Ash Peak district. They sold that to B.B. Adams for $10,000 on time payments which was never collected. The property changed hands so fast and so often that Pa forgot just who owed him the money.

The Apache Box property produced plenty high grade ore and they got a fair price for it, but it was so far from the shipping point, and so many people had shares, shares that Pa had given them, that when the profits were divided there wasn't much for anybody. Pa never was cut out for a millionaire.

I don't know if anybody in the world is more superstitious than a miner. When Pa's claims at Ash Peak were stolen, deliberately taken from him, they claim it hung a siwash on the mine. Maybe it did at that.

The mine had been running about two years, I reckon, it was located in 1897 I think, when the first sign of this siwash showed up.

Joe and Will Phillips, Pa's nephews, were working in the mine. Will was shift boss and Joe was powder monkey. Joe was due to come home for his regular two weeks rest. My two sons, just lads, Ernest and Ralph, and Hugh Phillips, a brother to Joe and Will, went to the mine to bring Joe home. They were within about a half a mile from the mine when the explosion took place.

The hoist was an old fashioned affair run by a man and a horse. The boys heard the boom, and seen smoke, earth and rocks shoot into the air. They seen the horse, hoist horse, sail into the air, and the hoist man done likewise. The horse went up and came down, laid there a minute or two then jumped up running like the furies were after him, he wasn't hurt much.

The hoist man was just a mass of human flesh, smashed to a pulp, when they found him. Will Phillips and eight or nine more men were trapped in the mine. Joe Phillips and another powder man were blown to such tiny bits that what was found of them was buried in a cigar box.

The powder magazine was underground, to be handy I reckon. Joe and the other man had gone in there to get some powder for blasting. No one will ever know just what happened to cause the explosion.

My son Ernest was sent into Duncan to give the alarm, but he was scared so bad when he got here that no one could get heads or tails of what had really happened. His eyes were as wild as a maniac and he kept waving his arms and moaning "The mine's blowed up! The mine's blowed up! Everybody out there is killed. Joe's killed! Will's killed! Oh my God!"

The poor boy was almost insane for months afterward, even to his dying day he couldn't bear to even talk about it.

The trapped men were rescued in about three days. They were a sorry sight to see. Will staggered out with his clothes hanging in rags and his shoes torn off his feet, his hat brim was around his neck. He looked like a mad man. The others didn't look any better, and they were almost starved to death.

The mine closed down then and stayed closed for several years. It has reopened under new ownership several times since but something always seems to happen to close it down. Maybe it's the siwash after all.

The ore is there, vast fortunes of it, but there have been fortunes spent there too trying to make more fortunes. I think the only real profits that have been realized from that mine had been made since it reopened in 1936. They have lost several men in one way or another, and had one rather serious cave-in that trapped five men for forty eight hours or more. It is practically closed now. Looks like the siwash is busy again.

I have raised two sons and one daughter. My dear boy Ernest died in 1908, and my precious son Ralph went to the World War and came home to us gassed so bad that he never recovered, but, thank God he died on his own soil. He dropped dead on the streets of Duncan, 1926.

Old Tombstone
*(AHS #99938)*

## Mary Willis Richards

Interviewer: Roberta Flake Clayton
Snowflake

First thing in the morning she helped milk the cows, then out came the spinning wheel. Four skeins of yarn was Mary's task each day but Sunday, week in and week out. She did this in order that her Mother would have plenty for weaving the cloth that was made into clothes for the family.

She married Joseph, a man nine years older, in Salt Lake City and returned to Mendon where they made their first home. Three fine boys were born here.

One day, like lightening from a clear sky, came the call for the little family to leave their happy home, their kindred and friends and go out into the wilds of Arizona to help colonize.

On April 20, 1876 they arrived at the settlements on the Little Colorado River. The first companies having arrived the March before. Such a barren desert-looking country they found. Not a tree for miles except an occasional cottonwood on the river.

There were four colonies or camps as they were called; Lot Smith's, Ballinger's Lakes and Allen's camps. They were called after the man that presided over each. Later these places were named Sunset, Brigham City, Obed, and Saint Joseph.

The Richards family lived first at Lake's Camp or Obed. Immediately after arriving they went into United Order. Mary and her husband were very well fitted with provisions, cows, chickens, etc., and had they not turned all they possessed into the Order, would have been very well fixed for pioneers.

The women took turns cooking and washing dishes. Then there were washings to get done in wooden tubs on homemade washboards with soap they had made with lye from cottonwood ashes. There were later great quantities of molasses to be made as bread and molasses was their diet.

At first they all lived in tents and wagon boxes with a large bowery where they met to hold religious services, and where they spread the long tables at which they all ate together.

In this camp there were sixty men and twenty women besides the children.

Soon they began building homes of rock which was near and plentiful. Mary had the joy and honor of living in one of the very first houses with a roof. Nearly all the houses in early days had dirt roofs, but not this one. Philip Gordon, a member of the colony who emigrated from Italy, understood the art of 'flag roofing', fitting large flat stones together as they would shed the rain. This was the kind of roof that sheltered the Richards family. Mary tells us that it was far superior to dirt as the mud did not run through and it did not leak no matter how long it rained.

In those early days when there were no doctors or nurses to welcome the stork that made frequent visits in pioneer home, some dear kind hearted woman with a love for humanity and a little knowledge of the human body had to qualify in each community as a midwife. Mary began at the age of 26 and for fifty-two years served in that capacity assisting and bringing hundreds of babies into the world.

When the fourth baby was expected, their house was not finished and the tent house was soaking wet because it had been raining almost constantly for two weeks. The men folk worked all night to get the roof on. Then they took the wet tent and hung it between her bed and the unplastered walls.

The baby arrived at dawn the next morning. She sent for two neighbor women; one a girl just married and the other the mother of one baby. She told them what to do and they did it. Thus was born her first daughter, and first Arizona baby.

There were many swamps near Obed, and when summer came almost the entire colony were stricken with malaria. It became so serious that the camp had to finally be abandoned.

Some of the people went to the other camps while others went to the southern part of the Territory where there were two Mormon settlements. The Richards family moved across the river to Allen's Camp. Here the fort was almost finished. The school house was competed and was used for all the public gatherings. Every evening all who were able gathered in this large room for the singing of a hymn and a prayer, after which the men planned their work and the women visited. It was a real social center.

While Mary was nursing in this wilderness country, her husband was taking the place of Doctor and Dentist, setting all broken bones and pulling all aching teeth.

In 1891 Mary's husband was called on a mission to England. He left his wife and nine children and gladly answered his call. He sailed on the S.S. Abyssinia. When about half way across the ocean, the ship, which was partly loaded with cotton, took fire. The passengers became panic stricken, but Elder Richards was calm and unafraid.

There was no wireless in those days, but just as it began to look very serious and hopeless, they sighted a German ship. They fired their signals of distress and the German ship hastened to their rescue and every passenger was taken aboard it. Before they were out of sight the Abyssinia sank.

Elder Richards's luggage was all burned and now must be replaced. He jokingly wrote his wife that they all went on a spree, meaning the German boat was named the Spree.

When he had been gone more than two years their fifteen-year old daughter May became seriously ill with typhoid fever. For three weeks the mother watched over her day and night, then she passed away. It took a month for her husband to receive word of their daughter's death.

## Ramona Rubio Richards

Interviewer: Romelia Gomez
Cochise County

Senora Richards, whose family name is Rubio, came to Bisbee in 1906 from Hermosillo, Sonora, at the age of 19. In Sonora Mr. Rubio operated a little grocery shop, which he closed up after deciding to bring his family to Bisbee. The Rubio family consisted of the Father, already well advanced in age, five daughters, and one son. Mrs. Rubio died in Mexico when Ramona was a small child.

On arriving in Bisbee Ramona immediately got a job as a seamstress in a dressmaking shop on Main Street. The owner was a Mr. Keans and his wife. Here she worked with five other girls, one a Mexican, besides herself. They all had plenty of work to do, cutting, sewing and pressing all day long, for there were many orders to be filled.

Their wages were $2.00 a day and they worked every day in the weeks but Sunday. Ramona liked her job very much, but it lasted only a year, after which the owner closed up the shop and moved to Mexico.

Her next job was working as a clerk in a little grocery shop on Naco Road. After that ended she worked as a domestic wherever she could find jobs open, also doing some sewing at home when people brought it to her home.

The Rubio family first lived in a rented house on Naco Road. When this house was sold they were obliged to move and went to live at Chihuahua Hill, living on this hill for many years in different houses.

Daily Life
*(Contentment 1896 Legends of America)*

The girls loved to dance and attended many dances at the K.P. Hall and at the Opera House on Opera Drive. There dances were attended by people of different nationalities and everyone had a gay time. The music was provided by different small orchestras, of which there were as few in Bisbee.

Being of Catholic faith, the Rubios attended church regularly at a little church located conveniently near their house on Chihuahua Hill. The priest from the Sacred Heart Church officiated here also and all the families on Chihuahua Hill and from Lowell went to this little church.

Besides going to dances and to church, Ramona and her sisters enjoyed taking long walks on Sundays up Zacatecas Canyon, which had only a few houses and was very picturesque. Although they had to pass the Brewery Gulch with its many saloons and drunkards to get to Zacatecas they didn't mind it as they were never molested in passing.

In 1910 Ramona married Mr. Richards, an American miner. He worked in the different mines of Bisbee earning $5.00 or $6.00 a day.

**Clara Mari Gleason Rogers**
Interviewer: Roberta Flake Clayton
Phoenix

In spite of hardships they arrived at their destination, Sunset Crossing (across the river from where Winslow now stands) with cattle, sheep, horses, seeds, etc., and lived in the wagons until the first crop was in and water on the land.

The order of Enoch was established, with Lot Smith in charge. The buildings were arranged and built on a cooperative plan. A large building in the center served both as a dining room and as a chapel. The kitchen adjacent was in charge of a man (the position in that day being too important for a mere women), but the women, three in number on a daily relay plan, did the work.

Food was sometimes scarce, but bread and sorghum molasses were staples. Because of this shortage, a rule was made that all food should be eaten from the plates. Any left would be reserved to those particular individuals at the next meal.

A cheese factory took care of the surplus milk, a tannery produced leather for buckskin clothes, shoes and harness. The latter not being very satisfactory however because the character of the tan permitted it to stretch. A saw mill cut sufficient lumber for all their needs.

The women were supplied with spinning wheels, a carding machine and loom, and made good substantial homespun. By filling in cotton warp with wool, a good linsey was made. As some were more efficient than others in spinning and weaving they exchanged work with those less fortunate.

In addition to this, all socks and stockings were knitted from the yarn. Nearly all could make their own candles when possession of form, these holding four, six, and twelve candles. They were made by first securely fastening the cotton wicking (which they bought ready-made) at the bottom of the form and filling the tin mold full of melted tallow, which when cool would easily slip out. Should the tallow stick to the mold, a little warm water poured over it would loosen them almost instantly. Kidney fat made the best candles. This distinction in light was very marked, when, as occasionally happened the candle supply ran out and they were compelled to use a “bitch” (a cotton rag string in a saucer of tallow.)

About this time Loce was assigned to the position of wood haul to the camp. He arose early and returned late with all he could haul. When the weather was extremely cold, the women waylaid him with axes and the wood sometimes literally failed to touch the ground.

In the summer they were transferred to the sheep range, and while engaged in that work on one occasion Mr. Rogers was impressed very strongly to move away from the place where they had made their camp. He paid little attention to the first urge to move, when a short time it was repeated it appealed to him with greater force. When it came a third time he was so impressed that although they had retired they got up and hurriedly packed their camping equipment and moved at once. Later they learned that their delightful camp had been a battleground between the Indians and U. S. soldiers, and an Indian had died in their newly built cabin.

Five or six years before this a Mexican employee had robbed his employers of about seven or eight thousand dollars in U.S. double eagles. A posse had formed and pursued him. He had hidden the gold, or lost it from his saddle, and when caught could not retrace his steps and find it, although he was hung until nearly dead to force a confession.

Mr. Roger’s sheep were on this range and while walking along the sheep trail one day he noticed a peculiar glitter on the oak leaves. On closer observation “the leaves” proved to be twenty dollar gold pieces. About ten feet away he saw one of the little mounds of rocks which had been made to make the ground as a guide to the searchers. That part of the country had been thoroughly searched. He tied the ends of his coat sleeves, filled them with gold and hurried after his sheep. Arriving at the camp he notified the owner that the gold had been found and that he might have it by calling for it. So, the baby played with the gold pieces on the bed and rejoiced at the musical clink as they jingled together.

The owners had given Mr. Rogers a handful of the coin which counted out to be two hundred dollars.

## Lousea Bee Harper Rogers

Interviewer: Roberta Flake Clayton
Phoenix

We arrived at Hackberry on the 24th of December, 1880, Christmas Eve and ate our Christmas dinner at this place. We had special dishes, molasses cake and homemade candy, cooked on the camp fire. We entered Phoenix on the first of January 1881 with skinny horses, the last end of provisions and some of us shoeless. I know I had on a pair of my Mother's old shoes and I would hide my feet if anyone came. My Father spent his last dollar and fifty cents for a sack of flour at the old Smith Mill between Tempe and Phoenix.

My father was persuaded to go to Lehi by Henry Clay Rogers, who was doing blacksmithing for C. T. Hayden at that time. He would come to our camp by the river, a short distance from where he was working, and tell us the most terrible stories about the varmints and reptiles. We could almost feel them crawling up to the light of the camp fire. We would jump once in a while thinking we had a scorpion or centipede crawling round our neck. But he was so jolly and friendly we fell for him right away. My father took his advice and traded for a forty acre tract covered with mesquite trees so thick and full of thorns we could hardly get through.

But, the best piece of land was in Lehi. We bought this piece of land from David P. Kimball who lived in nearer the town site. We were just one mile west from the center of Jonesville, now Lehi. Although we raised some of the most wonderful melons which weighted from ten to thirty pounds and our garden stuff couldn't be beat. We had to give credit to my Mother for she and the boys raised them while my father freighted.

Our stretch of land was right on the bank of the Salt River, a powerful river at flood time, and the Indian trail from their village to Tempe. This was terrifying to the white people who did not understand the ways of the Indians. At this time the Indians were drinking a mescal beverage, which they made from a plant in the mountains. Way into the night they would keep the trail hot with their whooping and yelling, it sounded to us like war whoops.

Many a time while left alone while my father was away freighting my Mother gathered us children into the bedroom, which was just a covered wagon, and prayed for the Lord to protect us and to bless us with a comfortable feeling that we might get our wanted sleep and rest.

At that time the storms were terrible. One time the lightning struck right before our eyes and close to the corral. It struck and busted a large mesquite tree all to pieces. Another time we were huddled together in our bedroom, my father had gone to Mesa on Old Pony, a riding horse we owned. The thunder and lightning was terrible, the rain poured down in sheets. My Mother had us children round her in our little nook asking the Lord for protection and to bring our father home safely. It seemed like the roar and crack of the thunder would cut the words right out of her mouth and our ears would fill up until we could hardly hear her.

In a little while the storm subsided and my father came riding in on little Old Pony and yelled, "Mother Lousea are you all safe? Thank God for that, for I was afraid you would be all washed into the river. Why, in the Mesa as I was coming long the water was up to Pony's knees and where did it all go to? It was terrific, the worse I have ever seen. Oh, I am so happy we are all together."

At this time our home consisted of a tent, two covered wagon boxes and a big shed that my father had built. We raised grain alfalfa, figs and had a nice vineyard besides our garden stuff.

My father got so he could spend more time at home while his brother did the freighting so he built a one room house of adobe, flat roof, and Mexican style.

How my Mother and I did fix that room up! We swiped some of Dad's boards and built us a cupboard and wardrobe and covered the dirt floor with straw, and a homemade carpet. It was driven down into the ground with pegs and how we enjoyed that room. We also had three weddings performed in that beautiful room, my own and my two sisters.

**Minnie Alice Wooley Rogers**
Interviewer: Roberta Flake Clayton
Navajo County

As there was a family of nine children each had to assist in providing for the family, and Minnie's girlhood was mostly spent in working for other people. When she was so small she had to stand on a chair while washing dishes, she would often go to help the neighbors. She didn't mind doing dishes, strange as that may seem. She would tend babies for busy mothers, who, because she was so dependable were never afraid to leave them alone with her.

For her services they would give her 5 or 10 cents. When she was 12 she did the work of a family consisting of a sick mother and eight children. For this service she received the sum of fifty cents a week.

She was never idle. Two summers were spent away from home drying fruit. In the evenings she would spin or knit. One of the diversions was for two or three of her girl friends to being their spinning wheels over and have a contest to see which could spin their amount of yarn first. The last one through had to make the molasses candy for the others.

Her Mother always joined in the fun, while her father would parch corn for the girls while they worked. This was only 'field corn' but seasoned up with butter and a little salt the girls thought it was very good.

On November 6, 1879, when she was seventeen years of age she married Davis Rogers. In company with the family of her husband's father, Samuel H. Rogers, and two other families, the

Wests and Wardells, they left for Arizona to join the pioneers who had gone previously to make a home in that desolate waste inhabited by Indians and outlaws.

Two of the brothers of Davis, Smith D. and Amos, had come to Snowflake in the fall of 1878 and had built a one room log house on the hill south of town. Into this room this family of about 15 people moved. The wagon boxes, with their bows and covers, served as sleeping quarters for the families, and were the only privacy afforded.

Arizona was famous for its terrific sand storms in those early days. After one of these blows, which usually lasted through days and nights, had overturned one of these covered wagons the boxes were removed from the running gears and placed on logs or stones on the ground where the wind could not have such force.

After the wagon that had been blown over was righted it was discovered that many articles of apparel had been carried away by the wind; among them hats belonging to Minnie and one of the other girls. Minnie's was never recovered. Sarah found hers at the mouth of the canyon over a mile away.

## Virginia Smith Scheerer

Interviewer: Helen M. Smith
Cochise County

Our home in Turkey Creek had been the Chenoweth's. Father still used the house as it was when they had lived there. It was a two-roomed log house with a fireplace, the first fireplace I had seen. The windows were simply holes in the wall with a window made of wood which swung inward and was held in place at night with a heavy bar. This was for protection against Indians and wild animals.

There was no stove, but fireplace cooking was nothing new to Mother. She made the finest kind of bread in Dutch ovens. The fame of her cooking soon spread over the country. She had brought dried yeast cakes with her, and no doubt the scarcity of yeast bread at that time was one thing which made it so appetizing.

She cooked one of the best steaks I have ever tasted. She first seared them on a spider over hot coals, then placed them in a Dutch over where they were cooked so tender as to almost melt in one's mouth. Another item of food was her pies, also Dutch oven cooked.

Mother had the true pioneer spirit, for she immediately set about to make a home in the wilderness. She planted trees, garden, flowers. She had bees brought to her at the earliest opportunity. She had a special place in her heart for cucumbers, of which she made a brine pickle which simply couldn't be beaten. People came for miles for a slice of her yeast bread and a cucumber pickle.

She ordered a stove in November, the next time any of the folks went to Tombstone. It reached Tombstone sometime in April.

Soon after my arrival I met Jacob Scheerer, whom I afterward married. He had come to Tombstone in 1860 from California, where he had been working at a saw mill. In Tombstone he bought three ox teams and everything necessary for freighting. Soon he was hauling logs, etc, from the saw mill near us. It was not long until he purchased a half interest in the saw mill, although he had bought his freighting equipment on credit and had no capital whatever. Freighting was a lucrative profession in those days. It had taken him only a short time to pay his debt and have enough capital to start another venture.

After we were married he bought a place in the Sulpher Springs Valley which became known as the Double Rod. There was abundance of grass on this place and the few Mexican steers with which he started soon became a large herd through the purchase of small herds of cattle from various residents of the valley and elsewhere. I remember that he received several small herds from John Slaughter. He still continued his freighting, which was quite profitable.

Soon he sold his share of the saw mill. Things were not going so well in the partnership and he thought it best to free himself from too many entanglements. About this time he returned to Kansas where his parents were and where he bought several pair of good mules to replace the oxen for hauling. The mules and all his freighting equipment he sold to a company in Mexico for hauling ore, after his own freighting days were over.

Soon came a halt to the prosperity which had seemed to attend our cattle business. There came a drought which almost cleaned us out. Our herd had dwindled to almost nothing when the drought broke. This proved only a temporary setback. Mr. Scheerer was often spoken of as the best manager in the territory, and I almost believe he deserved the compliment. In only a few years we were again prosperous. We bought more and more land, or leased it. Our herds grew rapidly.

All this time Mr. Scheerer was freighting and raising cattle I held down the place at home. I did my work, cooked for the cowhands, transient visitors, and even on occasion, outlaws.

We had two children, Pearl and George; also at the time Mr. Scheerer's younger brother, George, and his family. They were with me for more than a year, once, and on shorter occasions several times.

When the children had to attend school I was faced with quite a problem. I had neither time nor inclination to attempt their schooling myself. We tried boarding them out in Tombstone, which by then had become quite a quiet town. We tried letting them learn by themselves. Finally I had to live in Tombstone myself during the school term, which was much shorter than the term now is.

When our daughter Pearl had finished school at last she secured employment in the Company store in Bisbee. She had worked only a very short time when a proposed trip back to Kansas by my husband would have left me alone on the ranch. Pearl asked for a two week vacation that she might stay with me during his absence.

I had a large, old-fashioned range with a reservoir on the side with which to heat water. It scarcely held enough and I augmented my hot water by keeping a huge black kettle filled with water on the back of the stove. There were two small tabs on the rim of the kettle which held the lid on. I was used to this kettle, but Pearl was not. We bathed in a large tin tub, in the kitchen. Pearl was preparing a bath for herself. She lifted the kettle of water from the stove, and in attempting to pour it she loosened the lid. The steam burned her hands, and she dropped the kettle of water into the tub, spilling most of it on one leg as she did. She was burned quite severely, it being about six months before she could walk. Of course that was the last of her job.

**Rosa Talbot Schuster**
Interviewer: Edward J. Kelley
Tombstone

My husband and I moved to Tombstone early in 1881. Later on the miners struck for higher wages. The mine owners were a hard headed bunch who shut the mines down and fought it out with the men. Some of the workers made threats which gave the mine owners sufficient excuse to ask for military protection.

The garrison of Fort Huachuca was moved in here and we were under martial law for a month. By the time the strike was settled the water had risen in the mines until they were pretty well drowned out. By the time they were unwatered and work resumed the price of silver had dropped from the old ratio of 16 to 1 and the men never again made the big money of the early days.

Who was the most distinguished man associated with the camp in those days? Well, there were hundreds. Almost every man wore mustachios like Texan cow horns and beards were in style. The tin horn gamblers usually trimmed theirs and slicked 'em down with grease or wax. The cowmen let them wander where they would. Anyhow, they all looked more masculine and impressive than the smooth faced rascals of today. Oh, you mean what particular one I admired. I think the Reverend Endicott Peabody would be that man.

He came from Boston and had a string of letters like an alphabet hitched onto his name. This was his first ministry. He was a good mixer and because of his readiness to oblige at all times was liked by everyone.

I remember when we were securing donations to build St. Paul's. The committee stood outside the Crystal Palace saloon while he walked in to secure contributions. Wyatt Earp was dealing faro. How do I know it was faro? Should I blush? By mere walking down Allen Street in those days you could see and hear everything. The Bird Cage was at one end and a church at the other.

Anyhow the Reverend made known his mission. Promptly Earp counted out a stack of gold twenties. "This is my profit for today," he said as he handed them over. Then he went with the minister to the roulette, poker and other games and all donated as liberally.

They were really pleasant about it and invited Endicott Peabody to have a drink. He had a glass of wine with them while they ordered what they wished and then the committee proceeded to the other houses in their order.

A short time ago I dropped into the Crystal Palace with a subscription list for the Church. I have known most of the boys there since the day they were born, but how some of the other church members frowned on me for doing it. I still feel chilled. It seems I am unorthodox, unethical and impetuous and will fill an early grave.

However I note with pleasure that the Reverend Endicott Peabody is yet hale and hearty and still going strong at the head of a big eastern school. In the meantime he has not only officiated at the marriage of the President of the United States, but also at the marriage of the President's two sons. Some distinction for Tombstone and an old Tombstoner, I think.

After St. Paul's was built two of its most prominent members, Charley Leach and George Parsons, sat directly in front of me one Sunday. Both were sleepy eyed and heavy lidded as they had just left an all night poker game wherein Leach had won quite a sum from Parsons.

Mr. Parsons was asked to pass the plate. When he reached Leach, that pillar of the church placed a silver dollar in the box, but Parsons did not move. "Come again. Ten percent of last night winnings is the ante," he said.

Leach fished out a golden twenty and added that to his contribution, meanwhile whispering, "I'll have to win this back from you during the week."

On Saturday Dr. Peabody went down to Charleston to make collections and round up a congregation for the services he was going to hold on Sunday there. In the largest saloon he stepped up to the faro table, introduced himself and asked them all to be present at Sunday services. It was a tough bunch in a tough saloon in a notoriously tough town.

"Are you going to bring your gun?" growled one of the toughest.

"Are you going to bring a doctor?" added another bad egg.

"Better bring an undertaker," said a third.

None of them had cracked a smile. They were giving him "the works", as the Pastor's accent always betrayed the Bostonese before he spoke five words. They loved to scare sky pilots.

But the sky pilot did not scare. "Boys, I sincerely hope you be as happy and healthy Monday morning as I will be at that time. All of you," he laughed at them.

During the night one of these hecklers was shot and the other two lost their stacks. Anyhow, every hoss thief, smuggler and high-grader in Charleston mingled with the regular church attendants at services the next day, and the contributions amounted to over seventy five dollars.

About twelve years ago Dr. Peabody and his wife came out to Phoenix to assist in the consecration of St. Paul's Cathedral there. On their return trip they stopped over in Tombstone some days to review the old scenes he remembered so well.

Candidly, Mrs. Peabody told me she thought it was the most God-forsaken place she had ever seen, but the Doctor had the time of his life revisiting the whole countryside. One of my greatest treasures is a letter from the Reverend Endicott Peabody written June 12, 1934.

No, Tombstone was never a really tough camp as some people seem to think. Mr. Schuster used to assure me that if you were handy with a gun, was careful to say little at all times and kept an eye out behind as well as in front, you were pretty safe.

Of course a lot of bad men came here at different times who would pirouette around with a gun in their hand and act the bully for awhile. But, sooner or later there always cropped up someone a mite faster who would eventually down the first bad actor, and in turn, be downed by a faster man later. And so on and so on, ad infinitum as Dr. Peabody would say. Boot Hill got them all in due time, so you see we were a well conducted camp.

## Marie Annanettie Hatch Shumway

Interviewer: Roberta Flake Clayton
Navajo County

We were all pretty much in the same circumstances, poor. Yet the Fathers and Mothers felt happy and willing to go ahead and colonize as best they could. At that time all food stuff and other necessaries had to be hauled from Albuquerque, New Mexico by team and wagon.

My father homesteaded a farm about two miles from the town of Taylor. After much hard work and we had gotten the water to irrigate with, times began to be better. At least we had more to eat. Father got a few cows and a small herd of sheep.

My baby sister being several years younger than myself made it necessary for me to work and play with my brother just older. We were especially good pals. One of our tasks was to care for the sheep. One cold winter day a wildcat frightened the sheep scattering them. Then what a time we had wading in the snow to gather them before night.

On reaching home I sat down by the fireplace to warm my feet which by this time did not feel as cold as when out in the woods. I immediately began to remove my shoes and stockings knit from woolen yarn. To my surprise some of the skin from my feet came off with the stockings. Frozen, yes, and for three weeks or more brother Bert had the task of the sheep by his own lonesome self.

There was other outdoor work that I could do to help and it made me happy, such as strip the cane and feed the molasses mill when my brothers were too busy doing other things.

Father owned and operated a mill, making molasses for the neighborhood. One time the boys overdid the thing and cooked a boiler of juice to candy. Then what a jolly good time we had with a hay rack load of boys and girls coming from town to the candy pull.

Besides the outdoor duties I could help my Mother to provide light by making candles, also by making lye soap, brooms and other things the pioneers had to provide for themselves.

Our house was of logs, two rooms, not much furniture. At that time most of our evenings as a family were spent at home. These to me were happy times. Mother was a gifted singer so some evenings we would sing hymns and old time songs; sometimes scripture readings and games. One game was called the game of authors. This was a deck of cards with the pictures and names of authors such as Henry Ward Beecher, Nathaniel Hawthorne, John Quincy Adams, Harriet Elizabeth Stowe, Longfellow, Dickens and others. This was instructive as well as entertaining.

We made rag carpets and in them Mother contrived to have a number of bright colors, obtained from berries, roots and bark. Our curtains were kept clean and fresh so all in all it was anything but drab and dull.

I attended school for several terms. Our school terms were short and it was necessary that even the children help in every possible way in the settlement of this new country. Their schooling of necessity was meager. Later, I attended the dances and other social affairs of the community.

As young folks at that time we had a lot of good wholesome fun and frolic. True, no cars to ride in; we were in luck to find a wagon. Then when luck prevailed we would go riding. We generally had four spring seats with four couples. Perhaps the boys would sing to entertain, then maybe the girls, then again if we all knew certain song we would have a chorus together.

I soon was attracted toward my boy friend, James J. Shumway, and after a year of more of courtship we were married December 9, 1887. Arizona had always been our homeland. We have had a large family, eight boys and six girls. Two of the girls died in infancy, twelve living to man and womanhood. The passing of one son, who was killed on the 2 of June 1933 in the Richfield Oil Plant at Long Beach California, was one of the greatest sorrows of our lives, being doubly so as he left a dear little wife and six small children.

We had two sons enlist in the World War. One was overseas in the midst of the battle, coming home to us unhurt. The other was released from Camp Funston, Kansas just ready to leave for overseas when the Armistice was signed.

## Lannie Mitchell Smith

Interviewer: Roberta Flake Clayton
Navajo County

A wagon box was a poor house compared with a comfortable brick home, but Lannie made no complaint to living in one the first year of their married life.

They had their meals with Jesse's brother, Joseph W. and wife, Nellie Marsden, who welcomed them into their log house. Jesse and Lannie had no time to build as they spent the winter teaching school. Lannie did her part of the house work before and after school. Jesse worked with his father's family on the farm, etc., and after the spring planting was in he hauled logs from the mountains for their house. Lannie went with him on occasions.

Joseph Fish hewed the logs and as soon as the walls and part of the roof was up of their two room house, they moved into it and finished it as they could.

And now happened one of the incidents that showed what a mental strain the girl wife had been laboring under. As cold weather came on next winter a fireplace was started in one end of the front room. James C. Owens of Woodruff laid it up of adobes that had been frozen but which appeared to have been dried out.

He reached the ceiling just when he noticed some of them softening and he thought that a fire in the fireplace would dry them out. Jesse went out to get wood and Lannie crawled under trellises and what not to start the fire. As she blew the flickering fire Mr. Owens called from above, "Look out!" She dodged back just in time to escape being caught by the avalanche of mud that was to have been the fireplace. Then surged up in her the disappointment that she could not control, and she burst into tears.

It was a queer sight that met Jesse as he returned with the wood. There stood Mr. Owens trying to console his sobbing wife who insisted she was not hurt, she was just heartbroken at the thought of not having a chimney to the fireplace so they could keep warm. Mr. Owens said he would build one of rock, which Jesse hastened to haul and the house was completed--and Lannie was comforted.

### Betty Spicer

Interviewer: Helen M. Smith
Cochise County

Tombstone was considered quite a wild and wooly place, but nothing unusual happened to us while there. All the excitement seemed to be stirred up among a class of people to which we did not belong. Ordinary persons were as safe on the Tombstone of that day as they are today.

There were bad men in plenty, horse and cattle rustlers, smugglers, and the like. There was a great deal of smuggling going on in those times. Mexicans smuggled money across the line to buy goods, and then smuggled the goods back. White men stole cattle in Mexico and ran them across to the United States. That sort of thing was quite usual and accepted.

We made no attempt to get a start in cattle, believing that the rustlers made such an attempt impracticable. My husband hauled wood for a living during several years.

In 1887 we went to Phoenix but stayed there only a short time, traveling on to Flagstaff country. There we got a chance to contract the hauling of lumber to Phoenix in partnership with another man. I decidedly did not like the looks of this other man, and begged my husband not to undertake partnership with him. But, my husband laughed at my fears.

The children and I traveled with my husband in his trips back and forth in our covered wagon, as did the family of his partner. We had some great times in this travel. I remember making a low chimney of rocks over which I placed a piece of tin, then building the chimney higher with another piece of tin over it. I put fire above and below the pieces of tin and put my bread between them. In this manner I could cook bread which was really good to eat. We used sometimes to be able to find wild currents with which we made most excellent pies.

My fears of my husband's partner soon took a definite form. They quarreled on several occasions. It seemed to me that the partner, who said his name was Whittaker, was a man of violent temper and emotions. One night after we had retired to sleep in our wagon, his partner called to my husband to come out for a minute as he wished to discuss certain things with him.

I begged him not to go, but he only laughed as he pulled on his pants and went out. I listened breathlessly for a few minutes, and soon heard voices raised in anger. I rose quickly and started to dress. About that time I heard the sound of a dull, sudden blow, and then a moan from my husband.

When I reached his side Whittaker had left camp, escaping on one of our own horses. He had struck my husband over the head with a large shovel. He died before morning and I was left alone in the desert with five children and the family of my husband's murderer, and the birth of my sixth child only a few months off.

Whittaker's wife left the country and nothing was heard of her for some time after. Whittaker could not be found until five years had elapsed, three of which he spent in prison for another offense.

Then he was caught and brought to Prescott for the trial of the murder of my husband. His wife was wanted as witness, but could not be found. We learned that he had not been in communication with her since his flight. He did not deny the killing, but pleaded self defense. He showed old knife scars on his body, which he had told us were the results of Indian fights, and claimed that these scars came from previous encounters with my husband. There was only my word against his, and he was given seven years for manslaughter, only four of which he served, being freed on pardon.

I learned that Whittaker afterward went to the vicinity of Tombstone where some of his wife's relatives were living and hauled wood for the mines. He was killed there when he was thrown from a high piled load of wood to the ground between the wagon and the mules. One of which kicked him in the head as he fell. And so he died as my husband had died, of concussion from a blow to the head. This was in the vicinity of Bisbee. I heard that his wife was not aware of his death until some months after.

After my husband's death I took up my residence in Phoenix. I lived in a long adobe house between Jackson and Madison Streets. It was owned by an old man, Linville, who was a pioneer of the region. I remember that Mr. Linville's Father had buried a considerable sum of money on his place, and after the Father's death the family dug up the whole place looking for it, but so far as I learned, with no success.

Phoenix looked much as Agua Prieta does now—a few adobe houses and dirt roads. They were just putting in the doors and windows in the Luhrs Hotel when we arrived. I lived ten years in Phoenix, being acquainted with the whole population for a part of that time. I lost a child while there with diphtheria. We worked hard to make a living, the older children helping as much as possible. Fortunately times were good and so I was able to get by.

I saw all kind of life while there. Indians were plentiful, the women in bright colored calico dresses with a sort of cape affair made of men's bandana handkerchiefs sewed together. The women loved these in various colors; the men in blankets and white men's britches and shirts. I have seen dead horses hauled across the river from Phoenix and the Indians immediately skin and eat these animals. They were furnished smoked meat by the Government, but fresh meat seemed to be a necessity with them.

I was in Phoenix when the Edmonds act, requiring marriage between all men and women living together, was passed. It brought some difficulty to parts of the town, and to some of the Mormons who resided in the vicinity.

In 1890 there was a parade destined to show the progress of the locality. I remember that they had an old Indian, naked except for a breech cloth, squatted on a pile of sand under a greasewood bush, with a young Indian from the Indian school, decently clad, and working for a contrast.

In Phoenix I married the second time. My husband was Sam Bailey, who served four years as constable there, and was a charter member of the Elks Club of Phoenix. We were afterward divorced, and he died later.

I came to Tombstone in the nineties, again, but did not stay there for long. For awhile we lived in Safford. I had a queer experience while there. Believing that I possessed some psychic power, and as a way of earning money to support my children, I had taken up fortune telling when first a widow. The profession I have followed off and on since.

At Safford a young man came to me one night to have his fortune told. I read the cards, and saw some shooting, two men killed and one wounded. I told him of this, and he told me that he and an older man had come into Safford to rob the bank, but he was fearful after what I told him and would not go on with the project. I told him that if he would abandon it I would say nothing. I also advised him to go home, where I saw a grey-haired Mother waiting for him. He admitted that this was true also. Whether his story was true or not, I never saw him again, and there was no bank robbery.

When my children were grown I married again, Mr. William Spicer, with whom I made my home in Douglas where we lived until his death in September of this year.

**Mary Kirby Stocks**
Interviewer: Roberta Flake Clayton
Navajo County

Mary's carefree days were of short duration because at the age of fifteen she became the wife of Edward Stocks and as nature would permit the mother of eleven children. The family was so poor that she went out in the field after the grain was cut and hauled and gleaned wheat which she sold to get cloth to make clothes for her unborn babe.

In the year 1870 they moved to Arizona settling at what is now Linden. Broken in health, it was thought that the change might do her good. Her husband only remained here a short time returning to his family in Utah. This left Mary entirely on her own resources with a large family of small children to provide for.

Living in a sod house with a floor of the same material, she had a fireplace to give light and warmth in winter, and a place to cook in summer. She was away from all her family and associates, located on a dry farm that had to be cleared and fenced, near the Reservation of the most treacherous Indian tribe in the west. This was quite an experience for this English woman.

She used to tell of how she spent almost an entire night parching corn for her two eldest sons, only little fellows themselves, to take with them as their only food while they were out in the cedars cutting post and building fences around their field. If the winter before had plenty of snow and the rains came right, good crops of corn and beans and squash could be raise. But, if not as frequently happened, then the food supply was low.

As soon as the boys were old enough they herded sheep for $10 per month. In the bleak cold winter with frozen ears and feet they stayed with the herds, many times nestling up to the warm wooly bodies of the sheep to keep from freezing to death. Yet, how willingly and uncomplainingly they did this work that the mother might buy flour occasionally and the necessities—salt, soda and sometimes sugar.

One Christmas feast consisted of a big whole wheat pie baked in a milk pan, no shortening but a filling of pumpkin, the latter donated as a present from a neighbor. It was a rare treat.

After many years of struggle the family moved to Show Low. Poverty had done much for them. It had created a bond of unity, self sacrifice, and willing service. As the sons grew older they did what they could to make life easier for the Mother who had done so much for them.

While she never neglected her own she found time for anyone who needed her care. Either a natural aptitude or necessity, or both combined, made of her an excellent nurse and in her home was a supply of herbs, roots and barks the medicinal qualities of which she knew and used for the healing of her family and her neighbors.

## Eliza Ellen Parkinson Tanner

Interviewer: Roberta Flake Clayton
Snowflake

During these days of '76 and '77 many of the strong able bodied well-to-do men were being called to settle Arizona, Nevada and Idaho by the leaders of the Mormon Church. Henry Martin Tanner was called to Arizona, so with his bride made preparations for the journey into the barren wastes of Arizona. The trip lasted eleven weeks and was filled with hardship.

Finally on May 1, 1887, the Tanners settled in the Old Fort at St. Joseph (now Joseph City) built as a protection against the Indians. However, the people believed it was better to feed the Indians rather than fight them.

The settlers here were living in the "United Order", which meant that they lived as one large family. Each separate family had its sleeping quarters but all ate at the same big table. Each one was assigned his or her special work – the women taking turns doing the cooking and other tasks.

Henry was to look after the cattle, and was away much of the time. Eliza was very homesick and lonely and for the first few weeks wore her bonnet all the time so that no one would see the tears she could not check.

The cattle were taken out to Mormon Dairy, near Flagstaff, in the summer time and the women who could make butter and cheese went out there. Eliza was an expert at both so she spent much time out there. Not only at these was she efficient, but at spinning, weaving, knitting, sewing and as a cook and housekeeper she was unsurpassed. She was always busy as it gave her less time to think of her family and friends so far away. She would wash the wool shorn from the sheep, card, spin it and weave it into cloth or knit it into stockings. When clothing could no longer be used for wearing apparel, it was torn into one inch strips, these were sewed together then woven into carpets.

With fresh, clean, straw underneath, to make it warmer and softer, the new rag carpets were stretched and tacked down on the floors. No woman was ever prouder of her imported Turkish rugs than were the pioneer women of their own stripped or "hit and miss" homemade rag carpets.

Everyone who ever lived on the Little Colorado River knows the problem they had trying to settle the red, brackish water sufficiently for use. It was hauled from the river two miles away in barrels on low sleds. Plaster of Paris and buttermilk were used to settle it. Probably six inches of clear water could be carefully dipped from the top of the barrel, then the remainder would have to be emptied and the process repeated. In spite of this terrible handicap, Eliza's laundry always looked white and clean.

In 1886 the Tanners moved to their homestead, about a mile east of the Fort. Their home was only partly finished, but Eliza was glad to have a home of her own.

There were no Doctors and the women helped each other during sickness and death. The men became quite expert at setting limbs, extracting teeth, etc., and no one was ever too busy to help another who was in need.

## Rebecca Reed Hancock Tenney

Interviewer: Roberta Flake Clayton
Snowflake

When she was less than two years old she was brought to Arizona by her Mother and the older members of the family. One evening, after they had made an early camp, Rebecca and one of her older sisters went out to hunt cedar berries and pine gum. She got tired and thought to return to the camp alone. When she came to the road they had left she started back over the road they had traveled that day, and trudged on and on looking for the camp. When the sister returned and Rebecca was not with her great excitement reigned. Everyone set out on the search. Finally her little footprints were found in the dusty wagon tracks, but her brother Joseph followed her for two miles before he overtook her. When she returned to camp she was seated upon his shoulders and greeted all with a happy smile.

The family reached Taylor, Arizona on New Year's Day 1889. As soon as she was old enough, Rebecca started the village school. Rebecca was the twelfth child in the family, and was allowed to do pretty much as she pleased. Her Mother was a nurse and spent much of her time with the sick. The child was left to visit and play with her little friends, to wander through fields and over hills.

When she got large enough she used to go to the field and help her brothers with the crops. Especially did she like hay hauling time. It was such fun to tromp the sweet smelling alfalfa, and then to ride to the barn on a mountain of it.

The farmers used to haul their surplus hay to Fort Apache or Holbrook. One day the Hancocks had their wagons loaded high with baled hay. Two of the brothers were going to take it but one was sick and there seemed to be no one else. Rebecca was enlisted to drive the extra team. One of the horses, old Cap, was a balky rascal, and the Puerco Arroyo seemed to be his favorite place to do it. Rebecca had something to worry about from the time she left home until the stream was safely reached and crossed, which it was for once old Cap pulled his share of the load through the quicksand.

When Rebecca was eleven years old her sister and her intended husband were going back to St. George, Utah to be married. They decided to let Rebecca go along. Frank M. Perkins, besides being the successful lover, was the owner of a fancy team of horses. When only a few days travel from home they camped for the night and hobbled out the team. What was their amazement when they looked for the horses next morning to find them gone, hobbles and all.

Mr. Perkins hunted until past noon but no trace of them could be found. While the poor stranded people were trying to decide what to do, along came some men driving a bunch of Indian ponies. They stopped and very solicitously inquired what the trouble was. Upon being told they generously offered to loan the travelers a pair of their ponies to work until they reached the next settlement; which was about a week's travel away with a good team.

The offer was accepted and arrangements were made to leave the team at Moab. There was a young man by the name of John Lewis along. He volunteered to return to Taylor and get a team belonging to Mr. Perkin's brother and join the party at Moab. After these arrangements were made the men rode away, in a different direction from that taken by Lewis, and also away from the road taken by the family of Rebecca.

The journey was resumed but the little rats of ponies were balky, small, lazy and everything that would tend to aggravate anyone. Frank was on his best behavior, and moving at all was better than staying in camp. They plodded on and after many days reached the settlement where they stayed until help came from home.

While they were waiting they learned positively that the men who loaned them the team had stolen theirs, and that this span of ponies and the others they had from the Navajos.

**Ida Elizabeth McEwen Tompkins**
Interviewer: Robert Flake Clayton
Phoenix

In early days in the settlement of new places, the school teachers had rather an envied place. Theirs was not to cope with the elements, try to make a home of a wagon box, gather the doable weeds for food and do many things that the housewife did. They were just to teach the three R's to the rising generation keep themselves looking fit and do the finer things. Ida Elizabeth McEwen was a "school marm" the second teacher in the Prendergast District in Phoenix, Arizona.

The inducement and a desire to see the West were too great so she came landing in Phoenix on San Juan Day, June 23, 1885.

There was always a fear of Indians, so when she awoke one morning in Maricopa station and saw about 25 or 30 big Indians in gee-strings and bright red bandanas around their heads she was about frightened to death. She learned from the conductor that they were army scouts and were peaceable. She was quite relieved. A light spring wagon was waiting in Maricopa station to bring them to Phoenix as the train did not come any nearer than Maricopa at that time. The trip was made in about 6 hours.

In order to teach in Arizona Ida had to pass an examination. Arizona was noted for years for its strenuous examinations and though Ida had taught for six years before coming here she failed to pass. Nothing daunted, she made preparation to enter school as a pupil that fall.

She gave one day a week and her time nights and morning for board and room in the Jar Irvine home where she was treated as a daughter. The remainder of the time before school started was spent in working in a dressmaking and milliner establishment. Here she made $2.50 per week, but learned many valuable lessons in these arts.

Professor D. A. Reed was the teacher to whom she went when school started and she had no trouble passing the examination the next June. She was promised a school, but through some misunderstanding or otherwise, a man was given the same school. He only lasted until the Christmas Holidays and then she took it, becoming the second teacher in the Prendergast district. There were nine pupils when she began and thirty-five when she finished two years after.

In the first school there were four children belonging to one family. They had to come four miles to school. The eldest boy of this family told the teacher that his father didn't want his children taught any new fangled notions. They were not to study geography because he knew the world was flat and that settled that. Miss Ida said all right, his wishes should be obeyed. The children heard her tell the others how, when a ship was approaching you saw the top of the sails first. They went home and told their father that and he said it was true. Little by little he became convinced the teacher was right. Ida thinks diplomacy one of the greatest requisites in teaching a country school.

When she came West, Ida brought a lot of yard goods and had her dresses made here. There were excellent dressmakers here at the time. None of these dresses were suitable for the wedding gown, however, so she sent $75 to a friend with whom she had boarded in Omaha to buy the trousseau. There were 18 yards of 27 inch ottoman silk in the dress, which was made with short pointed basque, overskirt and puckers. The basque had 20 steel cut buttons down the front which cost $4.50 a dozen. The side panel of the overskirt was covered with cut bead pasamentrie. The little hat, shoes, hose, gloves and purse were a rich cinnamon brown, the color of the dress.

One of the practical neighbor women lamented the extravagance said, "Why that outfit cost you a whole month's wages. With that amount you could have bought you a good cow." To which Ida responded, "I expect to have lots of cows in my day, but only one wedding dress and it shall be one I can always remember with pride."

Ida and her lover were married on her Mother's wedding anniversary, March 25, 1887, in the Old Calvary Baptist Church in Phoenix. The reception was a grand affair and lasted all day and most of the night. There were over 100 guests invited. There was roast turkey and everything that goes with it. Everyone had a good time, and wished the happy young couple a long and prosperous life.

George's father had a homestead of 80 acres at Aqua Caliente and to this went the bride and groom. She drove two old mules and a spring wagon while holding a parasol over her head for shade. She followed the plow and sowed the first grain down there, carrying it in her apron.

Her experiences as a farmer's wife were very strenuous ones. At harvest time she would cook four meals a day for the men. Seventy five to a hundred pounds of meat and a hundred pounds of flour were cooked by her each week, these with the other food was no small amount of work. During this time she was also having her six children and rearing them.

## Sarah Ann Salina Smithson Turley

Interviewer: Roberta Flake Clayton
Navajo County

Saline was the third in a family of thirteen and when her services could be dispensed with at home she went with her father from Holbrook to Fort Apache driving her four or six horse teams with as great ease and skill as did her father or older brother.

Mr. Smithson and his eldest son claim to have hauled the first that went into Fort Apache on wagons. Until the advent of the railroad and a forwarding station established in Holbrook the freight for the soldier post had been carried on mule back from Manuelito, New Mexico. After the railroad was completed the men with teams had steady work hauling supplies as long as the Government maintained a fort there.

Another adventure she had was during the St. Johns War. This war was between the Cattlemen and the Mexican Sheep men. Already a number had been killed on both sides. The Greer boys were large cattle owners and had been having lots of trouble with the Mexicans. At this time the feelings ran very high and the Greers had to be away from their ranch so they sent to Woodruff for Saline to come and stay with their sister, Mrs. Blassingame.

One evening the women saw Mexicans riding around the place at some distance. Mrs. Blassingame decided it would not be wise for the two of them to remain there alone, so they started out to walk to Mr. Nat Greer's ranch which was six miles away.

Mrs. Blassingame was ill which necessitated their walking more slowly so that it was sunrise before their destination was reached, and they found only Mrs. Greer and her two little boys there. For three weeks these women and the two children were there alone. Sometimes the men would come in before daylight to get supplies, and often Saline would walk to a designated place and leave food or any news they might have.

Each woman had a six shooter, and during three nights when the Mexicans were prowling around the ranch, Saline armed herself and sat at one of the windows all night ready to shoot should the Mexicans attack the house.

At the time of the robbery of the Arizona Mercantile store in Woodruff, Saline was selected to spread the alarm to the men who were all working in their fields a short distance from town. She remembers feeling like she was flying rather than running as she leaped the irrigation ditches in her excitement. But neither the outlaws nor the money were heard from again.

During the early days in Woodruff the Smithsons kept the travelers, and many times when all the other beds were occupied, Saline and her mother would give up theirs and sit by the fire all night knitting or crocheting to keep awake.

When Saline was seventeen she took her team and wagon and with other members of her family drove to Utah where she took a course in sewing, and for twenty years did custom work, both in men's and women's clothing. During part of this time she was employed by the largest store in Holbrook to make print dresses and baby clothing. As a sunbonnet maker she gained a reputation that brought orders from far and near from ladies who valued their complexions.

These were hard years for the people of Woodruff who depended on irrigation to raise their crops. Almost every year the dam would be washed out of the river, and they hardly knew where the next meal was coming from. Then the men would have to go away from home to seek employment and the work at home would have to be done by the women and girls.

Saline was 21 years old when her mother died leaving seven unmarried children to her care. The eldest was twelve and the youngest a pair of twins sixteen months old.

Saline says she had done every kind of work on the farm, but running the modern machinery. She has plowed, cut, raked and hauled hay. She would hire out at 25 cents a day binding grain behind the men who cut it with a cradle. If anyone wanted whitewashing and housecleaning done, she did it, taking anything they could afford to pay. Besides all the other work she took in washing and wove hundreds of yards of carpet, anything she could do to help her father support the family she did willingly.

After her father died she married a widower with a large family. She was again called to be a mother to another motherless family and, strange coincidence the babies were twins, husky boys of six.

She was blessed with only one little child, a baby girl, and she was permitted to keep her for only 26 short months. No woman was ever more proud than this 42 year old mother.

## Ida Frances Hunt Udall

Contributed by her daughter Pauline H. Smith to
Interviewer: Roberta Flake Clayton
Navajo County

She passed through trying times in St. Johns. A lawless element settled there. She always shuddered at the memory of the night when two men were lynched just across the way from her home, the groaning, the oppressive gloom, was not conducive to much that should accompany one's honeymoon.

In the spring of 1887 her husband moved her to the Milligun ranch, near Springerville. It was here she felt the joys of young motherhood, even though borne amongst much adversity. The high altitude and cold winters told dreadfully on her health. She had never been too robust, a heart affliction due to bad health had prayed on her as she bore her six children. Her husband being a church man of the Mormon faith, and a colonizer, was away from home a great deal, which left the rearing and caring for the children mostly to her.

She soled their shoes, barbered their hair and made every article of clothing they wore until they were nearly grown. She made butter and cheese for sale, raised chickens and a garden each year. While at the same time she cooked for hired men. Her family consisted of a daughter, the eldest, and five sons.

Not withstanding her frail body, the multiplicity of her every day duties, she always found time for the refinement of life. There were petunias blooming in the window, or mignonettes in the yard. On the wall hung pictures, the frame of which she had fashioned from pine cones. The Mexican house, in which she lived, often ran tubs of water through its leaky roof, yet she never gave up the yearly going over its ceiling and walls herself with the white wash brush. The rag carpet on the floor had taken hours of her time.

On the Sabbath day she was often seen in the cart with its shafts drawn by one horse, accompanied by her children and their cousins on the way to the school house, one mile distant. Or, perhaps she walked another time. There a Sunday school class would be taught by her or a choir practice conducted.

It was approaching Christmas. The nearest store was at Springerville, four miles away. There were no Mail Order Houses and Parcel Post rates. Circumstances had prohibited that trip up to within a few days of that long looked for day. On the morning when the shopping was to have been done a most violent winter blizzard set in and stopped them. Christmas morning came with no Santa Claus. In the other part of the big Mexican house lived Aunt Ella and her children. The middle door was opened; Aunt Ella's Havilland China was brought down from the high top shelf of the cupboard, which had been hauled over Lee's Back Bone into Arizona. Aunt Ella, with her gift for cooking and dainty serving, prepared cocoa, a dainty delicacy to be served only to distinguished guests.

David, the Father, to revive memories of his childhood visits from the good old Saint, prepared a "sugar teat" for each child in lieu of the stick candy from Mr. Becker's store. The "sugar teat" was made by putting a spoonful of sugar in a square of clean white cloth and securely tied. This was sucked by the children. It was greatly disdained by big sister Pearl, then nearly ten years of age, who could not restrain her bitter tears of disappointment until Aunt Ida brought out the guitar and sang all the old Christmas carols.

This was an incident where Ida's vivacity and cheer and Aunt Ella's culture and art saved Christmas from being a dull disappointment to some little marooned mountain children and their jolly, fine daddy.

After years of crop failures, due to prolonged droughts, the mortgage on the farm was foreclosed. It became necessary for this woman, in connection with her devoted husband, to make another start in life.

To make this new start they decided to apply for a homestead entry in the Greer Valley, twenty miles below St. Johns. David had been a mail contractor, carrying the mail in buckboards from Holbrook to Springerville. In this valley he could establish a mail station while he homesteaded. Ida's boys might care for the teams while David was away on business pertaining to many things.

As the boys grew older they carried the mail over these treacherous rivers and washes and across the sandy flats. The mail station soon became, out of necessity, a way side inn for travelers to stop over night on their way to St. Johns and Springerville

The charm and open hospitality of Ida's nature made all classes at ease, forgetful of the primitive conditions under which she was living having to haul water for culinary purposes for more than a mile.

The anxiety over young sons detained by raging torrent, caused by some cloud burst of rain, or of facing the long cold ride in winter, one day following another, together with hard work and privations and loneliness proved too much for Ida's physical resistance.

It was in 1902, when they moved onto their homestead and established a Post Office, called Hunt. She camped under a cedar tree until a rude lumber house could be constructed around her. That year, the 1st day of May, six inches of snow fell before the roof was yet over her head.

## Annie Catherine Hanson Whipple

Interviewer: Roberta Flake Clayton
Navajo County

At the age of seven her schooling began with Johnnie Pace as her teacher. This only lasted one season as her father was called to help settle the new country of Arizona. After some delay they made the journey settling first at Show Low. Their first home in this land was a one room log house with no window and a blanket for a door. The wagon boxes were removed from the running gears and put on logs and served as bedrooms for the children.

Her father obtained employment at Fort Apache. What provisions were attainable he got for his family, but it was many miles to the nearest store and so the family had to depend largely on what they could raise or produce themselves. As their farm was dependent on the rains for moisture the crops were very uncertain. The bread was mostly made of corn meal and much of the time was unleavened.

There were a few families living round in the woods on their farms, who gathered together each Sunday for Sunday School and Church. Catherine used to look forward to those times when she could wear her calico dress and bonnet to Sunday School. She says, "My bonnet was made of light figured calico Mother had brought from Utah. It was starched with flour starched so stiff it would not bend, and when I was not wearing it, it was hung on a certain peg on the wall.

On Saturdays all the brass kettles, tin pans, and tin cups had to be scoured and shined, and the knives and forks also. That was one of my chores. That done then came the weekly bathing. I would get the old copper boiler and fill it with water on the stove to heat, bring in the wooden tub. Sometimes it would leak and we would pour a tea-kettle full of hot water in it to sack it up so we could use it to bathe in.

I usually started in with the baby and put about three through the bath before I changed the water. We had a large piece of soap to scrub them with. It was a luxury if we had a bar of white laundry soap from the store.

My father did all the shoe mending, and sometimes Mother took the tops of her shoes and cut them down and sewed them on the machine and made shoes for the children.

My father made his own shoe lasts of wood and made wooden pegs to tack on the soles with. He cut shoe laces from tanned sheep skin.

In the Summertime Father and the boys wore for socks a square piece of cloth torn from some old worn out garment. They would set their foot on the rag, cornerwise; pulling the front corner over their toes and crossing the sides over the top of the foot, then slip their feet into their shoes. We could not buy socks. Mother tried to have a pair of home knit ones for each for Sunday, but yarn was hard to get. What she had she had spun from wool. Sometimes we would gather the green hulls from walnuts to color the yarn."

Candy pulls, choir practice and dances were the only forms of social amusement. There were so few people that all had to participate, young and old alike. Girls of fourteen were grown young ladies. Catherine had just turned fifteen when she was married. The wedding took place in Snowflake, October 11, and the next day she and the happy young bridegroom, Charles Whipple, started on their honeymoon by team, to their old home in Utah. There were two other families along.

When they got to Provo, Utah, where her husband was raised they decided to remain for the winter as it was too cold to attempt the return trip. Here they decided Catherine should go to school while her husband worked. This was a new experience for her, but she made the most of her time.

When school was over she went out where Charley was cutting ties and lived in a tent. Her chairs and furniture were dry goods boxes, but she made a home of it.

At the end of a year they decided he should remain and work, as he had a good job, and Catherine should return home on the train. This was in the fall of 1887. She came back on the train, her first experience in that mode of travel.

It was a year before her husband joined her. She lived with her parents in the meantime. Charley had built a little home before they were married. When he came back they moved to it and began making a home of their own. Her father had given her a cow and they bought two more. Her Mother gave her half a dozen hens. That summer she made butter and raised chickens, supplied the house and the clothes with the money from these.

One of the unusual experiences they had was one night while camped near Fort Apache, they, in company with Charley's brother Edson and his wife, attended an Indian dance. They had not been there long when an old squaw with a papoose tied to her back came and tapped Charley as an indication that she wanted to dance with him. But, he would not go. Soon another came with the same result. Then the Whipple boys decided to dance with their wives. This greatly amused the Indians, and the old musician nearly beat the head out of his tom-tom keeping time for them. After they had finished the Chief came to them and told how honored the Indians felt that the pale face would dance with them.

## Rowena Celesta McFath Whipple

Interviewer: Roberta Flake Clayton
Navajo County

When three years old she was afflicted with rheumatism from which she suffered intensely. It left her with her limbs drawn up. She was placed in an iron cast and kept there for almost a year. By the end of that time her legs were sufficiently straight that she could go on crutches and when she was eight she could get around without them. However, she was very stiff in her knees and hips and one leg remained shorter than the other; another result of the rheumatism was the loss of sight of one of her eyes.

Mr. McFath was a carpenter and moved his family around to wherever he had employment, coming to St. Johns, Arizona, December 23, 1880.

After living in St. Johns about two and a half years Mr. McFath got a logging contract at Flagstaff and took his family along. There they lived in a tent and a wagon box.

While the family lived in St. Johns "Aunt Rene" went to school for two terms. The first to Edmund Richardson in a small adobe used also for a church, and the other in a one room log school house to Mrs. Annie Romney. There were perhaps a hundred pupils at this school, and about half of them were Mexicans. The benches were made of logs split in two and with legs made of short poles. No nails were needed for those benches.

There were very few books to be on hand and chances for an education were very poor. Only reading, writing, history and geography were attempted.

In those days parents had to buy the books and pay tuition. This was a hardship when the family consisted of thirteen children as did the McFath family. Besides their own children there was Emily Jane Hopkins, whose father had given her to the McFaths when her mother died and left her a tiny baby.

Mrs. McFath's own first son died about the same time and in as far as was possible little Emily Jane took the place of it and Mrs. McFath was a true mother to the little girl.

The first real sorrow that Rowena ever had was when on their way to Arizona the Father sent for his child and told the parties to bring her back even if they had to steal her. He was finally persuaded that the McFaths could do better by his child than he could and permitted her to stay with them. She and Rowena were always the best of pals.

The first wedding "Aunt Rene" remembers was in St. Johns. It was that of Joseph Patterson and Emma Richie. It was a grand affair with "pass around" and all. The ball room had only a hard earth floor, but what mattered as long as the hearts were light and they could dance by Joe McFath's fiddling.

Tragedy played its part in these early memories and the night her grandfather Tenney was shot while trying to bring about peace between the Green boys and some Mexicans will ever remain in her memory.

Her friendship with Ned Whipple ripened into love and on the 2 of January, 1884, "just to begin the right" they were married.

The wedding dress was made by her Mother. It was of gray wool material, and contained 14 yards. It was trimmed with blue satin and was made in the latest fashion with basque, pleated skirt overskirt and puckers. All of the people for miles around were invited, and came. A supper and dance followed. They made 30 gallons of molasses beer for the occasion. "A person could have drunk the whole 30 gallons and not got drunk."

After the wedding Ned took his bride to Show Low to present her to his family. They remained a month returning to Alpine where they built a one room house of quaking aspen logs. In this humble little home her first child, a baby girl was born.

Living here about a year and a half then they moved to what was known as Adair. Here they homesteaded. Her husband built a fort for their protection if attacked by Indians. This was used as a dance hall in those early days and people would come from all over the county in their wagons or on horseback and stay a day, or a week, at a time.

"I never kept a hotel", says Aunt Rene "but many a night we had beds spread all over the floor. I never charged but for one meal in my life, and I've always been ashamed of that. It was after one of these big celebrations we had so often and everything in the house was eaten. A Mexican came and wanted something to eat and I took his fifty cents and sent it to the store to get something to feed him."

Molasses was substituted for fine sugar and corn for flour. When foodstuffs were scarce, they did without, or made something to eat out of what they had. That was the test of a good cook, and she was that. She was also a seamstress and for many years made all the clothes for her family. Beside that she knit all of their socks and stockings.

In 1903 the family moved to Show Low and finally built a good home there. In their excavating they found they were on a large Indian ruin. From this they got many valuable relics such as stone tablets, bone needles, stone hammers, bracelets, rings, earrings, beads, turquoise, and many beautiful ollas.

This collection they later sold for $1500.00 and with their son Joe for a driver took a trip to Florida, through the South, then home by way of Washington D.C.

Nor only did she care for her own sixteen children, the last a pair of twins, but when her eldest daughter died and left five little ones, their Grandmother gave them a home and did for them as her own until the Father married again.

In 1913 when the U.S.A. entered the World War she sent four sons, John a Marine, Joseph in the Artillery, Columbus in the Infantry and Will a Sailor. The fifth signed up ready to go. She is especially proud of the record made by her boys.

Columbus was in the front lines 87 days. He swam a river with his clothes and cartridges on and rescued a drowning comrade. For his bravery he was given the Croix de Guerra. Once in the wire entanglements he lost his gun, but soon found another that the owner would never need again. He crossed a valley thirteen times in one day under fire. One of his companions was killed by his side when they had taken refuge in a shell hole. He was wounded in the foot but never reported it. He was in the service two years to the day.

Joe was in the Army of occupation in Germany. He was at the front fifty-four days. The brothers only met once, and then for only about five minutes.

Will was operated on in San Francisco for appendicitis. A letter came from him stating he was not well and was trying to get a leave to come home for a few days before going overseas. A short time later a telegram came saying he was seriously sick, and 20 minutes later another saying he was dead.

John got a ten day furlough and brought his brother's flag draped body to his grief stricken Mother. He also brought messages from Will's buddies and a cigar box filled with nickels and pennies they had contributed as a love token. He had been in the service four months. His body was brought home on his 28th birthday, July 10, 1918.

One of Joe's most thrilling experiences was when a corporal he was detailed to move a large supply of ammunition. With airplanes circling around over head, dropping bombs occasionally, it was no wonder some of the men became panicky. He promised them if they would obey orders they would be spared, and they were.

In 1920 a cataract formed over her remaining eyes and from May 1921 to October 1922 she was totally blind. She was not idle one moment. She always waited upon herself, washed dishes, made beds and did numerous household tasks, made 23 rugs, crocheted hundreds of yards of lace, some out of very fine thread, and very complicated designs. She also pieced four quilts, one each for her unmarried sons. She went to Salt Lake City to have her eye attended to. She was in the hospital for ten days, but it was a month before she was permitted to see.

Her son Aaron seems to have inherited from his carpenter grandfather some of his ability in the handling of woods. Among his Mother's prized possessions are two dressers, a book shelf and a dining room table all made of seasoned red cedar. The table is very unique; the top is formed of 75 pieces artistically arranged. It has eleven sides, one for each member of the family at the time it was made. This precious boy was killed while helping install some machinery near Mesa. He was trying to place a heavy belt with a hammer handle when it was wrenched from his hand and forced through his throat. He lived for 19 hours thereafter. He left a wife and two children.

Two years and ten days after John brought the body of his brother Will home, he was brought home for burial. He died of heat prostration in Phoenix.

She has buried her husband and eight of her sixteen children, yet she never complains is always cheerful and happy. "Part of the time we only had bread and gravy, sometimes gravy without the bread, but gravy still tastes good to me, and we never had hard times, never bought a readymade article for myself nor any of my family."

## Artemesia Stratton Willis

Interviewer: Roberta Flake Clayton
Navajo County

In 1878 my father moved his family to Snowflake, Arizona. In this place I spent my younger days. My parents gave me all the advantages of schooling that they could. The schools were very poor in those days, and I never went to school longer than three months of the year. I was taught to be honest, truthful, true to God, to my parents, to myself and others.

The people had to work together to protect themselves from the Indians and lawless men and anger that existed. Often the cry would go out that Indians were on the warpath and our fathers, brothers and sweethearts would have to leave whatever they were doing, take their firearms and stand guard. Often the Indians would steal cattle, horses, and whatever else they could.

During the sacrifices, trials and hardships, we had our pleasures and enjoyments. We tried to get as much out of life as we could. One of our chief amusements was to get a team of horses and hitch it to a hay rack and go for a ride. Our picnic lunches would consist of popcorn, molasses candy and molasses cake.

Our clothing was mostly handmade. When we could get enough calico for a dress, we were very proud. We always kept it for our best dress. I never had a hat, only when I gathered whet straw and my mother braided the straw and made the hat. If I were lucky enough to get a ribbon to put around it I felt that I was dressed up.

Most of the people lived in one room houses made of logs, usually with dirt floors. When anyone got the lumber and put down a floor we had a dance. Our music consisted of one violinist or "fiddler" and a guitar player. We enjoyed ourselves very much. A man by the name of Don Clayton and his wife were among the fortunate ones to have a lumber floor. They would let the young folks help them take out all the furniture and let us have a dance. After the dance was out we would put everything back where it was and go home rejoicing at what a wonderful time we had.

## Nancy Cedenia Bagley Willis

Interviewer: Roberta Flake Clayton
Phoenix

I went with my father to the fields to kill crickets that were destroying our grain. I have followed my Mother to the willow patch where she burned the willows for ashes to make our soap. When I was older I went out on the hillsides and dug the roots of oose, or Amole as the Mexicans call it, which were excellent to use in place of soap.

I have been lulled to sleep many a night by the busy hum of the spinning wheel as I sat in the corner of the old fireplace watching the sparks fly upward while Mother spun and reeled the yarn to be woven into cloth for our clothes. Our shoes were made by the one shoemaker in the town. Ugh! I fancy I can still smell the horrid old vats where the leather was tanned.

Then there was the school house; the slab benches without any backs. We had one little first reader for the whole class. It too was backless. Our slates were shaped from the slate rock that was found nearby. The sly glances, the smiles cast upon the little boy who was fortunate enough to have some kind or a knife to sharpen pieces of the slate stone for us to use as pencils.

When I was four years of age my father was called with others to help keep Johnston's Army back when they were going to exterminate the Mormons. That left my Mother, with the aid of a small neighbor boy, to drive our one yoke of oxen. Mother put our few belongings into the wagon. She permitted me to take my little kitten along. That was a great comfort to me.

When the people left their homes they thought never to see them again as they were to be set on fire as a last resort to keep the enemy from occupying them. That did not become necessary and after a short time the owners returned. When we returned, and saw our little white-washed adobe house my childish joy knew no bounds. I gave vent to my feelings in a shout of joy which was echoed through the room. But I had heard so many stories of soldiers, mobs, Indians that I was always afraid and the sound of my voice in the empty room startled me so that I ran to my Mother screaming.

It was ever a fear. Again the school house with its bullet holes through the door. Again a scene of confusion and fear as a regiment of soldiers was seen to form in line on the public square in front of the school room. The teacher lost all control of the children who crept under the benches as we saw the soldiers with their guns and sabers glistening in the noonday sun.

In the beautiful month of May, 1870, with his parents and other relatives we stared for Salt Lake City. On the 31 of May I became the bride of Merrill Willis. We visited with friends and relatives and upon returning to Toquerville; Merrill built us a comfortable home. Three sons were born to us there.

In 1877, a call came to my father to go to Arizona to help build that new country. I pleaded with my husband to go that I might be with my Mother. Merrill sold our home and farm. With two new wagons, white-topped carriage, fine teams, one year's provisions, ten cows and calves, we started on this journey on April 12, 1878.

We spent our first winter in Arizona in our wagon boxes. A ridge pole along the center and the wagon covers stretched tightly kept out most of the moisture. I was sorry that I had had to cut up our brown ducking tents to make the little boys suits, but they had to be clothed and there was nothing else. Then there was the little log house with factory cloth for windows, and its shake roof and floors.

There wasn't much time to devote to house building. Water and tillable land do not always lie adjacent. The hundred acres Merrill Willis had taken up were three miles from Show Low Creek. Ditches had to be dug from it to the land. Fences had to be built and the land cleared. It took fourteen years of hard toil for him and his three little boys to get everything as they wanted with alfalfa, pasture, orchard and garden plot. In the meantime a larger, more pretentious frame house had been built. This had porches on it.

Here the family was very happy each boy had his own calves and colts. Cedenia had her flowers and always her bee hives. The Willis family shared with their neighbors the barley bread. Flour was prohibitive at twenty dollars a sack.

On the twenty-fifth day of June, 1880, a beautiful baby girl came to our house. We named her Mary for my mother. How we loved her. My three little boys had whooping-cough at the time and our precious baby contracted it. Two months later on August 25, 1880, as the sun was sinking in the Western horizon our little family knelt around a freshly made grave where we had laid our treasure. This was our first parting by death and her little grave was the first one in the town of Taylor, Arizona.

## Emma Eliza Bryon Wyatte

Interviewer: Kathlyn M. Lathrop
Duncan

When I was fifteen Father bought a rather large plantation several miles from the home farm, and as my Mother had all she could do to take care of her home, tend the cows, pigs, chickens, make garden and care for six children and her aged, ailing Mother, I went to the plantation with Father to do the cooking for him and for ten to fifteen hired hands.

Besides cooking on an open fireplace and keeping house, I done the washing and ironing. We ironed with heavy andirons, heated on an open fire. I milked five or six cows twice a day, raised pigs and chickens, and made a garden; then found time to piece quilts, make rag rugs, and knit stockings.

When I went to school, or to church, or to town I carried my knitting bag along and knit as fast as I could every minute I had time.

At age seventeen I married George Washington Wyatte in Covenington County, Alabama. I already knew all the duties of a housewife, but I must admit there was certainly a lot about marriage that I didn't know. Mothers taught their daughters to work, keep house, cook and sew, but they considered it not only a disgrace, but dangerous to the morals of young womanhood to teach them anything about marriage. I raised a family of ten children, nine of them were born in Alabama and one in Arizona, five are living, and the others have gone to their rest, along with their father. Mr. Wyatte died in 1925 in Franklin, Arizona.

We started west in 1899. We came by train to Stanford, Colorado, and although we had a little money it seemed hard to get another start like we had at home.

When we lost our seventeen-year-old daughter in Colorado, we just couldn't stay there any longer. So in the winter of 1901 we headed for Arizona Territory.

We were on the road one month and five days, in the dead of winter. I dipped up snow and melted it to wash our clothes along the road. It was a miserable trip, with eight youngsters to look after, besides the stock to tend, and the weather was so cold.

We landed at Fort Thomas, Arizona, in time to put in a crop. But the bugs simply cleaned us out that year; off about twenty or thirty acres of wheat we got two sacks of grain.

We thought we had lean years back in Alabama but it was nothing compared to the first five or six years at Fort Thomas. At times it looked as if we were going to starve in spite of everything we could do, but we made it through, and none of us really went hungry.

Fort Thomas is near the San Carlos Indian Reservation. Those were the first Indians we ever knew very much about, we found them peaceable, friendly and mighty good neighbors.

As I said before the first years at Fort Thomas were mighty lean, besides bugs, grasshoppers and worms, we had a drought to contend with, and crops just couldn't produce.

Then we were about to give up in despair, we raised a bumper crop and the market prices went up; we began to "get on our feet" again. In another few years our struggle for existence seemed to have come to an end.

Oh no! One's "troubles" never really crease you know! But when financial worries let up, even temporarily, you feel that life is worth the living.

# CHAPTER FIVE
# Wild Beasts, Indians and Outlaws

*No weaklings could conquer the desert, the Indians, the wild animals, and live and develop a country; it took brave men and women who were unafraid of hard work and difficulties.*

*Ellen Malmstrom Larson*

The pioneers' battle for survival included more than meeting the needs of basic subsistence: food, water, shelter. The lack of food and water, horrendous weather and the most primitive of living conditions were enough to test the strongest person trying to eke out an existence on the frontier. Yet, nature and mankind conspired to make frontier life even more miserable and success more challenging.

Pioneer women faced dangerous beasts. They fought battles against invasions and attacks from poisonous snakes, bears, wolves and other wild life that claimed the land for their own. Added to that were the Indian attacks, and the threat of outlaws which were not singularly unique events, but part of everyday life.

Frequently the women were alone, responsible for their lives, the lives of their children, and the protection of the homestead. Because pioneer men, who were not ranchers or shopkeepers, took any job they could find, they often were away from home for long periods. The Mormon pioneer husbands often answered the call from their church to go on Mission. These Missions were to places far from their families, often as far away as Europe or Asia, and they were absent from their families for years.

The frontier was a wild, undisciplined, and mostly lawless land. Outlaws roamed the territory. They seldom attacked the pioneers, but ranchers were victims of rustlers, businesses were pray to robbers, and illegal acts were all around them. The saddest for the pioneers was when the law breakers were members of their own family. But, life on the frontier was hard, and it broke some weaker humans.

The pioneers faced continual and repeated attacks from the Native Americans, whose land they had encroached upon. Often the Indian attacks were rooted in the frustrations of reservation living and confinement. Added to this toxic mix were the wild beasts. Wolves, snakes, bobcats, and other native inhabitants claimed the right to the land and everything on it.

While the beasts were always dangerous, and the association with outlaws was nebulous, the Indians were not always a menace. In some instances they saved the lives of the pioneers by giving them food and shelter. But, they were always a presence to be reckoned with.

In this chapter the women tell how they survived some of these horrendous dangers. Many of these events took the lives of friends and family. The survivors were not always unscathed. They reveal how these encounters left their mark on them both physically and emotionally. Some of these reports will put a chill in your heart, but all will make you marvel at the tenacity and courage of the pioneers.

### Elizabeth Adelaide Hoopes Allen

Interviewer: Roberta Flake Clayton

Often the Indians would enter the settlement and take liberties and commit depredations which were unwarranted. On one such occasion, while her husband was away getting their winter supply of wood from the canyon, two Indians strolled into their yard, entered the house, ordered her to give them something to eat. Her nature was not of a nervous type so while some women under like circumstances might have been frightened, she displayed no timidity. She was preparing them a hand-out when she noticed one's gaze riveted on her rifle, which was hanging on the wall.

As he took a step toward the gun she saw his intentions, drew the gun herself. He immediately grabbed the hatchet out of the wall and raised it as if to strike. She gave him an unexpected shove. It was so forceful that it landed him outside the door on a board with a nail in it where he parted with a bit of goopy colored blanket.

As it is the nature of the red man; his admiration for her bravery recompensed him for the humility he had received. The Indians took themselves off without dealing her any more trouble.

## Edna Price Armbrust

Interviewer: Alfred E. Downing

Their homestead was located in the little valley which is now covered by Lake Mary, an artificial lake created about 1906. As their arrival there came after the Indians had been subdued, life was quiet and uneventful except for some of the Indian scares which so often resulted from accounts of earlier nerve-shaking incidents.

A band of Indians out hunting came upon their home one day while Father Price was away. Mrs. Price, taking no chances, closed the doors and warned the children not to show themselves.

The Indians came prowling around acting suspiciously, peering in the windows, but showing no hostilities. Finally Mrs. Price cautiously opened the door and gave them some of the bread she was baking that day to induce them to leave.

Edna Price, by then Mrs. James B. Armbrust, recalls a similar scare which seemed based on more substantial grounds. Mrs. Acker, teaching at the water tank twelve mile south of Flagstaff, saw a whooping band of Indians coming toward the school one afternoon, and not taking any chances, herded the pupils under the floor of the school.

The guttural comments of the Indians as they searched the school convinced the teacher that she had saved herself and the children from at least minor indignities by hiding before they arrived.

In 1900, Mr. Price purchased a farm on the east side of the Verde River near Camp Verde and settled permanently. During the next years he freighted between Prescott and Flagstaff, most of his hauling being for the pioneer Wingfield store in Camp Verde. By this time the Indians were becoming reconciled to confinement on reservations, and Mrs. Armbrust recalls her curiosity regarding those whom her father hired to work on the farm for fifty cents a day. They clung to their old tribal customs, however, and it took the Price family some time to become accustomed to hearing the noise of night-long ceremonial dances held to drive out sickness. Only a few years ago Mrs. Armbrust saw at short range one of the weirdest of these, the Devil Dance, performed every fifteen years. It depicts the exercising of the evil spirit by the savior of the people, the good spirits.

### Clara Armstrong

Interviewer: G. W. Reeve

The Border Ranch, which was run by the Armstrongs, was located in a very wild part of the country, and as they observed the usual Western courtesy of hospitality to all coming through, they had many visitors of the wild and lawless type stop over with them.

Mrs. Armstrong told me of one occasion when there was quite a large crowd of men stopping over night with them, some of the talk almost brought on a "free for all" shooting match.

After supper while all were sitting around the fire, the conversation drifted around to the subject of Billy the Kid. Mrs. Armstrong did not know the names of half of her guests, (not the real names at least), and did not know that Pat Garrett, the killer of Billy the Kid, was among them. In fact several of the men did not know this. And, during this conversation one of the men, evidently a hero worshiper, spoke up and said, "Well I would just like to meet the man that killed Billy the Kid. I would like to shake hands with him."

Mrs. Armstrong spoke up and said, "Well then, I have my opinion of YOU. I have no respect for ANY man who would travel with Billy the Kid, or any other man, share his grub and bed, and while he was sleeping pull a gun and shoot him in the back. In my opinion a man that would do a low down, dirty trick like that is just too low to be named."

There was a terrible silence after that outburst, and several of the men shifted their positions, and it looked as if there was going to be a split of the men into two sides and a shootout.

After a few minutes of watchful suspense Pat Garret said, "Mrs. Armstrong, I am Pat Garrett." Mrs. Armstrong replied, "What I said still goes, Mr. Garrett, you or any man who would take advantage of another man who trusted you in such a way, is just too low to be named, and I would hate to meet you where I had no protection. Mr. Garrett, some day, some kid is going to get you, just the way you got that poor boy, and I hope it will be soon."

The subject was dropped then. No serious trouble developed from the conversation.

Afterward, one time when Pat Garrett was trying to beat a young man by the name of Wayne Brazell out of his place, and the young man saw that Garrett was intending to shoot him down because he could not run him off, this young man beat Pat Garrett to the draw, and killed him, but he did not have to shoot him in the back as Garrett had shot Billy the Kid. Only part of Mrs. Armstrong's prediction came true.

## May Bates

Interviewer: Helen M. Smith

We saw much of the Apaches while we lived in Globe. Since Father was away much of the time, it was left to Mother to cope with them as best she could. Her best always seemed sufficient. The Indians had of course been tamed somewhat before this, but they still went on the warpath at times in small groups and committed minor depredations whenever they thought they could get by.

Fort Thomas was some distance away, and they could often do their deviltry and be back on the reservation before we could get word to the troops at the fort. One day when Father was gone, a runner came to our cabin and told Mother that the Apaches were on the warpath, and that all the women and children were to collect in a corral which was in a little hollow among the hills not far beyond the mine.

There were few men in Globe at the time, but those who were there were to collect all available ammunition, and would patrol this corral and vicinity until the danger was past.

Mother refused to go, saying that the corral was too available to the Indians, who could easily creep up on it under cover of the brush and rocks, or attack from the hills which surrounded it. When asked what she would do, she answered that she would remain home and protect herself as best she could. She would not change her mind and remained at home where she did not so much as glimpse an Indian. Sometime during the night, however, she thought she heard a faint noise, which may have been the gunfire as the Indians rushed the corral. All the women and children were massacred, and only one of two men escaped in the darkness.

I do not remember being scared of the Indians. Mother had me trained so that whenever I caught sight of an Indian I immediately ran to tell her.

I had a number of fine toys sent to me by our relatives in California, but I sometime left these toys lying around the door, and eventually they all disappeared, stolen by the Indians who constantly appeared around our cabin.

One day a group of Indians rode up to the bridge across the draw. One of these Indians came across with a flour sack in his hand and asked Mother if she wanted to buy some green coffee. The Indians frequently sold much of the food issued them by the government. He said the coffee was government coffee, and good. Mother asked him how much and he said fifty cents. She bought the coffee from him, and he still lingered.

"What do you want?" Mother asked. "You make me, my men coffee." He replied. Mother explained that she couldn't because there was no coffee parched, and it would take too long to parch it. "You make coffee for my men, I say." he said threateningly. "You git!" retorted Mother.

The Indian brought his gun to his shoulder and immediately Mother snatched it from him by the barrel, leveled it at him, and repeated her command for him to "Git." He got, back to the other Indians.

Mother had her own gun ready loaded and standing just inside the door, but she never had recourse to it unless driven. The Indians were more or less cowardly and the chances were good that she could handle them, but she thought there was little use in starting something that could result fatally for her if the Indians decided to fight.

After a powwow the chief came across the bridge, hands in the air. "Well? demanded Mother when he reached the door. "You give my man his gun", said the chief. Mother said she would if the rest of the gang would stay where they were. She broke the gun, removed the bullets, placed them in her apron pocket, and handed the gun to the chief with instruction to return to his men with his hands in the air, and that they were all to "git" and not come back.

One day I was playing just outside the door. Suddenly a big Indian appeared from the side of the house. He snatched me up and covered my mouth with his hand before I had a chance to make a sound. He started running with me, not across the bridge, but out to one side of the cabin and over a little hill. I could not scream, but I could kick and twist and I managed to hamper him considerable in his escape. Mother had a queer feeling about me, and looked out and saw I wasn't there; the next object that met her gaze was this big Indians, naked except for a gee-string, disappearing over the hill

Mother started running after him at top speed, not even pausing to get her gun. She was almost up with him when he looked back and saw her. He tried to increase his speed, but I was no light weight, and Mother caught up with him.

The wind was blowing hard, and the two flaps of his gee-string were blowing back between his legs as he ran. Mother made a grab, grabbed the flaps of both blowing back between his legs and gave them a violent jerk.

The force of the jerk swung him half around, and he almost fell. "You give me my baby!" She cried. "No," he grunted sullenly, "Me take to reservation. Keep in wigwam." Mother began kicking and hitting him, all the time trying to pull me from his arms, as he grunted sullenly. Mother said she never knew why he didn't use his tomahawk, his only weapon, on her, but he didn't. At last she told him her husband and some other men were coming, were just over the hill, and he would be killed if he did not immediately surrender the child. Whether he believed the story or whether he just thought he had bit off more than he could chew, he released me. Mother and I returned home.

Eventually the mine closed down, and the Arthur family decided to return to California. Some of Geronimo's tribe were on the warpath, and we were warned that it was dangerous to attempt to travel. We started any way and when it was time to camp for the night we were near a camp of Indians on the reservation.

Father asked the chief for permission to camp there, which he readily gave, and sent squaws to carry wood and water for us. We were too heavily loaded, and Father gave the chief a mattress and his son a violin, which the boy had seemed unable to leave. He also gave the Indians other heavy articles which he thought would need to be discarded.

We camped there several days and while we were there witnessed the funeral of an Indian boy who had been bitten by a rattlesnake. A platform was built and raised in the air to some height. The boy was laid on the platform, together with such of his belongings as could be placed with him. His horse and dogs were killed and placed under the platform, as also other articles too large to be placed on the platform with him. Indians remained around this platform all night, and kept up a howling which sounded much like coyotes from a distance.

### Catherine Barlow Burton

Interviewer: Roberta Flake Clayton

Kate spent some time living on a ranch. She was very timid and especially of Indians. She kept an eye out for them all the time. One day, however, when only she and her baby were on the ranch alone she looked around the corner of the house and there were two Indians with their long black hair hanging around their shoulders, and attired only in gee-strings. She knew they were Apaches. What should she do? The nearest neighbor was half a mile away. She had some grapes out drying. She gave the intruders some and told them to take as many as they wanted; but they only ate a few and went away.

### Mary Elizabeth Greenwalt

Interviewer: Kathlyn M. Lathrop

Our son Homer got into trouble and had to be sent off to a reform school; our son Harry followed in Homer's footsteps—always into some devilment of some kind. In a few years, he too, had to be sent to a reform school. Our daughter Flossie fell into disgrace and left us. Our youngest daughter, Florence, married against our will and died within a few months. We then had only our baby boy, Willie, left to us.

Then Homer came home from the reform school, got married and took to heavy drinking. Three years later he was shot and killed by an officer of the law who had known him all his life. They call it justified homicide. He left a wife and two children and a third child was born about a week after his death.

Harry came home and got married. He deserted his wife and two children and was sent to the penitentiary for bigamy. Then he was killed while trying to make a getaway on a moving freight train.

Ed married his own blood cousin, I blame Granny McCullock for that marriage, and after fifteen years of marriage, he killed his wife and another man, and cheated the law by hanging himself in prison.

## Mrs. Y. Garcia

Interviewer: E. S. Upton

In 1868 Mrs. Garcia's father was chased by Indians from what is now Forpaugh to Cullen's Well. He was obliged to cast away every possible article to lighten weight, including part of his clothing, to get the greatest possible speed and save his mount.

## Sarah A. Packer Higgins

Interviewer: Helen M. Smith

I remember one queer incident while we lived there, an incident which I would not believe if I had not seen it, and which I never could get my husband to accept.

Both he and my sister's husband were absent. I was doing the housework and my sister was irrigating. Suddenly she rushed into the house breathlessly, closing the door behind her hastily. She looked frightened.

"What is the trouble?" I asked her hurriedly, the thought of Indians in the back of my head.

"A snake," she replied quickly. "It followed me to the house and is after me now. It ran under the house when I ran in!"

"Well it can't get in. That is one consolation," I answered.

She looked at a knothole in the floor. "I'm sure it will come through that hole. I tell you it was after me," she said stubbornly.

I had scarcely got the words out of my mouth when the snake thrust its head through the knothole. My sister turned pale, I grabbed one of the babies asleep in the room and pushed her before me into the other room, closing the door firmly behind us. Here we stayed until the return of the men. We heard snake in the other room for a few minutes, but no trace was to be found when the men searched. My sister was firmly convinced that the snake had been in pursuit of her, and it was some days before she forgot her fear.

Bryce was another very small settlement. We had our little adventures there too. The children slept on a pallet on the floor, which I habitually placed just in front of my trunk, of which I was very proud. One morning in taking up the pallet I discovered that, whereas the children had slept in front of the trunk, a large rattlesnake had slept behind it.

Another snake adventure occurred while my husband was irrigating. He always kept his pants legs down while irrigating, while everyone else I ever saw rolled them up. I remonstrated with him without avail, since he always said he didn't want to get his legs sunburned. This habit of his probably saved his life on this occasion. An enormous rattlesnake struck at his leg with such violence that it required a very determined effort to loosen its fangs from the leg of his overalls. After that I never mentioned his rolling up his pants legs while irrigating.

On another occasion we had quite a scare. A mad wildcat came through the one door of the house, frothing at the mouth, clawing and scratching at everything with which it came in contact. We were lucky enough to avoid being bitten while leaving the house to the cat. We made a most hurried exodus and I got the children to a place of safety. Mr. Higgins was away from home. Eventually the cat left the house.

Our experience was repeated in one or two other homes, and men finally mounted horses and rode the cat down, killing it. However, such experiences were common enough to pioneer families, and nothing to get excited about after all.

## Miriam Dalton Hancock

Interviewer: Roberta Flake Clayton

On June 2nd, 1881, word came for us to go to Taylor at once as the Indians were on the warpath. Lyman then went out to hunt the horses and came across the Indians just north of Snowflake Camp. He left the horses and hurried back to let the other settlers know that the Indians were almost upon us. I had everything packed in the wagon ready to go to Taylor, but had to leave it all and start out on foot with my husband."

We were soon joined by the Angles and all went to where the Brewer brothers lived, got them together, and went to the Mortensen Ranch. By now there was quite a group of men and they considered themselves safe. There they remained over night.

The next morning Lyman and some of the men went to where we were living and all we had left was what we stood up in. The Indians had destroyed or taken everything. They killed the chickens, broke the stove, tore up all the books but one, the Book of Mormon, tore up our pictures, and carried the remainder of our belongings away.

While in Williams Valley," says Mrs. Hancock, "we were driven into town again by the Indians. This was the worst ordeal I ever went though. We didn't know what minute the Indians would come and kill us. The men stood guard for two weeks. We didn't gain anything by going to New Mexico but another son whom we named Charles Levi, so we returned to Pinedale.

"When our first baby was about a year old a band of Apaches came to our house. There were about twenty of them. Before we knew it they had come right into the house. My husband's gun stood in the corner. The Indians wanted to look at it, but he would not let them near it. Finally the leader of the band walked up to my husband, lifted his hat up and peered into his face. He then said, "Me sabe you." He was the Indian Lyman had found wounded in Water Canyon, about 3 years before, where he had been shot by the soldiers from Fort Apache; and had been taken to Mother Hancock's home in Taylor where she nursed the Indian until he was well and able to travel.

Then she divided what food she had with him and he left. As soon as the Indian recognized Lyman he began talking very fast to the others and they all went out of the house and the leader took two deer from the saddle and gave them to us."

Another time, after Mrs. Hancock had been away for some time, upon her return to Pinedale, an educated Apache named John Williams, came to see her and in gratitude told her she was all the same as his mother because she had fed him when he was a little boy and told her he would never forget her for her kindness.

## Loretta Ellsworth Hansen

Interviewer: Roberta Flake Clayton

The ranch was near the reservation and the family lived in constant fear of the Apaches. There were frequent uprisings, fighting even among themselves. One of the worst was enacted during a "tulipi" party when Chief Petone and two other Indians were killed, and two other seriously wounded. These Mr. Ellsworth took to his home and nursed back to life. One of them was Alssaya who became Chief in Petone's stead. By this act of kindness, Rettie's father and family were looked upon with gratitude by the Indians, and they and their belongings were pretty safe unless from renegade bands. The most dreaded of these were Geronimo's the very mention of whose name caused terror in the hearts of women and children and filled even the bravest man with fear and anxiety.

One of these raids was in 1881. A fort was built and all of the ranchers and people living in nearby communities gathered in. Rettie says "None were injured, but I will never forget the nights of terror I spent thinking every sound was Indians coming to murder us. I never told of my fear, but I am sure the others were as frightened as I was. We would hear of ranchers and travelers being horribly murdered, and didn't know but what we might be next. I remember I would make light of my Mother's fears while at the same time I would be terrified. With the capture of Geronimo the Indian trouble quieted down."

When she was seventeen Rettie promised to become the wife of Hans Hansen, Jr. as fine a young man as she had known since coming to Arizona. One September 29th, 1885, they and her brother Frank, and his betrothed, Edna Merrill, started on their wedding journey to St. George, Utah.

"One morning, way out on the desert, the boys were greasing the gear wagon, we girls at the other, washing dishes, when we found ourselves completely surrounded by large prairie wolves. We lost no time climbing into our wagon, and the boys killed wolves as long as their ammunition lasted. It was a thrilling sight to see about fifty large wolves lined up like soldiers. At the sound of the gun they would jump back a few paces still facing us, then would step forward again. The howling of the wounded and the firing of guns finally frightened them away.

**Lousea Park Harper**

Interviewer: Roberta Flake Clayton

In 1849, after living in the old fort for two years, they were called by President Brigham Young to go with other saints and settle on the Provo River. Here again a fort was built for their protection and all lived in it. The Indians were very troublesome helping themselves to anything they could steal and carry away. They also tried to steal some cattle at one time. They got possession of some which they drove away so fast that they got overheated and died. Lousea's husband, John Harper, and other men followed the Indians, overtook them, recovered the carcasses of the cattle and took them home. The hides were used to make shoes for the family and the tallow to make candles to furnish lights for their homes.

"Our stretch of land was right on the bank of the Salt River, a powerful river at flood time, and the Indian trail from their village to Tempe. This was terrifying to the white people who did not understand the ways of the Indians.

"At this time the Indians were drinking a mescal beverage which they made from a plant in the mountains. Away into the night they would keep the trail hot with their whooping and yelling. It sounded to us like war whoops.

"Many times while left alone while my father was away freighting, my mother gathered us children into the bedroom, which was just a covered wagon, and prayed for the Lord to protect us and to bless us with a comfortable feeling that we might get our wanted sleep and rest. We would certainly be glad for the light of day and would wake refreshed.

"At that time the storms were terrible. One time the lightning struck right before our eyes and close to the corral. It struck and bursted a large mesquite tree all to pieces and another time we were huddled together in our little bedroom. My father had gone to Mesa on Old Pony, a riding horse we owned. The thunder and lightning was terrible, the rain poured down in sheets. My mother had us children around her in our little nook asking the Lord for protection and to bring our father home safely. It seemed like the roar and crack of the thunder would pull the words right out of her mouth and our ears would fill up until we could hardly hear.

"In a little while the storm subsided and my father came riding in on little Old Pony and yelled, "Mother Lousea are you all safe? Thank God for that, for I was afraid you would be all washed into the river. Why, in Mesa as I was coming along the water was up to Pony's knees and where did it all go to? It was terrific, the worst I have ever seen. Oh, I am so happy we are all together."

## Carmen Hillman

Interviewer: Romelia Gomez

An incident which illustrates this exciting period of Bisbee's early days concerns three Mexicans who held up an elderly lady on Chihuahua Hill, thinking she had money. They struck her a blow on the head, then encountered her son whom they shot at, but fortunately missed him. He somehow managed to take their gun and chase them away, after which he notified the police.

The three would-be bandits, enraged and baffled in their attempt to get money, met an old Frenchman on their way up to Zacatecas Canyon. Venting all their rage on this poor man they slit his throat, for which crime they were later arrested and sentenced to prison.

## Virlinda Jennings

Interviewer: Kathlyn M. Lathrop

I recall it was on Christmas eve, before my 19th birthday (1864), shortly after dark. It was on the light of the moon and a cold North wind had sprung up and was whistling like ghosts around the house and soughing through the trees.

I felt lonesome somehow and did not want to go to bed early. I piled on a lot of pine knots on the fireplace, put on a pot of lye soap to boil, set the boys to picking their boots full of seeded cotton, and sat down to my spinning. When the children picked their boots full, each night, I would let them go to bed and not before. They had to help me you see, even little Bucky, not quite two years old, picked his little shoes full each night.

Bucky had begun to nod, he almost always did before he got his shoes filled, and I started to pick him and put him to bed, when I heard the hoot of an owl outside. I almost froze in my tracks, I knew what that meant, it was not an owl, it was Indians, and Davy and Henry both knew it too.

I seen Davy glance up at a crack where the chinking was out by the fireplace, he did not make a sound, just looked at me and went right on picking cotton as if he had seen nothing at all; even children had to be brave in those days. I glanced at the crack and seen a pair of eyes staring in at me.

I pretended not to see those eyes, I just picked the baby up and kicked a rag rug out of my way, the rug was over the trap door to the tunnel, and laid little Bucky on the rug right by the door. Then I scolded the boys, real loud, for not getting their boots full sooner, they understood me perfectly.

I then kicked up the fire real bright and began stirring the boiling soap as hard as I could. Then I picked up a quart cup and skimmed the foam from the soap and carelessly tossed it through that crack, the foam I mean. There was a blood chilling yell and a terrible commotion outside. There must have been a hundred Indians out there from the noise they made.

When I threw the soap Davey jumped up and grabbed the baby while Henry jerked open the trap door. Both boys darted into that dark tunnel and jerked the door down behind them. I had schooled them in what to do in case of an attack like that and I knew they would try to do it.

I seen another pair of eyes at that crack and threw some more soap, another, another, and another. I just kept right on with my soap throwing and counting out loud, and thinking about the children. "One, two, three' four," I counted in betwixt thoughts, "Will Davy make it from the tunnel, five, six—to the gates—seven—will Henry—eight—stay in the tunnel—nine—with the-ten-baby-will the soap-eleven-hold-twelve-out-thirteen, fourteen-until-fifteen-help comes."

Well I kept that up until I had counted nineteen Indians that I had thrown soap in their eyes. I was wondering why they did not break into the cabin or why they did not set fire to it, but I guess they were too scared. Indians you know are a superstitious lot. They might have thought it was some kind of a fire God in there.

Just as I was about to count twenty, the trap door flew open and ten men from the fort arrived. I counted "twenty" threw my cup down and grabbed my rifle and shoved it through that crack and began to pull the trigger. Nobody spoke; the men just rushed to the gun holes in the walls and began shooting.

In a very little while everything was quiet outside, and the men decided we had better get to the fort while the getting was good, if it still was; them red devils were a tricky lot you know. The first thing I remember saying to the men was that I couldn't have held out more than one more Indians, as I had used all the soap but about one cupful of scrapings. When I got to the fort I found my three children safe.

Next morning the men captured twenty soap-blinded Indians in the woods, and they had killed fifty or more.

Yes, Arizona was still a little wild 'n wooly when we came here, but all the Indians had been corralled on reservations by that time, all but one half-breed called the Apache Kid. I never did seen him myself, but he holed up in a Canyon near our place once when the soldiers or a posse, was after him for killing somebody over here near Safford, Arizona. He stayed there several days.

None of my boys was ever outlaws that I know of, and I don't know just why they didn't kill that Indian when they knew he was there. But my boys said they was not being paid for killing anybody, and besides he had done us no harm.

I tried to argue with them that he had killed white people and that he was just an Indian, but they argued that he was half white also, and the world hadn't given him a right to live a civilized life, and if he had killed it was for a reason other than just the merciless shedding of white blood.

The only Arizona outlaw I ever knew personally was a fellow called Lee Woods; his right name was Lee Wright, so I learned in later years. He had a hideout away up on the mountain above our ranch, and he has stayed at our house lots of times.

He had a young wife named Ellen; I guess she was his wife anyway. She ran away from him once and came to our house and was there almost a week before he came after her and took her off to El Paso, or someplace else. They said they were going to El Paso to be married by his right name. I never seen either of them since then.

I heard a few years ago that an officer by the name of Lee Wright had been killed by a woman outlaw named Irene Schroder over near Phoenix. I suppose it was the same Lee Wright that I had know to be an outlaw at one time. I learned that Ellen Wight died over here in the Greenlee County hospital several years ago. She and Lee were divorced at the time they said.

## Olive Jewell

Interviewer: Helen M. Smith

We were not molested by Indians ourselves, but murder by them was of frequent occurrence all around us. They could not attack settlements, but killed and robbed when one or two persons could be caught alone. There was the murder of the two Wright brothers by Indians while the brothers were trying to recover some stolen horses.

Once two freighters were killed and their wagons burned very close to us. There was a Mr. Merrill and his daughter killed a short distance from Solomonville by Indians. Two years later during a 4th of July celebration by the Mormons of the community, the whites and the Indians were having a tug of war. Mrs. Merrill was present, and she saw her daughter's dress on an Indian girl. There were a great many questions asked but no one could find out who had killed Mr. Merrill and the daughter.

## Ellen Jane Parks Johnstun

Interviewer: Roberta Flake Clayton

There were three wagons; one had a four mule team, and the others four oxen, the rest were handcarts. Indians would come whenever we were near their land to trade with us. One of our teamsters was a Scotsman and we called him Sandy. One time he had been bothered a lot with them and not having any goods to exchange for a pair of beaded moccasins, thought to get rid of them by saying he would trade me for them. The Indians were very pleased and would not change the trade. Three Indians followed us for three days and I had to be hidden to keep them from stealing me. Another lesson learned.

We first built an adobe fort where we lived for many years. The Indians were very poor in this part of the country. Some children were so thin you could see the workings of the intestines. We had to feed them once a week with thin mush. They were so hungry they would eat it with fingers while it was almost boiling hot. This of course made us short of provisions. One day an old buck tried to steal my towel from over the wagon bow. I saw him and grabbing a fire shovel splattered it until he let go. He wanted it for a gee string. Andrew Gibbons saw me and he said "lay it on, Ellen." Towels were not so easily gotten in those days.

**Rebecca Steward Kartchner**
Interviewer: Roberta Flake Clayton

After a month of just such luck we came into New Mexico. There we found a bunch of wild Navajo Indians and they gave us lots of trouble. They would follow us all day trying to steal a horse, mule or oxen. At night the men would stand guard taking turns always keeping awake.

Both cattle and camp had to be guarded. They would sneak up so easy a cat couldn't hear them. Sometimes when the women would raise their bake oven lids, the Indians would grab the bread out of their hands, take our coffee pot and get away.

There were so many of them standing around we could hardly walk and they were full of lice. That is what we had to contend with from the time we got into New Mexico until we got out. We were so happy when we crossed the line into Arizona.

**Caroline Marion Williams Kimball**
Interviewer: Roberta Flake Clayton

The Skull Valley Indians were quite troublesome in those days. On several occasions while Father had charge of the ranch, Indians stole large herds of stock. Father took part several times in trying to subdue the Redskins.

Mother was a very brave woman. Many times the Indians would come when she was left alone. They would talk very mean, but Mother would give them something to eat and always had a prayer in her heart asking the Lord to bless and protect her.

One day when Father was home they decided they would like to practice shooting at a target. While Father and Mother were practicing, twenty young Indians heard the shooting and came over to the house and asked if they could shoot at the target too, and Mother let them.

They all tried to see who could hit it, but Mother was the best shot among them. They all cheered her and told her she was good at shooting. Therefore, she always thought they respected her and seemed afraid to say or do anything out of the way around her.

**Amy McDonald**
Interviewer: Helen M. Smith

The fear of Indians was constantly with us. I think I may say that the first fifty years of my life were lived in that dread. Even after all danger of Indians attack was a thing of the past, it required many years for me to convince myself of the fact.

We had almost reached our stopping place on the Gila, being only one day out, when a party rode into our camp. There was a posse of men, accompanied by two women, both of whose husbands had just been massacred by the Apaches. That was my introduction to my new locality.

There was a women in the neighborhood who had had two husbands killed by Indians, and had been a captive with her two daughters. During her captivity her baby was born. The three were afterward removed from the Indian encampment by a body of soldiers. We never knew when our turn would come.

One night we heard a rustling in the corn patch, which we knew was Indians stealing corn. We kept very quiet while my brother made preparations for defending us should the Redskins attempt to molest us. We hoped that they would confine their depredations to the roasting ears. My brother had an old cap and ball six-shooter which he prepared as quickly as possible. It took about half an hour to load it, after which it would shoot six times before another half hour became needed for reloading. We remained up all night expecting attack, but none came. In the morning we discovered that the cows had broken into the corn!

I knew “Black Jack” Ketchum personally before he ever came to Arizona. His home as a boy was in Tom Greene County, Texas. He had no mother, which probably explains why he became wild. The cowboys who worked on his father’s place razzed him considerably. This did not help his disposition to improve. He was always rather overbearing, probably to cover up an inferiority complex. I believe that he would have turned out to be a good cowman but for his losing his mother when a baby.

## Mary Ann Smith McNeil

Interviewer: Roberta Flake Clayton

The Indian Chief Petone became angry at the Thanes and some of the other families. He said, "They lie, no good." He told John that he was going to scare them out by telling them that Geronimo was coming to fight. But he told John to sit down—"he no lie, heap good man, sit down, Indians no hurt." So we stayed. Everyone else left. I wanted to go but John wasn't afraid of the Indians, so he stayed and took care of his crop, also the crops of the other people, then in the fall the men came back to gather theirs."

I did lots of sewing for the squaws. Their skirts had ten yards of material in each one, besides trimming by the yards. I had to use my own thread. I used up two boxes that I had brought from Utah. When it was all gone I could not sew anymore and I was glad of it for they pestered me continually to sew for them.

One day an Indian man came and asked me to make him a shirt. I told him I was sick and couldn't. He kept coaxing me so I told him I had no thread. He got awful angry and called me names he had learned from the soldiers at Fort Apache. John told me I had better make him a shirt. The summer of 1880 the Indians gave us a war scare. It was about the middle of August.

Mr. McNeil and the Indians were great friends. He was never afraid of them, but the children and I were. He and Moses Cluff helped the Forest Dale Indians build a fort. It was a hollow place made in the top of a hill. They lowered barrels down into the fort, where they were hiding their food, squaws and papooses.

The San Carlos Indians came up to fight the Apaches. There was three or four hundred of them, and they were painted and wearing skeins of red yarn around their heads. They turned their horses loose in our corn field. John left me and the children while he went to take care of the corn and fix up the fences. We were nearly scared to death.

The Indians came up to the house. We had a watermelon patch in front of the house. They came and asked me for some. I traded a melon for three skeins of yarn. They soon stopped wanting to trade and took to helping themselves not only to the melons, but to things I had in the house. They took my butcher knife, cups and all my soap and everything else they saw that they wanted.

The children clung to my skirt and we were all trembling with fear. Soon they began to leave. John came back and said there had been a dispatch sent by Charlie Cooley to Fort Apache for help and the officers and soldiers came to settle the trouble. The San Carlos Indians went back. They had no fight but it was an awful scare we got.

**Sarah McNeil Mills**
Interviewer: Roberta Flake Clayton

During the summers spent at Forest Dale the Indians camped near and made themselves at home at the abode of the McNeils. Even Petone, the chief of that particular tribe was a frequent visitor. One day Mr. McNeil jokingly told the man that he could have Sarah for his wife. None of the family thought of it again until one day when Sarah was alone in the house Petone came, and taking her in his arms said she was to be his squaw, and when she was a little older he was going to steal her.

Sarah lived in constant fear that someday he might make his threat good so it is no wonder that she was much relieved and happy when a year or two after this he was killed in a "tulipi" brawl with two other Indians.

When the shooting died down a runner came with the news of the killing, and to get help for the three who were wounded.

Sarah had to satisfy herself and went back to the bloody scene with her father and others, and sure enough there was Petone, lying dead with three bullet holes through him, and with one of his squaws sitting at his head, and another sat his feet, moaning and crying as only an Indian can.

He was not Sarah's only Indian suitor. Later a young brave, known to all as Mike, who lived near them and worked for a neighbor, began casting "sheep's eyes" at Sarah. When the work of the day was over and the children of the village would gather to play games such as "hide and go seek", which Mike called "tugagole", he would take delight in finding Sarah's hiding place, but if he was blinding, he would always let Sarah in free.

Sarah says of him, "He was a jolly lad with never an unclean thought, so we were always glad to have him join in our games. One day he asked my mother how many horse she would take for me. Knowing he had only two horses and not dreaming he was in earnest, she laughingly told him three. What was her surprise a few days later to see Mike come riding one horse and leading two other, the new one, a black mare, he had appropriated from a white man, Dave Savage.

Although thwarted, Mike was undaunted and soon learned that wives were sometimes won without the aid of horses, so he began in this manner. "Sairih, me no likie Injun gel, me likie Meei-can gel. Ingen gel too muchie stink."

When he proceed to press his suit Sarah told him she could not marry him because Indians were mean to their squaws. She had seen a few Indians women with their noses cut off as far as the bone, and others with slashes across their forearm. Mike told her he would not cut off her nose because she would not be untrue to him, and that only those that talked back to their husbands got their arms cut.

Because he had stolen the horse he was sent back to the Reservation. After Sarah became the wife of Mr. Dan Mills, Mike came back and asked Mrs. McNeil where Sarah was. She told him and he said, "Sairih marry Dom. Et makie me cry. Maybe me kill Dom."

Not more than a year later he met Mr. Mills and said, "I gata marry, gata leetle boy, too. Maybe you likie giv him sack of flour and pirty red hankchier to tie round his head." Dan had forgiven his rival and was glad to give the new born chieftain a sack of flour and a red handkerchief.

Sarah recalls the battle in which Petone was killed. The Indians were very fond of a drink they made called "tulipi." Corn was mashed and covered with water, then left to ferment, and when it had "plenty kick" they would drink it with the effect that while it lasted, they owned the world.

On this particular occasion a squaw had been at the home of the McNeils and left her baby strapped to his carrier. Mrs. McNeil was at a neighbor's house when the shooting began and Sarah, fearing some of the Indians might see the baby and think they had stolen it, and also being alarmed for their safety because the bullets were flying around, sent her brother Dan for her mother.

He had only gone a short distance from the door when a loud shot was heard and he ran back into the house with his hands on his head, yelling at the top of his voice, "I'm shot in the head." Sarah was frightened then in earnest, but upon examination, found it a false alarm.

As Sarah was telling this story she laughed at the memory of the Indian who came to give the alarm of the battle and to get help. He ran so fast that his "gee- string stood out straight in the back."

### Annie Moore

Interviewer: Helen M. Smith

We saw Indians occasionally, but they were pretty well subdued before I came out. The closest I came to any real adventure with them was at Hunsaker's farther up the canyon. I had gone up there to spend the night with the family. They had a large, two-story adobe house, with their barn and out buildings across a fairly deep gully. The rest of the household slept down stairs, but the guest room was upstairs in the corner of the house facing the barn.

During the night the dogs make a great deal of fuss about the barn, and although the family tried to quiet them several times, they kept it up. There were no animals about the barn except the horse I had ridden, which was in the corral.

Things were apparently all right the next morning, but before noon some men rode in who were looking for horses stolen by Indians. They had trailed the Indians to the Hunsaker place. Then everyone noticed moccasin tracks all around the corral.

Why they didn't take my horse I don't know. I made a great to do about the whole thing to my folks, saying I knew that if the Indians had known I was upstairs in that corner they would have shot me sure.

### Eleanor C. Roberts Morris

Interviewer: Roberta Flake Clayton

For twelve years her husband served as Head Scout in the Indian trouble, which repeatedly broke out. He had many thrilling experiences. At one time he left his home and dear ones expecting to be back within twenty-four hours, but his party of perhaps a dozen men were cunningly lured on and craftily led into a box canyon where they were kept bottled up for 18 days. They were finally rescued from a starving condition by U.S. soldiers.

Years afterwards, when peace had been restored, a former Navajo leader said he crept so near their camp that he recognized Hyrum, who had at one time come to the Indian Village and with Eleanor's help had cared for his sick Indian baby saving its life. This Indian had slipped away and carried word to the soldiers.

On the Hualapai Desert, while journeying on, the children had been allowed to walk beside the wagons for a change, when all at once from over the near foot hills a band of Indians were seen riding swiftly toward the company.

Hyman was riding a horse that day and all children were quickly piled into wagons. The train was closed up nearer and every man was told to have his guns ready if needed, but not too plainly in evidence.

His early day training stood him in good need now. As the Indians approached, he rode out to meet them waving a white kerchief as a signal of peace, when to the great joy of all it was found to be a friendly band of Hualapai's selling pine nuts. You can believe they soon disposed of all they had, trading them for flour and other things.

In 1883, the Apache Indians went on the war path and threatened to wipe out Mesa and Jonesville (now Lehi), but the Pima and Maricopa Indians said the white men had been their friends, and they now would help them.

The formed a line of defense out east on the desert, which they maintained for days, but the Apaches never made the attack. This time the Indian men wore nothing but a breech clout, or gee-string, and had much paint on their bodies, and the women wore a wrap around made of about 1½ yards of calico wrapped closely under the arms.

## Fannie Gordon Nelson

Interviewer: Unknown

It was less than a year later, I think, when the Apache Indians did go on the warpath up in that neighborhood and killed our nearest neighbors, Charles Sixbey and Joe Bonguis. Bob Sixbey got one arm broken by being shot through the arm. Even though suffering with such a terrible wound he walked into Payson to a doctor. The Indians took all the horses they could capture.

Then, bout 1882, the Apache Indians attacked more of our friends who resided about 23 miles from our place in Cherry Creek, and about 25 miles from Globe. The family's name was Middleton. Henry Moody and George Turner were killed and Moody and the Middleton family narrowly escaped death. Indians used to come by our ranch in bunches, once and twice a year, but always seemed peaceable, and never tried to harm any of us.

Our good friend, Al Sieber and the scouts finally got all of the mean Apaches. Often when passing Al would make camp at our ranch and was well known and well liked by the old timers.

## Lucy Bedford Phillips

Interviewer: Kathlyn M. Lathrop

About the earliest thing I can remember clearly, is when I was about seven or eight years old, when the Indians attacked our neighborhood in broad daylight.

All the women and children in the neighborhood, except us and one other family that I know of—I don't recall just why Mother hadn't gone, or why she should have gone at that particular time-were gathered at the home of Mrs. John Friend that day.

The Friend home, having a high stone wall around the yard, served as a sort of fort during Indian uprising, but at this time there had been no report of Indians on the war path.

Mr. Friend had gone to Llanotown to bring Miss Florence Friend home from school for the summer. Father and the other neighborhood men were out on Buffalo hunt; they got big money for buffalo hides at that time.

It was along in the late afternoon when someone seen a bunch of horseback riders coming down the road toward the Friend home. Thinking it was the hunters returning, some of the women ran out to meet them. They discovered too late, the men were Indians in war paint.

They had no time to get back inside the yard, or to get the gates barred. They were just a bunch of terrorized women and children with no one to protect them, and no way of protecting themselves. But they must have put up a mighty battle, at that, as there were almost as many "good Indians" scattered around the place as there were slaughtered white people.

It was only about one and a half miles from our house over to Friends. We could hear the screaming and shooting, the women had guns, but the Indians used bows and arrows, and we could see the smoke and flames shooting upward when they fired the buildings, all but the house. No one knows why they didn't set that on fire.

Mother knew it was Indians, and she knew she could offer no help to the stricken women and children. She put us children in the cellar under the house and barred the doors. She could shoot as well as any man, so could Grandmother and my two aunts who were there. But the Indians must have been satisfied with what they done at the Friend house, or they went off in another direction, anyway they missed us that time.

I think it was seven women and children killed on the Friend premise in the house or in the yard, and Mrs. Friend was left for dead. They took about twenty women and children away with them, and young Temple Friend, a boy about my age, was taken along with the rest.

Mrs. Friend was shot with an arrow clean through her bowels. After they had shot her, an Indian came over to her and jerked the arrow up and down several times to see if she was dead. She knew everything, and the pain must have been terrible, but she didn't dare even moan. She knew when he jerked out his knife and skelped her, and still she didn't faint or anything.

After the Indians had gone she laid there in all that misery, hours and hours, it must have seemed a thousand years to her. Then long after dark, when she had managed to get the arrow out of her, she crawled a full mile to the house of another neighbor.

The neighbor woman had taken her children with her that day and had been working in her field down in the river bottom, and had come home about dark. She hadn't known anything about the Indians being there until she opened the door to Mrs. Friend.

They were all scared so bad that they ran off and left Mrs. Friend laying there on the dirt floor, all by herself again. They came to our house and Mother let them in and they were scared so bad they couldn't speak for hours. Mother didn't dare go to Mrs. Friend either. They thought she would be dead anyway by that time.

It was nearly morning before any of the men folk got in and brought Mrs. Friend over to our house. She didn't know anything by that time, but she was still alive. The ants had got in her wounds to add to her suffering.

The men folk went on the trail of these Indians. It wasn't hard to follow as they found it strewn with beaten, bruised and skulped bodies of children. Most of the older girls and women had been spared death for a much worse fate.

Mrs. Friend was eventually taken to a hospital in San Antonio where she got well and lived many years. Of course, the hair never did grow back on her skelp, and the scars on her face made her a frightful thing to see, but she lived.

Temple Friend was about seventeen when they found him and got him back from the Indians. He was a handsome young man, but he was as wild and uncivilized as any Indian. He looked like an Indian, being naturally dark and baked by the sun as he was.

The only word he knew in English was his father's name. I can't imagine how he remembered even that much. He didn't want to come home, didn't want to be civilized, refused to try to learn English. He kept trying to run away and go back to the Indians.

He became so savage and unruly that they had to keep him locked up like an animal in a cage. I think they were afraid he'd skelp somebody. I was scared to death of him myself, and I'd played with him when we were children. He never did become the least bit civilized; he died about three years later, like some wild beast in captivity.

A few months after the attack on the Friend home we got another scare. Uncle George Bedford and Father had started off on a hog hunt. We watched them go galloping out of sight. Then all of a sudden they came riding back in a dead run, like the devil was after them.

"Indians! Indians! Uncle George yelled, as they leapt off their horses and everybody grabbed guns, and Mother began shoving us children down the cellar steps.

Seven or eight Indians, not in war paint, came riding toward the house. The road ran right by our front gate, they slowed up, waved, and called out "How", then rode on. They paid no attention to the guns leveled at them from the doors and windows. The men could have killed every one of them, but Mother and Grandmother said, "NO, NO! Don't shoot They are not on the warpath, and if you kill them it might start another uprising".

Father and Uncle George sure wanted to kill them Indians. Next morning most every horse in the community was missing, then Father did rave right.

Then we moved to Llanotown. I was a grown young lady by this time. One night, a horse in our neighbor's corral began acting strangely, running around and around and snorting. Mother knew at once that the horse smelled Indians.

"That horse smells Indians, sure as we are born" she said. I thought she was just imagining things, as the Indians had been quiet a long time now.

Our two saddle horses and milk cow were kept in a corral down by the river, about a quarter of a mile from the house. The men folk were all away at the time, and nothing would do Mother but to go after our horses and cow. I went with her and we brought them to the house and locked them up in a shed room off the kitchen. Next morning every horse and cow in town that were not locked up was gone.

No one had seen any Indians, but there were unmistakable Indian signs. We couldn't be sure it was Indians though, as there were so many outlaws and rustlers around over the country who knew how to make Indians signs and lay their dirty work onto Indians.

## Clara Mari Gleason Rogers

Interviewer: Roberta Flake Clayton

Mrs. Rogers was again appointed as companion to her husband in sheep herding thereby releasing one man for more strenuous work. One day her husband was much startled at the sheep stampeding down the mountain side, and rushing up to see the cause of the disturbance came face to face with a large bear.

Being unarmed, Mr. Rogers stopped when the bear stopped, and they surveyed each other steadily for a little while. Then the bear dropped to all fours and withdrew slowly up the mountain, leaving him victor of the field and the spiritual uplift that "the true shepherd will give his life for his sheep."

## Minnie Alice Woolley Rogers

Interviewer: Roberta Flake Clayton

The first June they were here Davis, his wife, his father, and his father's wife took the cattle and went up to Phoenix Park where they had previously gone in March and planted a crop. Here the women made butter. It was a lovely location and would have been very pleasant had there not been the constant fear of Indians who were frequent visitors. They used to come and sharpen their knives at Father Rogers' grindstone and would often take delight in brandishing them over Minnie's head just to see her fright; though she tried hard not to show the fear she felt. She says she had to keep her mouth shut tight on these occasions to keep her heart from jumping out.

As was customary with the early settlers among the Indians, it was better to feed then to fight them and many a meal was given to them, also some of their best cattle. But, in spite of this when the Apache went on the war path, they spared nothing as was proven when they drove the Rogers' and all the settlers in the mountains from their belongings and took or destroyed everything. The precious bee hive carried over Lee's Backbone, and which had been taken to Phoenix Park with them, shared the same fate. Mrs. Rogers can't be blamed for hoping the bees retaliated.

Clara Rogers
*(LDS Church History Library)*

**Leonora Allen Russell**
Interviewer: G. W. Reeve

The few citizens of Globe were constantly on the lookout for Indian raiders, and there were a few scouts watching from the nearby mountain tops to warn the settlers when any Indians were coming toward Globe. There was also a small building that served as an arsenal, where the guns and ammunition were kept. This building was in the middle of Broad Street, located about between the European Hotel and the bakery.

In 1882, while visiting the mining camp of McMillan, Leonora's mother was struck on the head by an Indian tomahawk during an Indian raid there, and shortly afterward died in a hospital in Wilcox from the effects of this blow. Several people were killed in this raid.

## Rosa Talbot Schuster

Interviewer: Edward J. Kelley

In 1882, there was an Indian scare. The Apaches chasing prospectors and travelers right into town, but Indians were an old story and so this passed over soon. With Geronimo's capture we commenced to forget Indians and in but a few years we completely forgot there was such a thing. Which I think is odd for we were always compelled to keep the Apaches first in our minds if we cared to live any length of time.

I think the liveliest event was the lynching of Jack Heath early in 1884. Heath was said to be one of the six men who held up and robbed Bisbee a few months before, during which fracas a woman was killed. All six were condemned to be hung and Heath was sentenced to life. The Bisbee people approved the death sentence for the five, but angrily disapproved of the idea Heath was to be let off with only life imprisonment. They decided to make it six even by lynching Heath and an army of them came over in wagons and buggies as well as horseback for that purpose.

At first the Tombstone men resented the idea of outsiders coming in here to start a rumpus, and for awhile it looked as if there would be a battlefield around this house we are in, but when the local people remembered a woman had been killed by this gang, possibly by Heath himself, they veered around and helped the Bisbeeites. The Sheriff's office gave the man up without much of a struggle. I suppose their sympathies were with the voters, and Heath was hung right in town with much needless shooting and uproar.

Did I personally know Wyatt Earp, the old city Marshall? Of course, just as I knew pretty nearly everyone else in camp. A number of his relatives have visited me from time to time the past few years.

What did I think of him? Well, er, er, I guess he must have been just the man for the place. It takes a certain kind of a man to handle a certain kind of people, and he stayed for quite a while. You know we had a number of hard characters here in his day and he kept the lid on pretty well.

I cannot say I thought much of Doc Holliday and some of the rest of the crowd that Earp trained with. I have heard Mr. Schuster describe several occasions on which they crawfished when up against one of the real old timers.

## Betty Spicer

Interviewer: Helen M. Smith

Fred White was the first town Marshall, and was killed accidently while in discharge of his duty. There had been too much of the "shooting up the town" sort of thing, and officials were determined to put a stop to it. They decided that everyone must disarm while in town.

Curly Bill refused to do so upon his arrival in town, declaring that no one could tell him what to do or what not to do. When the Marshall attempted to disarm him by force, Curly started to tender him his gun, butt foremost.

There was an old trick known to bad men of that time by which one extended a gun in that fashion, and then quickly spun it on one finger until the muzzle pointed toward the other, when death was sudden and sure.

Wyatt Earp noticed the position of the gun, and grabbed Curly quickly from behind. Taken by surprise, Curly struggled, and his gun was discharged, killing Mr. White. Curly was tried, but was able to show that the whole thing was an accident, and was dismissed.

While in Tombstone we got acquainted with Buckskin Frank Leslie. He was quite an agreeable man when he wished to be, having a good voice and a fondness for singing, and being an interesting conversationalist.

It was after we left that Frank Leslie committed the murder which sent him a prisoner to Yuma. He was a bad gunman always, but usually took care to keep on the safe side of the law, or to be in such a position as to talk his way out of trouble. In this event, too, he thought that he had all things planned to escape the results of his misdeed, but he slipped.

He had been at his ranch in the Swisshelms with a young man named Hughes, and a woman. They were all drinking together, when the supply ran short. Leslie rode away to procure more. Upon his return he saw something in the conduct of his guests which made him suspicious. He shot both the woman and Hughes, leaving the latter for dead out on the hills. But, Hughes recovered enough to make a ranch, where he told the whole story. His evidence convicted Leslie and sent him to prison. I never learned what became of the man after his term was served.

We made no attempt to get a start in cattle believing that the rustlers made such an attempt impractical. My husband hauled wood for a living during several years.

At one of our camps an Indian rode up. After helping us to do some work on our wagon, he made signs that led us to believe he wanted sugar. When we offered it, he tasted it and shook his head. We then offered salt, upon which he nodded violently. We gave him most of our salt which he carefully tied up in his shirttail with a piece of string before riding on.

## Martha Jane Layne Stratton

Interviewer: Roberta Flake Clayton

The Indians were still bad. At one time they stole a white child and took it by the heels and knocked its head against a rock and killed it. Just a few days after this happened and while Mother was alone with her children, some Indians came to her home.

Seeing that Mother was alone and very frightened they picked up the baby and acted as if they were going to take it and treat it the way they did the other, but a prayer from the heart saved the baby. The Indians put it down and went away laughing at her fright.

## Janet Mauretta Johnson Smith

Interviewer: Roberta Flake Clayton

When the sight in her beautiful eyes became so dim she could no longer read or sew, she could tell stories of pioneer days and sing or recite to her grandchildren. They loved to hear her tell of her courage when at one time she was alone in those early days when Indians "went on the warpath", just she and her little girls when three Indians came with some cloth they wanted to trade for flour.

One of them had 3 yards of jeans he wanted to trade for 3 pans of flour. She got it for him but when he put it in his sack he decided it was not enough, and asked for more. This she refused to give him. Then he reached and took the cloth away from her.

In a flash she snatched it back, put it in a wooden chest, closed the lid and sat upon it. The three Indians stood and conferred with each other a few minutes then left the room, returning shortly with two more. She explained in detail the agreement to one of the new comers who seemed to be the chief, and when she was through he said, "Buena squaw! Heap brave!"

## Adelinah Quinn Taylor

Interviewer: Helen M. Smith

We had far more Indian scares in Safford than we had had on the way out. I never experienced anything of the sort personally, but in my part as nurse I often saw the results.

There was a man in the community who had got himself in bad with the law in Mexico, and had left hastily. He worked hard after he reached our locality to earn money enough to have his wife and baby brought out of Mexico. When he had enough money, he had a friend and wife travel out to Safford with his wife and baby. This company camped at a water hole near Safford on their last night out. Indians attacked them at dawn, killing both women and the man. The baby was covered by the feather bed, no doubt by accident, and the Indians never knew it was there. It was discovered by the rescue party, and first it appeared smothered to death, but it was revived by first aid treatment.

The posse followed the Indians with the aid of the Indian scout, and I am sure that they eventually got most of them, although they rode into an ambush the first thing and a young married man named Wright was killed.

An old man named Merrill, and his daughter, were also killed by Indians. The girl was getting ready to be married, and wanted money to buy finery for the wedding, and also a chance to buy the finery. The father started for Clifton with a load of produce, and the girl accompanied him for the purpose of purchasing what she desired.

They camped for the night, and the morning being cold, they decided to walk behind the team for awhile to warm up. Suddenly there was a shot, and the father fell, shot through the back. The daughter turned and threw her hands to her head in horror. She was shot through the breast and fell, still with her hands upraised. I helped dress the body, and I never before saw such a look of horror on a face as was on hers. The Indians had not molested the bodies, but had burned the wagon and run off the horses.

Mother went blind after we had lived for awhile at Safford. One evening she was alone in the house but for my sister Emma, the youngest of the family, and a little boy, a cousins of Emma's. The older ones of us were long since married, and Father was away. The three had just sat down to supper when two Indian braves rode up. They had been drinking, and still had a bottle.

They sat themselves down at the table and ate supper, and afterward began to look about the house, evidently searching for money. Mother had one lone dollar in the house, and when she saw that their failure to find anything was making them angry, she put the dollar where they could find it, by stealth. They became good humored, sat down at the table and commenced playing cards.

They had noticed Emma, who was only a little girl; had asked Mother for the "little papoose" to take to the reservation. Emma had it in her head to go for help from the beginning, but they had watched her so closely that she had had no chance to sneak out. However, soon after they sat down at the table, one of them became quite drunk, and the vigilance of the other relaxed. Emma motioned to her little cousin and they sneaked out. They ran three miles through the dark to the town itself, and barefooted. Emma knew that she was expected to look after "Ma", and she soon aroused the town. A wagon was made ready in short order, and Emma was the first to leap into the wagon. Men with guns drove as fast as possible to the house.

In the meantime one of the Indians had fallen under the table in a stupor, while the other appeared half "addled." However, he heard the wagon approaching and managed to drag his companion outside by the time the wagon had reached the place, all the time looking around dazed and saying "Where papoose? Where papoose?"

Emma leaped from the wagon and ran with bleeding feet to her mother. The Indians kept begging her, "Papoose tellum Indian good man." Emma stamped her foot, "I won't. John ain't been a good Indian tonight," she cried.

The men decided to allow the Indians to go since they had done no real damage and they feared the vengeance of other Indians should they punish them.

## Sarah Ann Salina Smithson Turley

Interviewer: Roberta Flake Clayton

Saline was the third in a family of thirteen and when her services could be dispensed with at home she often went with her father from Holbrook to Fort Apache driving her four or six horse teams.

On one of Saline's trips she wore a red calico dress trimmed with white braid. A young Indian, seeing her, was much pleased with her looks and offered one of the men of the company ten horses for her. The man, not realizing the harm he was doing, nor that an Indian never jokes about such matters, told him he could have her for two horses. The Indian rode away but soon returned, bringing the two horses and another Indian with him. The men were all out of camp caring for their teams. The prospective bridegroom motioned for Saline to get on behind him, and when she refused he tried to pull her out of the wagon. She put up a brave fight, but the Indian was determined.

She thought of her black whip, a weapon she had become pretty expert with in the management of her team, so reached down to get it from the bottom of the wagon. He then grabbed her by the back of the dress and was pulling with all his might when she raised up and gave both him and his horse a sharp crack with her whip.

The astonished horse plunged and ran and before the rider could get him under control and get back to the wagon, the men returned and her brother with pistol in hand ordered the Indians away.

When the men told the Commanding Officer of the incident, he at once saw their danger and told them they must not stop until they were off the reservation. This meant that they must drive all night, which they did. That was the last load of freight Saline took.

**Julia Ellsworth West**
Interviewer: Roberts Flake Clayton
Navajo County

"My girlhood was spent on a ranch. The country was new and we had many thrilling experiences. The Apaches had a drunken fight on the hill right close to our house. They killed three Indian men, one a Chieftain, and wounded another Chief. Father was a great friend to the Indians, he would feed them and give them wagon loads of squash. He tried to teach them that all men were brothers. One day he called Natzen a rascal. The sly old fellow patted Father on the back and said, "You my brother!"

Julia recalls the only death of the Mormon pioneers in this part of the country was caused by Indians when they murdered Nathan Robinson, the Uncle of the man she afterward married. He rose up to where they had killed a stolen beef, and they shot him and threw his body in Show Low Creek, covering all but one leg with stones. This foot stuck out of the water, and thus his body was discovered.

## Nancy Cedenia Bagley Willis

Interviewer: Unknown

Little Cedenia was naturally a sensitive and timid little child and to this day remembers with a feeling of resentment things that crushed her spirit, and with horror some of the tragic scenes of her childhood.

The schoolhouse door had bullet holes shot through it by Indians who were chained in there once and got the pistol from the young man who was guarding them.

Even in the night she would wake up shuddering and crying from fear of Indians. One of the most terrible sights she saw in her childhood is given in her own words. "It was ever the Indians, ever on guard, ever a revolver with a belt of cartridges worn by men. I witnessed a sad scene which can never be erased from my memory. A wagon being driven slowly to the schoolhouse, the bottom partly burned away. When they reached the building, two noble looking men were tenderly carried by friends and lain on those crude benches to have the arrows pulled from their breasts. My father was assisting but it was too much for him and he was carried fainting from the room. Such a sickening scene.

"A beautiful woman was taken from the partly burned wagon. She had been a victim of the dreadful massacre by the bloodthirsty Indians. The next day the funerals were held. The husband and wife were laid in one grave, the brother by their side. As the sweet strains of the violin and bass viol were wafted on the breeze their bodies were consigned. These were members of the Berry family.

"I shall never forget the journey of over 300 miles with only one other family and our hired man. Black Hawk was on the war path. Father was ever on the watch with his revolver handy, ready for use at anytime. One day at noon the little company was stirred by the blood-curdling yells and war hoops of a dozen Indians as they dashed down the hill into our camp. Father picked up his revolver from the wagon tongue where he had lain it to make a fire. Mother got in the wagon holding the gun cartridges while Sister and I got behind Mother. An overwhelming joy filled our hearts as the Indians, after a counsel among themselves, rode away.

## Lucy Jane Flake Wood

Interviewer: Roberta Flake Clayton

Jane was always afraid of Indians, as were most of the children in those early days, for they were taught that the Indians would steal and carry them away, as they sometimes did.

One day while she was very small, some of them came to the house. Jane was alone in the yard. The dog was trained to dislike the Indians, too, and when he saw them he started after them. They ran for the door and slammed the gate leaving poor little Jane outside. Her screams, and the barking of the dog soon brought her father to the door, and she was rescued.

# Additional Reading

Arizona WPA Writers' Project, *Arizona: A Guide to the Sunset State,* Hasting House, New York, 1940, pages 530.

Baker, Terri M, and Connie Oliver Henshaw, editors, *Women who Pioneered Oklahoma: Stories from the WPA Narratives,* University of Oklahoma Press, Norman, 2008, pages 226.

Bold, Christine, *Writers, Plumbers, and Anarchists: The WPA Writers' Project* in Massachusetts, University of Massachusetts Press, Amhurst and Boston, Massachusetts, 2006, pages 272.

Ellis, Catherine, H., *Images of America: Snowflake,* Arcadia Publishing, San Francisco, CA, 2008, pages 128,

Flynn, Kathryn A. with Richard Polese, *The New Deal,* Gibbs Smith, Publisher, Salt Lake City, Utah, 2008, pages 168.

Green, Elna, editor, *Looking for the New Deal: Florida Women's Letters during the Great Depression,* The University of South Carolina Press, Columbia, South Carolina, 2007, pages 243.

Hirsch, Jerrold, *Portrait of America: A cultural History of the Federal Writers' Project,* The University of North Carolina Press, Chapel Hill and London, 2003,pages 293.

Houston, Neal B., *Ross Santee: Southwest Writers Series #18,* Steck-Vaughn Company, Austin, Texas, 1968, pages 44.

Mangione, Jerre, *The Dream and the Deal: The Federal Writers' Project, 1935-1943,*Syracuse University Press, Syracuse, New York, 1996, pages 416.

Robolledo, Tey Diana, and Maria Teresa Marquez, editors, *Women's Tales from the New Mexico WPA: La Diabla a Pie, Arte Publico Press,* University of Houston, Houston, Texas, 2000, pages 454.

*Udall, Cameron, Images of America: St. Johns,* Arcadia Publishing, San Francisco, CA, 2008, pages 127.

# Name Index

# Place Index

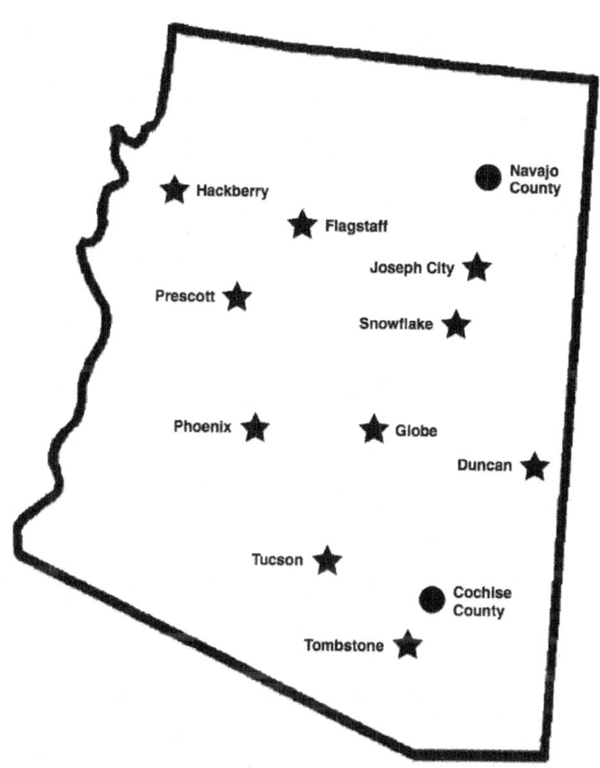
Hackberry
Navajo County
Flagstaff
Joseph City
Prescott
Snowflake
Phoenix
Globe
Duncan
Tucson
Cochise County
Tombstone

# Confessions of a Missouri Guerrilla:

## The Autobiography of Cole Younger

*This is an intelligent, articulate, Cole Younger—not the blood-thirsty desperado of myth. Now he tells HIS side of the story.*

*"On the eve of sixty, I came out into the world to find a hundred or more books, of greater or lesser pretensions, purporting to be a history of "The Lives of the Younger Brothers." I venture to say that in the whole lot there could not be found six pages of truth."*

***This then is YOUNGER'S version of the story***

**ISBN-13: 978-1-934757-30-7**
**180 Pages - 6" X 9" - Paperback - 9 Illustrations**

***www.FireshipPress.com***

CPSIA information can be obtained at www.ICGtesting.com
Printed in the USA
BVOW09s2054041114

373525BV00006B/34/P

9 781934 757956